Study Guide

for use with

Financial Accounting

Second Edition

Robert Libby
Cornell University

Patricia A. Libby
Ithaca College

Daniel G. Short
Miami University

Prepared by
Jeannie M. Folk
College of DuPage

Irwin
McGraw-Hill

Boston   Burr Ridge, IL   Dubuque, IA   Madison, WI   New York   San Francisco   St. Louis
Bangkok   Bogotá   Caracas   Lisbon   London   Madrid
Mexico City   Milan   New Delhi   Seoul   Singapore   Sydney   Taipei   Toronto

Irwin/McGraw-Hill

A Division of The McGraw-Hill Companies

Study Guide for use with
FINANCIAL ACCOUNTING

1 2 3 4 5 6 7 8 9 0 BBC/BBC 9 0 9 8 7

ISBN 0-256-25433-8

http://www.mhhe.com

PREFACE

This Study Guide was developed to help you study more effectively. It incorporates many of the accounting survival skills essential to your success. It is designed to accompany the second edition of *Financial Accounting* by Libby, Libby and Short, but is not a substitute for your textbook. Its purpose is to supplement the textbook by helping you learn.

Each chapter of the Study Guide contains the following sections: *Chapter Focus Suggestions; Read and Recall Questions; Self-Test Questions and Exercises; Solutions to Self-Test Questions and Exercises;* and *Ideas for Your Study Team*

AN ACCOUNTING SURVIVAL PLAN (Preview, Read, Recall, Test, & Review)

Before you read a chapter, preview it. Start by reading the *Chapter Focus Suggestions* included in the Study Guide, and the learning objectives which appear at the beginning of the chapter in your textbook. Next, thumb through the chapter, noting the names of each of the section headings. Finally, read the chapter summary, and the list of key terms at the end of the chapter.

Now that you know what to expect, start reading. As you finish reading each section of the chapter, answer the related *Read and Recall Questions* included in the Study Guide. Check your answers by referring to the related section in your textbook. If you were not able to answer all of the questions, read the related section of the chapter in your textbook again. If you can answer the *Read and Recall Questions*, you understand and can recall what you just read. To move that information into long-term memory, you'll need to practice and apply what you have just learned.

You can do this, in part, by completing the *Self-Test Questions and Exercises* included in the Study Guide. Test your vocabulary skills by matching the key terms with the textbook definitions. Complete the true-false and multiple choice questions, and check your answers in the *Solutions to Self-Test Questions and Exercises* section. Work through the exercises. Feel free to check an answer to one part of an exercise with the *Solutions* before moving on to another part. (And make sure that you complete all of the homework exercises and problems assigned by your instructor.)

Remember that you're not alone. Develop your own support system by forming a study team with three or four of your classmates. Each chapter of the Study Guide contains a number of *Ideas for Your Study Team*. You'll learn by discussion, and develop valuable interpersonal skills.

Use the Study Guide on a daily basis as you prepare for exams. The *Read and Recall Questions* can be used to review the essential concepts covered in each chapter. The *Self-Test Questions and Exercises* are likely to be similar to the materials you will encounter on exams. And don't forget to use positive self-talk as you visualize your success in this accounting class. You can do it!

I would appreciate your comments and suggestions. Please write to me at the following address:

Jeannie M. Folk, Associate Professor, Accounting
College of DuPage
425 22nd Street
Glen Ellyn, Illinois 60137
folkje@cdnet.cod.edu

TABLE OF CONTENTS

Title	Pages
Chapter 1 Financial Statements and Business Decisions	1 - 34
Chapter 2 Investing and Financing Decisions and the Balance Sheet	35 - 68
Chapter 3 Operating Decisions and the Income Statement	69 - 99
Chapter 4 The Adjustment Process and Financial Statements	100 - 126
Chapter 5 The Communication of Accounting Information	127 - 158
Chapter 6 Reporting and Interpreting Sales Revenue, Receivables and Cash	159 - 190
Chapter 7 Reporting and Interpreting Cost of Goods Sold and Inventory	191 - 221
Chapter 8 Reporting and Interpreting Property, Plant, and Equipment; Natural Resources;and Intangibles	222 - 250
Chapter 9 Reporting and Interpreting Liabilities	251 - 277
Chapter 10 Reporting and Interpreting Bonds	278 - 309
Chapter 11 Reporting and Interpreting Owners' Equity	310 - 336
Chapter 12 Reporting and Interpreting Investments in Other Companies	337 - 369
Chapter 13 Statement of Cash Flows	370 - 394
Chapter 14 Analyzing Financial Statements	395 - 426

CHAPTER 1
FINANCIAL STATEMENTS AND BUSINESS DECISIONS

CHAPTER FOCUS SUGGESTIONS

This chapter describes the process that businesses use to communicate financial information to investors and creditors. If you have not yet worked in a business setting, you will probably not be familiar with many of the terms used in this chapter. A listing of key terms appears at the end of the chapter. You will need to be able to define each of these key terms. However, you should also make sure that you are familiar with the other terms that are used in this chapter. These terms will be used throughout this course.

This chapter also describes the four basic financial statements that are used to communicate financial information and introduces you to the parties involved in the communication process. You will need to be able to recognize the categories of items reported on each financial statement and how the financial statements are interrelated. Memorize the equations for the four financial statements and practice preparing them. Knowing which items are reported on each financial statement will help you to understand how the financial statements are used by decision makers.

READ AND RECALL QUESTIONS

LEARNING OBJECTIVE
After studying this section of the chapter, you should be able to:
1. Recognize the information conveyed in the four basic financial statements and how it is used by different decision makers (investors, creditors, and managers).

THE OBJECTIVES OF *FINANCIAL ACCOUNTING*

What is the purpose of the Libby, Libby & Short *Financial Accounting* textbook? Which groups of readers is the book aimed at?

What do you expect to learn in this accounting course?

BUSINESS BACKGROUND

What do owners (often called investors or stockholders) hope to gain when they purchase a company? What risks do they assume?

Why do creditors lend money to businesses? What do they hope to gain? What risks do they assume?

— gain — interest ($)

— risks — if an entity

What functions are performed by Maxidrive's accounting system? Who uses the reports produced by this accounting system? (Hint: There are two major groups of users.)

How does managerial or management accounting differ from financial accounting? Which of the two is the focal point of this text?

REFLECTING BUSINESS OPERATIONS IN FINANCIAL STATEMENTS

What did Exeter Investors, Maxidrive's new owner, and American Bank, Maxidrive's largest creditor, use to learn more about the company before making their purchase and lending decisions? What assumptions did they make when they used this information?

What are the four basic financial statements?

The Balance Sheet

What is the separate entity assumption?

What is the purpose of the balance sheet? What is another name for the balance sheet? What is the time dimension of the balance sheet?

What unit of measure is used to prepare financial statements of companies located in the United States? What unit of measure would be used by a Canadian company?

Assets

Cash, accounts receivable, inventories, plant and equipment, and land are listed as assets on Maxidrive's balance sheet. What is an asset? How are assets initially measured on the balance sheet?

What is the cost principle?

Why did American Bank and Exeter assess Maxidrive's assets? Why are assets so important? If Maxidrive goes out of business, can its assets be sold for the amounts listed on its balance sheet?

Liabilities And Stockholders' Equity

How is a liability created? How is owners' equity created?

What is the basic accounting equation? What is a company's "financial position?"

What is a liability? How do liabilities arise?

If Maxidrive is not able to pay its debts, what action can its creditors take?

What are the sources of stockholders' equity? (Hint: There are two sources.)

What is another term for stockholders' equity? Why is the amount of Maxidrive's stockholders' equity so important to American Bank? Does the amount of stockholders' equity represent the market value of a company as a whole to its owners? Why or why not?

The Income Statement

What is the time dimension of the income statement? What other names are given to the income statement? What does the income statement report?

What does Maxidrive's net income measure? What is the income statement equation?

Revenues

What are revenues? When should revenues be reported on the income statement?

Is it appropriate to wait for the receipt of cash to record revenue? Why or why not?

Expenses

What are expenses? When are expenses reported on the income statement?

Is it appropriate to wait for the payment of cash to record an expense? Why or why not?

Net Income

What is net income? What other terms are used to describe net income? What term is used if total revenues are less than total expenses? What if total revenues equal total expenses?

Statement of Retained Earnings

What information is reported on the statement of retained earnings?

Does net income increase or decrease the balance of retained earnings? Does the declaration of dividends increase or decrease the balance of retained earnings? What is the retained earnings equation?

What is the time dimension of the statement of retained earnings? Does the time dimension of this financial statement match that of the balance sheet, income statement or both?

Statement of Cash Flows

Why aren't reported revenues always equal to the amount of cash collected from customers? Why aren't reported expenses always equal to the cash paid out during the period?

What is the purpose of the statement of cash flows? What is the time dimension of this statement?

What are the three primary categories of cash flows in a typical business?

What is meant by "cash flows from operating activities?"

What is meant by "cash flows from investing activities?"

What is meant by "cash flows from financing activities?"

What is the cash flow statement equation?

Notes

There are three types of notes (or footnotes) to the financial statements. What type of information is provided by each?

The Fraud

What three types of errors did Exeter find in Maxidrive's financial statements?

Determining the Purchase Price for Maxidrive

What factors did Exeter consider when deciding on a purchase price for Maxidrive?

What is one method that is used to estimate the value of a company? How is the value of a company computed using this method?

Maxidrive overstated the amount of its net income. Assuming that the purchase price paid by Exeter was determined by taking net income times the price earnings ratio, did Exeter pay too little or too much for Maxidrive?

RESPONSIBILITIES FOR THE ACCOUNTING COMMUNICATION PROCESS

What does the decision maker need to understand before using accounting information?

What is auditing?

Generally Accepted Accounting Principles

Why were the Securities Exchange Acts of 1933 and 1934 passed by Congress? What function is performed by the Securities and Exchange Commission (SEC)?

Companies incur the cost of preparing financial statements and bear the major economic consequences of their publication. What are the potential economic consequences? (Hint: There are at least three.)

Is there one set of generally accepted accounting principles in use throughout the world?

LEARNING OBJECTIVE
After studying this section of the chapter, you should be able to:
3. Distinguish the roles of managers and auditors in the accounting communication process.

MANAGEMENT RESPONSIBILITY AND THE DEMAND FOR AUDITING

Who is responsible for the information that is presented in a company's financial statements?

What three steps can be taken by managers to ensure the accuracy of the company's records?

What is the role of an independent auditor? What is the purpose of an audit?

The owners and managers of Exeter were misled by the information presented in Maxidrive's financial statements. What is the best protection available to users of financial statements?

ETHICS, REPUTATION AND LEGAL LIABILITY

What is necessary if financial statements are to be of any value to decision makers?

Why do independent auditors adhere to a professional code of ethics? (Hint: There are at least two reasons.)

How prevalent is financial statement fraud? How are many financial statement frauds first identified?

Is it reasonable to expect that auditors will uncover all frauds?

Types of Business Entities

What is a sole proprietorship? What are the characteristics of this type of business?

What is a partnership? What are the characteristics of this type of business?

What is a corporation? What are the characteristics of this type of business?

What is the dominant form of business organization in the United States? Why is it the dominant form?

CHAPTER SUPPLEMENT B
Determine whether or not you are responsible for this supplement.

Employment in the Accounting Profession Today

What requirements must be met before an accountant may be licensed as a Certified Public Accountant?

What are the three types of services performed by accounting firms?

What types of functions are performed by accountants employed by profit-making business enterprises? By accountants employed in the public or not-for-profit sector?

SELF-TEST QUESTIONS AND EXERCISES

MATCHING

Match each of the key terms listed below with the appropriate textbook definition:

E 1. Accounting
H 2. Accounting entity
M 3. Accounting period
O 4. Audit
J 5. Balance sheet
K 6. Basic accounting equation
L 7. Financial Accounting Standards Board
C 8. Notes (footnotes)

D 9. Generally accepted accounting principles
G 10. Income statement
A 11. Report of independent accountants
N 12. Report of management
I 13. Securities and Exchange Commission
F 14. Statement of cash flows
B 15. Statement of retained earnings

A. A report that describes the auditor's opinion of the fairness of the financial statement presentations and the evidence gathered to support that opinion.

B. A statement that reports how net income and the distribution of dividends affected the financial position of the company during the accounting period.

C. Supplemental information about the financial condition of a company, without which the financial statements cannot be fully understood.

D. The measurement rules used to develop the information in financial statements.

E. A system that collects and processes (analyzes, measures, and records) financial information about an organization and reports that information to decision makers.

F. A statement that reports inflows and outflows of cash during the accounting period in the categories of operations, investing, and financing.

G. A statement that reports the revenues less the expenses of the accounting period.

H. The organization for which financial data are to be collected (separate and distinct from its owners).

I. The U. S. government agency that determines the financial statements that public companies must provide to stockholders and the measurement rules that must be used in producing those statements.

J. A statement that reports the financial position (assets, liabilities, and stockholders' equity) of an accounting entity at a point in time.

K. Assets = Liabilities + Stockholders' Equity

L. The private sector body given the primary responsibility to work out the detailed rules that become generally accepted accounting principles.

M. The time period covered by the financial statements

N. A report that indicates management's primary responsibility for financial statement information and the steps taken to ensure the accuracy of the company's records.

O. An examination of the financial reports to assure that they represent what they claim and conform with generally accepted accounting principles.

TRUE-FALSE QUESTIONS

For each of the following statements, enter a T or F in the blank to indicate whether the statement is true or false.

_T_ 1. The focus of financial accounting is on external users, whereas the focus of managerial accounting is on internal users of accounting information.

_F_ 2. The balance sheet is prepared to summarize the results of the company's activities over a specified period of time, such as one year.

_T_ 3. The basic accounting equation is often called the balance sheet equation.

_F_ 4. The balance sheet lists a company's assets, liabilities, revenues and expenses.

_F_ 5. A company's financial position can be determined, in part, by reference to the current market values of its assets as reported on the balance sheet.

_T_ 6. Stockholders' equity is the amount of financing that has been provided by the company's owners. (+ RE)

_F_ 7. The revenue earned from the sale of goods to a customer is always reported in the period in which the goods are paid for by the customer

_T_ 8. Revenues earned from providing services to customers are reported on the income statement in the period in which the services are provided regardless of whether or not the customers have paid for the services.

_F_ 9. An item is considered to be an expense as soon as the company has paid cash for it.

_T_ 10. Expenses reported in one accounting period may be paid for in another accounting period.

_F_ 11. The income statement sets forth the company's revenues and expenses and any dividends declared during the accounting period.

_F_ 12. The time dimension of a company's statement of cash flows is the same as its income statement and the time dimension of its statement of retained earnings is the same as its balance sheet.

_T_ 13. The price/earnings ratio is a measure of expected company growth.

_F_ 14. The FASB specifies the laws under which financial statements are prepared, and the SEC enforces these laws.

_T_ 15. The FASB actively solicits the input of the business community in the development of new accounting rules.

_F_ 16. Investors and creditors do not need to obtain an understanding of the company's operations if they are relying on financial statements that have been prepared in accordance with generally accepted accounting principles.

_F_ 17. If a company has implemented internal control procedures, decision makers can safely assume that no errors exist in the company's records or financial statements.

_F_ 18. If a company has implemented internal control procedures, its managers can safely assume that the company's assets are then safeguarded against any possibility of theft or embezzlement.

_F_ 19. The owners of sole proprietorships and partners in general partnerships are personally liable for the debts of these types of businesses; as a result, the businesses cannot be treated as separate accounting entities from their owners. *(Supplement A)*

_T_ 20. A corporation is legally separate from its owners; as such, a corporation is a separate business entity which must be accounted for separately from its several owners. *(Supplement A)*

MULTIPLE CHOICE QUESTIONS

Choose the best answer or response by placing the identifying letter in the space provided.

_C_ 1. When accountants refer to a "creditor" of a company, they mean the person or business that

    a. owns the company.
    b. owes the company money.
    c. loaned the company money or allowed it to buy goods and pay for them later.
    d. has reviewed the company favorably in the business press.
    e. takes care of the company's banking needs.

_e_ 2. Each of the following is one of the four basic financial statements except the

    a. income statement.
    b. statement of cash flows.
    c. statement of retained earnings.
    d. balance sheet.
    e. bank statement.

_e_ 3. The statement of financial position is another term for the

    a. income statement.
    b. statement of cash flows.
    c. company's bank statement.
    d. results of today's trading in the company's stock.
    e. balance sheet.

_C_ 4. An accounting period is

    a. exactly one year in length.
    b. one specific date in time.
    c. any specified time period.
    d. the time required to collect accounts receivable.
    e. the life of the entity.

_e_ 5. The balance sheet equation may be stated as

    a. assets = liabilities + owners' equity.
    b. assets - liabilities = owners' equity.
    c. assets - owners' equity = liabilities.
    d. assets + liabilities = owners' equity.
    e. a, b, or c above.

_a_ 6. All of the following items are classified on the balance sheet as assets except

    a. notes payable.
    b. inventories.
    c. land.
    d. accounts receivable.
    e. cash.

_c_ 7. Amounts owed by customers to the company for prior sales to these customers are reported on the balance sheet as _____, whereas amounts owed by the company to vendors or suppliers for goods or services are reported as _____.

    a. cash; cash.
    b. accounts payable; accounts receivable.
    c. accounts receivable; accounts payable.
    d. inventories; sales.
    e. sales; inventories.

_a_ 8. Assets are usually reported on the balance sheet at

    a. acquisition cost.
    b. market value on the balance sheet date.
    c. market value adjusted for any deterioration from storage.
    d. cost adjusted for inflation since the purchase date.
    e. expected selling price.

_d_ 9. Retained earnings is the amount of

    a. cash that stockholders may reasonably expect to receive as dividends in the future.
    b. earnings held for payment of executive bonuses.
    c. cash that will be left over after all of the company's liabilities have been satisfied.
    d. earnings kept, or reinvested, in the business, and thus not paid out as dividends.
    e. cash invested by the owners of the business.

_b_ 10. Revenues are reported on the income statement

    a. in the period in which an order is received from a customer.
    b. in the period in which the goods or services are actually provided to the customer.
    c. in the period in which cash is collected from the customer.
    d. any time the company receives cash.
    e. all of the above.

_e_ 11. All of the following are classified on the income statement as revenues except

    a. cash sales of goods to customers.
    b. credit sales of goods to customers.
    c. amounts earned by providing services to customers.
    d. amounts earned by renting property to others
    e. cash received when money is borrowed from a bank.

_b_ 12. Expenses are reported on the income statement

    a. in the period in which an order for goods or services is placed with a vendor or supplier.

    b. in the period in which the goods or services provided by a vendor or supplier are used to generate revenues.

    c. in the period in which cash is paid to vendors or suppliers for goods or services that have been purchased.

    d. any time the company disburses (or pays out) cash.

    e. all of the above.

_d_ 13. All of the following items are classified on the income statement as expenses except

    a. the cost of acquiring the merchandise that was sold.

    b. wages of sales staff.

    c. the Vice President's annual bonus.

    d. the cost of a parcel of land acquired for the construction of a new store.

    e. research and development costs on a potential new product.

_a_ 14. If revenues are less than expenses during an accounting period,

    a. a net loss is reported.

    b. no dividends can be declared or paid during the accounting period.

    c. dividends can be declared but not paid during the accounting period.

    d. net income results.

    e. none of the above.

_d_ 15. Net income is often called

    a. net earnings.

    b. profit.

    c. the bottom line.

    d. all of the above.

    e. none of the above.

_a_ 16. The statement of retained earnings indicates the relationship between

    a. the income statement and the balance sheet.

    b. sales and cash collected.

    c. beginning and ending cash.

    d. assets, liabilities, revenues and expenses.

    e. all of the above.

_c_ 17. The equation for the statement of retained earnings is

    a. net income - dividends = retained earnings.

    b. beginning retained earnings + net income + dividends = ending retained earnings.

    c. beginning retained earnings + net income - dividends = ending retained earnings.

    d. beginning retained earnings - net income - dividends = ending retained earnings.

    e. none of the above.

_C_ 18. The statement of cash flows is divided into the following categories:

    a.   cash inflows, cash outflows.
    b.   current, non-current.
    c.   operating, investing, financing.
    d.   assets, liabilities, equity.
    e.   revenues, expenses.

_b_ 19. The price earnings ratio (or multiplier) is computed as

    a.   dividends divided by market price.
    b.   market price divided by net earnings.
    c.   revenues divided by expenses.
    d.   stockholders' equity divided by net earnings.
    e.   market price divided by dividends.

_d_ 20. The notes (or footnotes) that accompany the financial statements

    a.   describe accounting rules applied in the preparation of the financial statements.
    b.   present additional detail about particular line items listed on the financial statements
    c.   present information about certain items not reported on the financial statements.
    d.   a, b, and c above.
    e.   are optional, and present any information the company would like to add to its financial statements.

EXERCISES

Record your answers to each part of these exercises in the space provided. Show your work.

1. What is the balance sheet equation? Apply that equation in each independent case below to compute the missing amount for each case.

	Case A	Case B	Case C
Assets	9400 (a)	$13,100	$6,500
Liabilities	$3,500	3,50 (b)	4,100
Stockholders' equity	5,900	9,600	2400 (c)

2. The balance sheet of Exeter Corporation contains the following items (in thousands). Mark each item as an asset (A), liability (L) or stockholders' equity (SE). Then, solve for the missing amount and prepare a balance sheet as of June 30, 19A.

L	Accounts payable	$350	A	Inventories	$175
A	Accounts receivable	300	A	Plant and equipment	650
A	Cash	200	L	Note payable	500
SE	Contributed capital	275	SE	Retained earnings	? 200

300
200
175
650
1325

350
500
275
1125

3. The income statement of Elegance Corporation contains the following items (in thousands). Mark each item as a revenue (R) or expense (E). Then, prepare an income statement for the year ended December 31, 19A.

E	Cost of goods sold	$225	E	Research and development	$ 12
E	Interest costs	40	R	Sales revenue	550
E	Provision for income taxes	20	E	Selling, general and administrative	110

Elegance Corporation
Income Statement
For Month Ended December 31, 19A

Revenue:
Sales $550
Total Sales $ 550
Expenses:

4. During April, the first month of the company's operations, Landon Inc. sold $150,000 to goods to customers for cash. In addition, Landon sold $350,000 of goods on credit to customers. Payments from these customers amounted to $130,000 during April; the remaining $320,000 had not been not received as of April 30th. How much revenue should Landon report on its income statement for April?

5. During October, the first month of the company's operations, Barbeton Corporation produced goods which cost $475,000. Goods with a cost of $375,000 were delivered to customers during October and $100,000 of goods were on hand at October 31. What amount should Barbeton report as costs of goods sold on its income statement for October?

6. What is the equation for the statement of retained earnings? Apply that equation in each independent case below to compute the missing amount for each case. Assume that it is the end of 19B, the second full year of operations for the company.

	Case A	Case B	Case C	Case D
Retained earnings, beginning of year	$4,500	$2,300	$3,500	(d)
Net income (loss)	575	(b)	3,100	$1,275
Dividends	275	990	(c)	925
Retained earnings, end of year	(a)	$2,500	$4,000	$600

7. During its first year of operations, Arbor Inc. performed landscaping services for which its customers promised to pay $315,000. Customers remitted payments amounting to $205,000 by the end of the year. Arbor paid $101,000 in cash for employee wages, $29,000 in cash for rent and $68,000 in cash for landscaping materials that had been used to perform its landscaping services. At the end of the year, Arbor owed $13,000 to one of its suppliers for landscaping materials that had been used during the year. Arbor has not yet paid its income taxes for the year. Its income tax rate is 25%. On the last day of the year, Arbor declared and paid dividends of $20,000. Required: (a) Determine the increase or decrease in cash during the year. (b) Prepare an income statement for Arbor's first year of operations. (c) Determine that amount of retained earnings that will be reported on Arbor's balance sheet at the end of its first year of operations.

8. Faxit Corporation began the year with $67,000 in cash. The company's statement of cash flows contains the following items (in thousands): Mark each item as a cash flow from operating activities (O), cash flow from investing activities (I) or cash flow from financing activities (F) Then, prepare a statement of cash flows for the year ended September 30, 19B.

___	Cash collected from customers	$1,000	___	Cash received from bank loan	$350
___	Cash paid for dividends	125	___	Cash paid for interest	75
___	Cash paid for income taxes	50	___	Cash paid to purchase equipment	325
___	Cash paid to suppliers	250	___	Cash paid to employees	425

SOLUTIONS TO SELF-TEST QUESTIONS AND EXERCISES

MATCHING

1.	E	4.	O	7.	L	10.	G	13.	I
2.	H	5.	J	8.	C	11.	A	14.	F
3.	M	6.	K	9.	D	12.	N	15.	B

TRUE-FALSE QUESTIONS

1. T

2. F - The balance sheet is prepared as of a certain date in time. The income statement and statements of retained earnings and cash flows cover a specified time period.

3. T

4. F - The balance sheet lists the company's assets, liabilities and its stockholders' equity.

5. F - Each asset is initially measured on the balance sheet by the total costs incurred to acquire it. Balance sheets do not indicate the current market values of the assets reported.

6. T

7. F - Revenues are normally reported on the income statement in the period in which the goods or services sold. The cash may change hands in a different accounting period.

8. T

9. F - Expenses are normally reported on the income statement in the period in which goods or services are used to earn revenues. This is not necessarily the same period in which cash is paid for the expense item.

10. T

11. F - The income statement reports only revenues and expenses. Dividends declared are reported on the statement of retained earnings.

12. F - The time dimension of both the statements of cash flows and retained earnings is the same as the income statement. The balance sheet is prepared as of a certain date in time.

13. T

14. F - The FASB develops accounting standards which are "generally accepted;" these standards are not law.

15. T

16. F - Investors and creditors need to obtain an understanding of a company's operations in order to understand the nature of the various items reported on the financial statements.

17. F - Internal control procedures can only safeguards against errors. Some errors may not be prevented or detected by a company's internal control procedures.

18. F - Internal control procedures can only safeguards against thefts and embezzlements. Certain frauds, such as those committed by collusion, may not be prevented or detected by a company's internal control procedures.

19. F - Even though a sole proprietorships is not a separate legal entities from its owner, it is still considered to be a separate accounting entity which are accounted for separately from its owner. The same applies to partnerships.

20. T

MULTIPLE CHOICE QUESTIONS

1.	c	5.	e	9.	d	13.	d	17.	c
2.	e	6.	a	10.	b	14.	a	18.	c
3.	e	7.	c	11.	e	15.	d	19.	b
4.	c	8.	a	12.	b	16.	a	20.	d

EXERCISES

1. The balance sheet equation is: Assets = Liabilities + Stockholders' Equity.

Case A

(a) = $3,500 + $5,900

(a) = $9,400

Case B

$13,100 = (b) + $9,600

(b) = $3,500

Case C

$6,500 = $4,100 + (c)

(c) = $2,400

2. The correct classifications of the items on the balance sheet are:

L	Accounts payable	$350	**A**	Inventories	$175
A	Accounts receivable	300	**A**	Plant and equipment	650
A	Cash	200	**L**	Note payable	500
SE	Contributed capital	275	**SE**	Retained earnings	?

Exeter Corporation
Balance Sheet
June 30, 19A
(in thousands of dollars)

Assets

Cash	$ 200
Accounts receivable	300
Inventories	175
Plant and equipment	650
Total assets	$1,325

Liabilities

Accounts payable	$350	
Notes payable	500	
Total liabilities		$ 850

Stockholders' equity

Contributed capital	$275	
Retained earnings *(see below)*	200	
Total stockholders' equity		475
Total liabilities and stockholders' equity		$1,325

To determine the amount of retained earnings, start by determining the total amount of stockholders' equity using the basic accounting: equation:

Assets = Liabilities + Stockholders' Equity

$1,325 = $850 + SE

SE = $475

Then, solve for retained earnings:

Stockholders' Equity = Contributed Capital + Retained Earnings

$475 = $275 + RE

RE = $200

3. The correct classifications of the items on the income statement are:

E	Cost of goods sold	$225	**E**	Research and development		$ 120
E	Interest costs	40	**R**	Sales revenue		550
E	Income taxes	20	**E**	Selling, general and administrative		110

Elegance Corporation
Income Statement
For the Year Ended December 31, 19A
(in thousands of dollars)

Revenues:		
Sales revenue	$550	
Total revenues		$550
Expenses:		
Cost of goods sold expense	$225	
Selling, general and administrative expense	110	
Research and development expense	120	
Interest expense	40	
Total expenses		495
Pretax income		$ 55
Provision for income tax		20
Net income		$ 35

4. Revenue is reported in the period in which goods are sold. As such, Landon should report total sales revenue of $500,000 on its income statement for the month of April. Total sales revenue was computed by adding cash sales of $150,000 and credit sales of $350,000.

5. Cost of goods sold expense is the total cost to produce the goods that were delivered to customers during the period. Barbeton should report $375,000, the costs of goods delivered to customers, as cost of goods sold expense on its income statement for the month of October.

6. The equation for the statement of retained earnings is: Ending Retained Earnings = Beginning Retained Earnings + Net Income - Dividends.

Case A

(a) = $4,500 + $575 - $275

(a) = $4,800

Case B

$2,500 = $2,300 + (b) - $990

(b) = $1,190

6. continued

    Case C

    $\$4,000 = \$3,500 + \$3,100 - (c)$

    $(c) = \$2,600$

    Case D

    $\$600 = (d) + \$1,275 - \$925$

    $(d) = \$250$

7. Increase or decrease in cash during the year (in thousands):

Collected from customers		$ 250
Paid to/for:		
Employees	$(101)	
Rent	(29)	
Suppliers	(68)	
Dividends	(20)	
Total cash payments		(218)
Increase in cash		$ 32

Arbor Corporation
Income Statement
For the Year Ended December 31, 19A
(in thousands of dollars)

Revenues:		
Sales revenue	$315	
Total revenues		$315
Expenses:		
Employee wage expense	$101	
Rent expense	29	
Landscaping materials expense *(68 + 13)*	81	
Total expenses		211
Pretax income		$104
Provision for income tax		26
Net income		$ 78

Ending Retained Earnings = Beginning Retained Earnings + Net Income - Dividends

Ending Retained Earnings = $0 (no beginning retained earnings) + $78,000 - $20,000

Ending Retained Earnings = $58,000

8. The correct classifications of the items on the statement of cash flows are:

O	Cash collected from customers	$1,000	**F**	Cash received from bank loan	$350
F	Cash paid for dividends	125	**O**	Cash paid for interest	75
O	Cash paid for income taxes	50	**I**	Cash paid to purchase equipment	325
O	Cash paid to suppliers	250	**O**	Cash paid to employees	425

Faxit Corporation
Statement of Cash Flows
For the Year Ended December 31, 19B
(in thousands of dollars)

Cash flows from operating activities:		
Cash collected from customers	$1,000	
Cash paid to employees	(425)	
Cash paid to suppliers	(250)	
Cash paid for interest	(75)	
Cash paid for taxes	(50)	
Net cash flow from operating activities		$200
Cash flows from investing activities:		
Cash paid to purchase equipment	$(325)	
Net cash flow from investing activities		(325)
Cash flows from financing activities:		
Cash received from bank loan	$ 350	
Cash paid for dividends	(125)	
Net cash flow from financing activities		225
Net increase in cash during the year		$100
Cash at beginning of year		67
Cash at end of year		$167

IDEAS FOR YOUR STUDY TEAM

1. Rewrite each of the definitions of the key terms that appear at the end of the chapter using your own words. Imagine that you are trying to explain each key term to a friend who has not taken any accounting classes. Then, get together with the other members of your study team and compare your definitions.

Accounting

Accounting entity

Accounting period

Audit

Balance sheet

Basic accounting equation

Financial Accounting Standards Board

Notes (footnotes)

Generally accepted accounting principles

Income statement

Report of independent accountants

Report of management

Securities and Exchange Commission

Statement of cash flows

Statement of retained earnings

2. Prepare a list of items that would be on the balance sheet of a typical college student. What are your assets? What are your liabilities? How would you determine your "equity?" Then, attach approximate or hypothetical values to each asset and liability listed. (Don't feel that you need to be too explicit about your personal finances.) Put your balance sheet into a form similar to Exhibit 1-2. (Instead of stockholders' equity, use one line called "equity.") Compare and contrast it with the balance sheets prepared by the other members of your study team.

3. Imagine that your study team decides to get together and start a new business to make some money next summer. First, decide what type of business you would operate. Then, decide you whether you should operate the business as a partnership or corporation. Discuss the advantages and disadvantages of each form of business. *(Supplement A)*

4. The accumulated amount of earnings less all dividends paid to the stockholders since the formation of the corporation is reported as retained earnings. Get together with the other members of your study team and see if you can agree on a company policy regarding the payment of dividends. Would you distribute all of the company's earnings each year as dividends? Why or why not?

CHAPTER 2
INVESTING AND FINANCING DECISIONS AND THE BALANCE SHEET

CHAPTER FOCUS SUGGESTIONS

The accounting terms and concepts covered in the next four chapters are introduced using the conceptual framework of accounting theory that was developed by the FASB. Chapter 2 begins the discussion of how the accounting function collects data about business transactions and processes the data to provide periodic financial statements. Emphasis is placed on transactions which affect only the balance sheet.

At first, you might want to approach this chapter by trying to memorize the recording of the business transactions that are presented. If you adopt this approach, you may encounter transactions in homework assignments or on an exam that differ somewhat from the ones that you have memorized, and you probably will not know how to record these transaction. You will be much more successful in this course if you try to understand the process itself. Use the transaction analysis concept that is introduced in this chapter to determine how a transaction affects the entity in terms of the accounting equation. As you analyze a transaction, carefully complete each step in the transaction analysis process. With practice, you will soon be able to analyze a variety of business transactions. This skill will come in handy throughout this course.

This chapter also introduces you to the concepts of debit and credit. Again, you should try to understand how debits and credits are incorporated into the transaction analysis model instead of memorizing the recording of selected business transactions. Continue to complete each step in the transaction analysis process as you prepare journal entries and use T-accounts to determine the impact of various transactions on the balance sheet. Again, with practice, you will soon be able to use journal entries and T-accounts to record a variety of transactions. *These skills are essential to your success in this course.* You will also need to know how to prepare a balance sheet and use the debt-to-equity ratio to analyze the balance sheet.

READ AND RECALL QUESTIONS

LEARNING OBJECTIVE
After studying this section of the chapter, you should be able to:
1. Define the objective of financial reporting, the elements of the balance sheet, and the related key accounting assumptions and principles.

OVERVIEW OF THE CONCEPTUAL FRAMEWORK

What group publishes the Statements of Financial Accounting Concepts that make up the conceptual framework of accounting? How does this conceptual framework relate to this *Financial Accounting* textbook?

Objective of Financial Reporting

What is the primary objective of external financial reporting? How are decision makers defined in the conceptual framework? What knowledge are decision makers expected to have?

Underlying Assumptions of Accounting

What is the separate-entity assumption? What is the unit-of-measure assumption? What is the continuity (or going concern) assumption? When would it be appropriate to violate the continuity assumption?

Elements of the Balance Sheet

What are assets? How are assets usually listed on the balance sheet?

Why are certain valuable intangible assets listed on the balance sheets of some companies, but not on the balance sheets of others? What is the asset recognition rule? How does the application of this rule determine which assets will be listed on a company's balance sheet and which will not be listed?

What is a liability? How are liabilities usually listed on the balance sheet? What are the two criteria that must be met before a liability is recorded?

What is stockholders' equity? What are the two major components of stockholders' equity? What do each of these components result from? What expectations (or hopes) do owners have when they invest in a business?

Financing Strategies

How is the debt-to-equity ratio computed? What does it measure? What is leverage? Why is debt financing considered to be more risky than financing with stockholders' equity?

At the end of 1995, Sbarro's debt-to-equity ratio was considerably lower than the average debt-to-equity ratio for the fast food industry. Was Sbarro's financing strategy more or less risky than that of its competitors? Why does Sbarro have such a low debt-to-equity ratio compared to its competitors?

What is the cost principle? How is cost measured under this principle? What are the advantages and disadvantages of the use of the cost principle to report assets on the balance sheet?

WHAT BUSINESS ACTIVITIES CAUSE CHANGES IN FINANCIAL STATEMENT AMOUNTS?

Nature of Business Transactions

There are two types of transactions: external events and internal events. What is a transaction? What is an external event? What is an internal event?

The definitions of assets and liabilities indicate that only economic resources and debts resulting from past transactions are recorded on the balance sheet. Has a transaction taken place if a contract is signed, but no cash, goods, services or property have changed hands yet? Why or why not?

LEARNING OBJECTIVE

After studying this section of the chapter, you should be able to:

3. Define an account and identify common balance sheet account titles used in business.

Accounts

What is an account? What is a chart of accounts? How is a chart of accounts organized? (Hint: Your reply to this last question should address each of the five types of accounts.)

Why don't all companies use the same chart of accounts?

HOW DO TRANSACTIONS AFFECT ACCOUNTS?

Why do business managers need to understand how transactions impact the financial statements?

Transaction Analysis

What is the basic accounting equation for a business organized as a corporation?

What is transaction analysis? What two principles underlie the transaction analysis process?

Duality of Effects

What is the duality of effects concept?

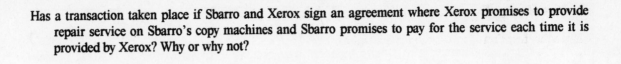

Has a transaction taken place if Sbarro and Xerox sign an agreement where Xerox promises to provide repair service on Sbarro's copy machines and Sbarro promises to pay for the service each time it is provided by Xerox? Why or why not?

Has a transaction taken place if a supplier ships goods to Sbarro in exchange for Sbarro's promise to pay for the goods? Why or why not?

Maintain the Accounting Equation

What are the four steps that are performed in the transaction analysis process?

LEARNING OBJECTIVE
After studying this section of the chapter, you should be able to:
5. Determine the impact of business transactions on the balance sheet using two basic tools: (a) journal entries and (b) T-accounts.

HOW DO COMPANIES KEEP TRACK OF ACCOUNT BALANCES?

What are the two important tools that aid in reflecting the results of transaction analysis and performing other financial analysis tasks?

The Direction of Transaction Effects

What is the direction of transaction effects rule?

What is the transaction analysis model? (Hint: Start with the basic accounting equation and then add the terms "increase" and "decrease" under each element of the basic accounting equation using the direction of transaction effects rule.)

The Debit-Credit Framework

What does debit mean? What does credit mean? (Add these two terms under each element of the basic accounting equation in your transaction analysis model above.)

Refer to your transaction analysis model. Do asset accounts usually have debit or credit balances? Do liability accounts usually have debit or credit balances? Do stockholders' equity accounts usually have debit or credit balances?

Are credits good? Are debits bad? What do these terms mean to accountants?

How can you remember which type of accounts increases with a debit and which types increase with a credit?

What is the equality check?

Analytical Tool: The Journal Entry

Where are transactions initially recorded? In what order? What is a journal entry? What is a compound entry?

Analytical Tool: The T-Account

What does the bookkeeper do after the journal entries have been recorded? As a group, what are the accounts called?

What is a very useful tool for summarizing transaction effects and determining balances for individual accounts?

What equation can be used to determine the balance of a T-account for financial statement purposes?

LEARNING OBJECTIVE

After studying this section of the chapter, you should be able to:

6. Prepare and analyze a simple balance sheet.

BALANCE SHEET PREPARATION

When can a balance sheet be prepared? When multiple periods are presented, where are the most recent balance sheet amounts usually listed?

SELF-TEST QUESTIONS AND EXERCISES

MATCHING

Match each of the key terms listed below with the appropriate textbook definition:

I   1. Account
L   2. Assets
C   3. Continuity assumption
S   4. Contributed capital
J   5. Cost principle
D   6. Debits
E   7. Credits
F   8. Journal entry
M   9. Liabilities
R   10. Primary objective of external
           financial reporting

O   11. Retained earnings
A   12. Report form
B   13. Account form
Q   14. Separate-entity assumption
N   15. Stockholders' equity
H   16. T-accounts
K   17. Transaction
P   18. Transaction analysis
G   19. Unit-of-measure assumption

A. This is a common balance sheet preparation form; assets are listed on the top and liabilities and stockholders' equity on the bottom.

B. This is a common balance sheet preparation form; assets are listed on the left side and liabilities and stockholders' equity on the right side.

C. Businesses are assumed to continue to operate into the foreseeable future.

D. The name for the left side of the account; represents increases in assets and decreases in liabilities and stockholders' equity.

E. The name for the right side of the account; represents decreases in assets and increases in liabilities and stockholders' equity.

F. An accounting method for expressing the effects of a transaction on accounts in a debits-equal-credits format.

G. Accounting information will be measured and reported in the national monetary unit.

H. An analytical tool for summarizing transaction effects for each account, determining balances for financial statement preparation, and drawing inferences about a company's activities.

I. A standardized format used by organizations to accumulate the dollar effects of transactions on each financial statement item.

J. An accounting assumption that requires assets to be recorded at the cash-equivalent cost, which on the date of the transaction is cash paid plus the current dollar value of all noncash considerations also given in the exchange.

K. An exchange between a business and one or more external parties, such as borrowing money from a bank, or a measurable event internal to a business, such as adjustments for the use of assets in operations.

L. Probable future economic benefits owned or controlled by the entity as a result of past transactions.

M. Probable debts or obligations of the entity as a result of past transactions which will be paid with assets or services.

44

N. The financing provided by the owners and the operations of the business.

O. Cumulative earnings of a company that are not distributed to the owners and are reinvested in the business.

P. The process of studying a transaction to determine its economic effect on the business in terms of the accounting equation: Assets = Liabilities + Stockholders' Equity.

Q. Business transactions are separate from the transactions of the owners.

R. To provide useful economic information about a business to help external parties make sound financial decisions.

S. Results from owners providing cash (and sometimes other assets) to the business.

TRUE-FALSE QUESTIONS

For each of the following statements, enter a T or F in the blank to indicate whether the statement is true or false.

__T__1. Assets are owned or controlled by the entity as a result of past transactions and have probable future benefit to the entity.

__T__2. For simplicity of presentation, individual asset categories reported on the balance sheet often include a number of assets with smaller balances which total the amount presented; the same is true for individual liability categories.

__F__3. Assets should be listed alphabetically when a balance sheet is prepared.

__T__4. Liabilities are listed on the balance sheet in order of maturity.

__F__5. Probable debts or obligations which result from past transactions are recorded as liabilities on the balance sheet only if the related amounts can be reasonably estimated.

__F__6. "Contributed capital" results when owners purchase stock from the company with no expectation of a return on the funds invested.

__T__7. Earnings that are not distributed to owners and are reinvested in the business by management are called retained earnings.

__F__8. Financing with stockholders' equity is considered more risky than debt financing because dividends must be paid to the company's stockholders on a quarterly basis.

__F__9. Assets are recorded at cost based on an arm's-length exchange with an external party; as a result, the balance sheet will always reflect the market value of the assets owned or controlled by the company.

__T__10. At times, important events which have an economic impact on the entity are not recorded in the entity's financial statements.

__F__11. All publicly-held companies must use the standardized chart of accounts developed by the FASB.

__F__12. The accounting equation must be in balance at the end of the accounting period, but does not necessarily need to be in balance after each individual transaction is recorded.

__T__13. Debit means the left side of an account and credit means the right.

__F__14. As a group, the accounts are called a journal.

T 15. A T-account is a simplified representation of a ledger account and can be used as a tool for summarizing the transactions effects and determining balances for individual accounts.

T 16. Purchasing as asset "on account" is synonymous with acquiring an asset "on credit."

F 17. The buying and selling of productive assets are categorized as financing activities.

F 18. Transactions must be measured precisely and objectively to ensure that the accounting results reported in the financial statements reflect exactly what happened during the period.

T 19. Accounting requires considerable professional judgment on the part of the accountant.

F 20. Because they spend most of the day recording repetitive, uncomplicated transactions, the work performed by accountants tends to be routine and clerical in nature.

MULTIPLE CHOICE QUESTIONS

Choose the best answer or response by placing the identifying letter in the space provided.

b 1. Providing external parties with economic information about a business so that they can make sound financial decisions is the primary objective of

    a. the Wall Street Journal.
    b. external financial reporting.
    c. news releases.
    d. financial analysts.
    e. external auditors.

c 2. The separate-entity concept maintains that a business must be accounted for separately from

    a. its owners.
    b. its owners, but only if the entity is a corporation.
    c. its owners, other persons, and other entities.
    d. other business entities only.
    e. other related businesses.

e 3. The continuity, or going-concern, assumption holds that a business will continue to operate

    a. at least until the end of the current fiscal year.
    b. for the life (lives) of its owner(s).
    c. into the foreseeable future.
    d. long enough to meet contractual commitments and plans.
    e. c and d above.

_e_ 4. A number of automobile manufacturers have published recalls of auto models containing seat belts that might fail under stress. Owners have been instructed to bring in their cars to have the seat belts replaced free of charge. The anticipated cost to the automobile manufacturers for replacing these seat belts should

   a. be ignored under the assumption that most of the cars are old, and if the belts have not failed up to now they probably will not do so; thus consumers are unlikely to go to the trouble of having the seat belts replaced.
   b. not be recorded because it cannot be precisely calculated.
   c. be recorded as an asset, then expensed when replacements actually are made.
   d. be recorded as each owner brings in a car and requests a replacement.
   e. be recorded as a liability because it resulted from past transactions, is probable and can be reasonably estimated.

_e_ 5. An event with an economic impact on the entity that is recorded as part of the accounting process is known as a(n)

   a. account.
   b. asset.
   c. external event.
   d. exchange.
   e. transaction.

_e_ 6. A transaction that is an external event can best be described as

   a. any event that happens outside of the business.
   b. any event that occurs outside the principal location of the business.
   c. any event that has an economic impact on the entity.
   d. anything involving persons not owning or employed by the business.
   e. an exchange of assets and liabilities between the business and one or more other parties.

_c_ 7. The duality (or duality of effects) concept states that

   a. there is more than one way of looking at any situation.
   b. there are two entities involved in every transaction.
   c. every transaction has at least two effects on the accounting equation.
   d. every transaction must be recorded twice; once in the ledger and once in the journal.
   e. every transaction has both good and bad aspects.

_c_ 8. Which accounts are affected if a fast food restaurant purchases paper napkins on credit from a supplier?

   a. Accounts payable and accounts receivable.
   b. Accounts payable and cash.
   c. Inventory and accounts payable.
   d. Inventory and accounts receivable.
   e. Inventory and cash.

_a_9. If the fast food restaurant pays the supplier for the paper napkins purchased on credit above, which types of accounts would be affected and what are the directional effects?

   a. Decrease an asset and decrease a liability.
   b. Decrease an asset and increase a liability.
   c. Increase an asset and decrease a liability.
   d. Increase an asset and increase a liability.
   e. None of the above.

_c_10. Which accounts are affected and what are the directional effects if the fast food restaurant purchases a new countertop, gives the supplier a cash down payment and signs a promissory note agreeing the pay the unpaid balance in 60 days?

   a. Increase cash, increase equipment, and increase notes payable.
   b. Decrease cash, increase equipment, and increase accounts payable.
   c. Decrease cash, increase equipment, and increase notes payable.
   d. Decrease cash, decrease equipment and decrease notes payable.
   e. None of the above.

_d_11. Journal entries are recorded in the journal in

   a. account order
   b. alphabetical order
   c. balance sheet order
   d. chronological order
   e. no particular order

_a_12. Increases to accounts on the left side of the accounting equation are recorded on the _____ side of the account and increases to accounts on the right side of the accounting equation are recorded on the _____ side of the account.

   a. left; right
   b. left; left
   c. right; left
   d. right; right
   e. any of the above could be correct under different circumstances.

_e_13. Which of the following is not true?

   a. A debit increases asset accounts.
   b. A debit decreases liability and stockholders' equity accounts.
   c. A credit increases liability and stockholders' equity accounts.
   d. A credit decreases asset accounts.
   e. All accounts are increased with debits and decreased with credits.

C 14. Which of the following sets forth the usual balances of asset accounts, liability accounts and stockholders' equity accounts, respectively?

    a. debit, debit and debit
    b. debit, debit and credit
    c. debit, credit and credit
    d. credit, debit and debit
    e. credit, debit and credit

a 15. A journal entry which affects more than two accounts is called a

    a. compound entry.
    b. double entry.
    c. general journal.
    d. internal entry.
    e. special journal.

d 16. A T-account is a simplified form of a

    a. balance sheet.
    b. customer invoice.
    c. journal entry.
    d. ledger account.
    e. purchase order.

EXERCISES

Record your answers to each part of these exercises in the space provided. Show your work.

1. The following economic events relate to a newly formed corporation which will operate a hardware store. Indicate whether or not the events would result in recording an asset on the company's balance sheet. If an asset would be recorded, indicate an appropriate account title and amount. Then, indicate the other accounts affected.

Event	Does an Asset Result?	Asset Account Title	Amount	Other Accounts Affected
The newly formed corporation issues stock for cash of $50,000.				
The company acquires equipment on account for $10,000.				
The company purchases a new delivery van with a sticker price of $27,999 by paying cash of $3,500 and signing a promissory note for $20,000.				
The company places an order for 50 lawnmowers for $100 each for delivery in three months.				
The company signs a contract for $55,000 for remodeling to be completed two months from now and gives the contractor a cash deposit of $5,500.				

The company pays $2,400 for insurance coverage for the next twelve months.				
The company's major stockholder purchases a computer for $2,500 for personal use from one of the company's suppliers.				
The company receives the lawnmowers; payment is due in 30 days.				

2. The following economic events relate to a newly formed corporation which will operate as a dry cleaner. Indicate whether or not the events would result in recording a liability on the company's balance sheet. If a liability would be recorded, indicate an appropriate account title and amount. Then, indicate the other accounts affected.

Event	Does an Liability Result?	Liability Account Title	Amount	Other Accounts Affected
The newly formed corporation issues stock for cash of $10,000.				
The company purchases office supplies on account for $1,300.				
The company purchases a new piece of machinery by paying cash of $400 and signing a promissory note for $2,000.				
The company places an order for 100 boxes of plastic bags for $30 each for delivery in 30 days.				
The company receives $2,500 from a local restaurant and agrees to dry clean its uniforms during the next six months.				
The company receives its telephone bill for $160 for the past month, but will not pay the bill until next month.				
The company borrows $20,000 from the local bank and signs a six-month note.				
The company receives the shipment of plastic bags; payment is due in 30 days.				

3. Pixar was formed in 1986 by Steve Jobs. The company, which develops and produces animated feature films, such as Toy Story, went public during 1995. The following table sets forth a partial listing of items recently reported on Pixar's December 31, 1996 balance sheet. For each item listed, enter one "X" to indicate the type of account and one "X" to indicate its usual balance. The first item has been completed as an example.

Account	Type of Account			Usual Balance	
	Asset	Liability	Stockholders' Equity	Debit	Credit
Capitalized film production costs	X			X	
Accounts payable					
Accrued liabilities					
Accumulated deficit (See note below table.)					
Cash and cash equivalents					
Common stock					
Film production costs payable					
Note payable to majority shareholder and accrued interest					
Prepaid expenses and other current assets					
Other assets					
Other receivables					
Property and equipment, net					
Short-term investments					
Trade accounts receivable, net					

Note: Even though the company was profitable in 1996, on a cumulative basis since the date of its incorporation in 1986, Pixar has not been profitable. That is, the total amount of net losses reported by the company have exceed reported net income. As a result, at the end of 1996, Pixar reported an accumulated deficit of approximately $15 million on its balance sheet. An accumulated deficit can be thought of as negative retained earnings. As such, the usual balance for the accumulated deficit account is the opposite of the usual balance of retained earnings.

4. Complete the follow table by indicating the amount and direction of the effect of each transaction (+ or -).

Transaction	Assets	Liabilities	Stockholders' Equity
A. Issued stock for cash of $14,000.			
B. Borrowed $15,000 from a local bank and signed a six-month promissory note.			
C. Purchased office supplies for cash of $2,500.			
D. Purchased inventory on account from a supplier for $8,300.			

E. Purchased $15,000 of equipment, paying $7,500 cash and the rest on account.			
F. Loaned $375 to an employee.			
G. Made $8,300 payment to supplier on account.			
H. Collected $375 on loan made to employee.			
I. Paid $8,500 to bank to reduce note balance.			
J. Collected $5,000 in cash from customers for services to be performed in the future.			
Ending balances			

5. Prepare journal entries for the transactions set forth in the prior exercise.

   A.

   B.

   C.

   D.

   E.

   F.

   G.

H.

I.

J.

6. Boardwalk, Inc. had assets of $64,000 and liabilities of $16,000 at the end of the year. What is the company's debt-to-equity ratio?

7. During the year, Rice Lake, Inc. purchased equipment and inventory totaling $13,000 on account from its suppliers. Rice Lake made payments on account to these suppliers in the amount of $6,800. At the beginning of the year, the balance in Rice Lake's accounts payable account was $5,000. What is the balance in Rice Lake's accounts payable account at the end of the year? (Hint: Use the T-account equation to determine the ending balance.)

8. During the year, Douglas Corporation's cash receipts amounted to $53,900 and the company made cash payments totaling $50,700. Douglas had $9,300 of cash on hand at the end of the year. How much cash did the company have on hand at the beginning of the year? (Hint: Use the T-account equation to determine the beginning balance.)

9. What does the entry for $2,000,400 in the T-account shown below most likely represent? What does the entry for $1,950,400 most likely represent? What is the balance in the account at 12/31?

Accounts Receivable		
1/1	$ 300,000	
	2,000,400	$1,950,400
12/31	$?	

10. Lisa and Charlie operate a yacht maintenance service which they incorporated as Reliable Yacht Repair, Inc. On April 1, 19B, the beginning of the season, the business had the following accounts and balances, in alphabetical order. All accounts have normal balances (debit or credit).

Accounts payable	$ 200
Accounts receivable	500
Cash (in bank account)	600
Computer	4,000
Contributed capital	6,800
Inflatable launch	4,000
Retained earnings	2,180
Maintenance supplies	80

A. Using the transaction analysis process outlined in the text [(1) identify the accounts affected, (2) classify each account as an asset (A), liability (L) or stockholders' equity (SE), (3) determine the amount and direction of the effect (increase (+) or decrease (-) on each A, L and/or SE) and (4) determine that the accounting equation remains in balance], perform transaction analysis for each of the transactions entered into by Reliable Yacht Repair during the period.

Transaction	Assets	=	Liabilities	+ Stockholders' Equity
1) Lisa purchased a new outboard motor for the inflatable launch for $1,500, giving the dealer a company check in the amount of $500 and a promissory note for the remainder, to be paid in four monthly installments beginning in 30 days.				
2) Charlie purchased $850 of maintenance supplies to be used in their business from a vendor on account.				

3) Lisa transferred $1,000 from their personal savings account into the checking account of the business.	
4) Lisa gave the local newspaper a company check in the amount of $200 to pay for an ad that was run on credit at the end of the winter season. (Consider this as a payment on account.)	
5) Last winter, Reliable delivered a yacht to Florida on account for a customer. The amount due from the customer was properly recorded at the time the delivery service was performed. The customer finally mailed a check for $500 to Reliable.	

B. Prepare journal entries for each of the transactions.

    1.

    2.

    3.

    4.

    5.

C. Set up T-accounts for the company, enter the beginning balances in the T-accounts, and then post your entries to the T-accounts.

D. Prepare a balance sheet for reliable Yacht Repair as of April 30, 19B.

11. The following is a partial list of Sbarro's transactions. For purposes of classifying the transaction for inclusion on the company's statement of cash flows, label each transaction as an investing or financing activity and as an inflow or outflow of cash.

_____   _____ Issued additional stock to investors for cash.

_____   _____ Borrowed money from a local bank.

_____   _____ Purchased productive assets.

_____   _____ Lent money to a franchisee.

_____   _____ Collected on the note signed by the franchisee.

_____   _____ Made a payment on the amount borrowed from the bank.

SOLUTIONS TO SELF-TEST QUESTIONS AND EXERCISES

MATCHING

1.	I	5.	J	9.	M	13.	B	17.	K
2.	L	6.	D	10.	R	14.	Q	18.	P
3.	C	7.	E	11.	O	15.	N	19.	G
4.	S	8.	F	12.	A	16.	H		

TRUE-FALSE QUESTIONS

1. T

2. T

3. F - Assets should be listed in order of liquidity.

4. T

5. T

6. F - Investors do expect (or hope) to receive two types of cash flows: dividends and gains from selling their stock in the company.

7. T

8. F - Interest must be paid on amounts borrowed; generally, there is no legal obligation to pay dividends to common stockholders. As a result, debt financing is more risky.

9. F - A disadvantage of the cost principle is that the continued use of historical cost on the balance sheet does not reflect any changes in the market value of assets owned or controlled by the company.

10. T

11. F - Each company would develop its own unique chart of accounts which conforms to the nature of its operations.

12. F - The accounting equation must be in balance after each individual transaction is recorded; as a result, it will be in balance at the end of the accounting period.

13. T

14. F - As a group, the accounts are called a ledger.

15. T

16. T

17. F - The buying and selling of productive assets are categorized as investing activities.

18. F - Not all transactions can be measured precisely and objectively; estimates often must be used.

19. T

20. F - The work performed by bookkeepers involves the routine, clerical part of accounting; accounting requires considerable professional judgment on the part of the accountants when complex transactions are analyzed.

MULTIPLE CHOICE QUESTIONS

1.	b	5.	e	9.	a	13.	e
2.	c	6.	e	10.	c	14.	c
3.	e	7.	c	11.	d	15.	a
4.	e	8.	c	12.	a	16.	d

EXERCISES

1.

Event	Does an Asset Result?	Asset Account Title	Amount	Other Accounts Affected
The newly formed corporation issues stock for cash of $50,000.	Yes	Cash	$50,000	Contributed capital
The company acquires equipment on account for $10,000.	Yes	Equipment	$10,000	Accounts payable
The company purchases a new delivery van with a sticker price of $27,999 by paying cash of $3,500 and signing a promissory note for $20,000.	Yes	Equipment (or van)	$23,500	Cash Note payable
The company places an order for 50 lawnmowers for $100 each for delivery in three months.	No			

The company signs a contract for $55,000 for remodeling to be completed two months from now and gives the contractor a cash deposit of $5,500.	Yes	Deposit	$5,500	Cash
The company pays $2,400 for insurance coverage for the next twelve months.	Yes	Prepaid insurance	$2,400	Cash
The company's major stockholder purchases a computer for $2,500 for personal use from one of the company's suppliers.	No			
The company receives the lawnmowers; payment is due in 30 days.	Yes	Inventory	$5,000	Accounts payable

2.

Event	Does an Liability Result?	Liability Account Title	Amount	Other Accounts Affected
The newly formed corporation issues stock for cash of $10,000.	No			
The company purchases office supplies on account for $1,300.	Yes	Accounts payable	$1,300	Office supplies
The company purchases a new piece of machinery by paying cash of $400 and signing a promissory note for $2,000.	Yes	Note payable	$2,400	Equipment Cash
The company places an order for 100 boxes of plastic bags for $30 each for delivery in 30 days.	No			
The company receives $2,500 from a local restaurant and agrees to dry clean its uniforms during the next six months.	Yes	Unearned revenue (or customer deposit)	$2,500	Cash
The company receives its telephone bill for $160 for the past month, but will not pay the bill until next month.	Yes	Accounts payable	$160	Utility expense
The company borrows $20,000 from the local bank and signs a six-month note.	Yes	Note payable	$20,000	Cash
The company receives the shipment of plastic bags; payment is due in 30 days.	Yes	Accounts payable	$3,000	Inventory

3.

Account	Type of Account			Usual Balance	
	Asset	Liability	Stockholders' Equity	Debit	Credit
Capitalized film production costs	X			X	
Accounts payable		X			X
Accrued liabilities		X			X
Accumulated deficit			X	X	
Cash and cash equivalents	X			X	
Common stock			X		X
Film production costs payable		X			X
Note payable to majority shareholder and accrued interest		X			X
Prepaid expenses and other current assets	X			X	
Other assets	X			X	
Other receivables	X			X	
Property and equipment, net	X			X	
Short-term investments	X			X	
Trade accounts receivable, net	X			X	

4.

Transaction	Assets	Liabilities	Stockholders' Equity
A. Issued stock for cash of $14,000.	+ $14,000		+ $14,000
B. Borrowed $15,000 from a local bank and signed a six-month promissory note.	+ 15,000	+$15,000	
C. Purchased office supplies for cash of $2,500.	+ 2,500 - 2,500		
D. Purchased inventory on account from a supplier for $8,300.	+ 8,300	+ 8,300	
E. Purchased $15,000 of equipment, paying $7,500 cash and the rest on account.	+ 15,000 - 7,500	+ 7,500	
F. Loaned $375 to an employee.	+ 375 - 375		
G. Made $8,300 payment to supplier on account.	- 8,300	- 8,300	

H. Collected $375 on loan made to employee.	+ 375 − 375		
I. Paid $8,500 to bank to reduce note balance.	− 8,500	− 8,500	
J. Collected $5,000 in cash from customers for services to be performed in the future.	+ 5,000	+ 5,000	
Ending balances	**$33,000**	**$19,000**	**$14,000**

5.

A.	Cash	14,000	
	Contributed capital		14,000
B.	Cash	15,000	
	Note payable		15,000
C.	Office supplies	2,500	
	Cash		2,500
D.	Inventory	8,300	
	Accounts payable		8,300
E.	Equipment	15,000	
	Cash		7,500
	Accounts payable		7,500
F.	Other receivables	375	
	Cash		375
G.	Accounts payable	8,300	
	Cash		8,300
H.	Cash	375	
	Other receivables		375
I.	Note payable	8,500	
	Cash		8,500
J.	Cash	5,000	
	Unearned revenue		5,000

6. First, calculate Boardwalk's stockholder's equity using the basic accounting equation:

Assets = Liabilities + Stockholders' Equity
$64,000 = $16,000 + X
$48,000 = X

Then, calculate the debt-to-equity ratio:

Total Liabilities / Stockholders' Equity = $16,000/$48,000 = 33%

7. The balance in Rice Lake's accounts payable account at the end of the year is $9,200 computed as follows:

Beginning balance + Effects on the increase side - Effects on the decrease side = Ending balance
$5,000 + $13,000 - $6,800 = X
$11,200 = X

8. Douglas Corporation had $6,100 of cash on hand at the beginning of the year computed as follows:

Beginning balance + Effects on the increase side - Effects on the decrease side = Ending balance
X + $53,900 - $50,700 = $9,300
X = $6,100

9. The entry for $2,000,400 most likely represents sales on account (or on credit) to customers. The entry for $1,950,400 most likely represents cash collections from customers on account. The balance in the accounts receivable account at 12/31 is $350,000 computed as follows:

Beginning Balance + Effects on the Increase Side - Effects on the Decrease Side = Ending Balance
$300,000 + $2,000,400 - $1,950,000 = X
$350,000 = X

10A.

Transaction	Assets	=	Liabilities	+	Stockholders' Equity
1) Lisa purchased a new outboard motor for the inflatable launch for $1,500, giving the dealer a company check in the amount of $500 and a promissory note for the remainder, to be paid in four monthly installments beginning in 30 days.	Inflatable launch + 1,500 Cash - 500		Note payable +1,000		

62

2)	Charlie purchased $850 of maintenance supplies to be used in their business from a vendor on account.	Maintenance supplies + 850	Accounts payable + 850	
3)	Lisa transferred $1,000 from their personal savings account into the checking account of the business.	Cash + 1,000		Contributed capital + 1,000
4)	Lisa gave the local newspaper a company check in the amount of $200 to pay for an ad that was run on credit at the end of the winter season. (Consider this as a payment on account.)	Cash - 200	Accounts payable - 200	
5)	Last winter, Reliable delivered a yacht to Florida on account for a customer. The amount due from the customer was properly recorded at the time the delivery service was performed. The customer finally mailed a check for $500 to Reliable.	Cash + 500 Accounts receivable - 500		

10B.

1) Inflatable launch   1,500
       Cash   500
       Note payable   1,000

2) Maintenance supplies   850
       Accounts payable   850

3) Cash   1,000
       Contributed capital   1,000

4) Accounts payable   200
       Cash   200

5) Cash   500
       Accounts receivable   500

10C. (T-accounts reordered in balance sheet order.)

Cash			
4/1	600		
(3)	1,000	(1)	500
(5)	500	(4)	200
4/30	1,400		

Accounts Receivable			
4/1	500		
		(5)	500
4/30	0		

Maintenance Supplies			
4/1	80		
(2)	850		
4/30	930		

Inflatable Launch			
4/1	4,000		
(1)	1,500		
4/30	5,500		

Computer			
4/1	4,000		
4/30	4,000		

Accounts Payable			
		4/1	200
(4)	200	(2)	850
		4/30	850

Note Payable			
		4/1	0
		(1)	1,000
		4/30	1,000

Contributed Capital			
		4/1	6,800
		(3)	1,000
		4/30	7,800

Retained Earnings			
		4/1	2,180
		4/30	2,180

10D.

Reliable Yacht Repair, Inc.
Balance Sheet
April 30, 19B

Assets

Cash	$ 1,400
Maintenance supplies	930
Inflatable launch	5,500
Computer	4,000
Total assets	$11,830

Liabilities

Accounts payable	$ 850	
Notes payable	1,000	
Total liabilities		$ 1,850
Stockholders' equity		
Contributed capital	$7,800	
Retained earnings	2,180	
Total stockholders' equity		9,980
Total liabilities and stockholders' equity		$11,830

11.

Financing	**Inflow**	Issued additional stock to investors for cash.
Financing	**Inflow**	Borrowed money from a local bank.
Investing	**Outflow**	Purchased productive assets.
Investing	**Outflow**	Lent money to a franchisee.
Investing	**Inflow**	Collected on the note signed by the franchisee.
Financing	**Outflow**	Made a payment on the amount borrowed from the bank.

IDEAS FOR YOUR STUDY TEAM

1. Rewrite each of the definitions of the key terms that appear at the end of the chapter using your own words. Imagine that you are trying to explain each key term to a friend who has not taken any accounting classes. Then, get together with the other members of your study team and compare your definitions.

Account

Assets

Continuity assumption

Contributed capital

Cost principle

Debits and credits

Journal entry

Liabilities

Primary objective of external financial reporting

Retained earnings

Report and account form

Separate-entity assumption

Stockholders' (or owners) equity

T-accounts

Transaction

Transaction analysis

Unit-of-measure assumption

2. Imagine that the members of your study team meet for lunch ten years from now and decide to go into business together. First, with the other members of your study team, decide what type of business you would operate. Then, individually, prepare a chart of accounts for your business. (Include only balance sheet accounts at this point.) Finally, get together with the other members of your study team and compare and contrast your charts of accounts.

3. Assume that the members of your study team work for an automobile manufacturer that installed seat belts, now known to be defective, in all of the automobiles that it sold during the last three years. Your employer has decided that the company must issue a recall to all of the owners of the cars in question and offer to replace the seat belts for the owners free of charge. None of the seat belts have been replaced yet. Get together with the other members of your study team and decide how you could reasonably estimate the potential cost to your company.

Then, use transaction analysis to determine how you would record the potential effect of this economic event on your company's accounting equation. Assign a logical name to the account that would be used to report the company's obligations to its customers under the recall, decide whether the account involved would be an asset or liability, and indicate whether the account would be increased or decreased when the obligation is first recorded. Then, indicate whether the account would be increased or decreased as the customers bring their cars in and the company replaces the seat belts. Compare your transaction analysis with that of the other members of your study team.

4. Assume that you recently discovered that a company whose balance sheet you are analyzing will only be in business for the remainder of this year. You realize that the balance sheet was prepared using the continuity (or going concern) assumption. How should the company's assets and liabilities be valued and reported on the balance sheet if the company's continuity is no longer assured? Get together with the other members of your study team and share your concerns. Consider using Sbarro's Balance Sheet as a basis for discussion.

CHAPTER 3
OPERATING DECISIONS AND THE INCOME STATEMENT

CHAPTER FOCUS SUGGESTIONS

Chapter 3 continues the discussion of how the accounting function collects and processes data to provide periodic financial statements. Emphasis is placed on concepts relating to the measurement of revenues and expenses and analyzing transactions which affect the income statement.

GAAP requires the use of the accrual basis of accounting for financial reporting purposes. It is important to remember that the timing of cash receipts and payments does not control the recording of revenues and expenses when the accrual basis is used; revenues are recognized when earned and expenses when incurred. The transaction model introduced in chapter 2 is completed in this chapter when revenues and expenses are added to the model. You should continue to complete each step in the transaction analysis process as you prepare journal entries and use T-accounts to determine the impact of operating activity transactions on the financial statements. You will also need to be able to determine whether an adjusting entry based on the transaction is required.

When cash is received before revenues are earned or paid before expenses are incurred, adjusting entries are often required at the end of the period to properly recognize (or record) the revenue earned or expense incurred during the period. Also, when cash is received before revenues are earned or paid after expenses are incurred, adjusting entries are often necessary at the end of the period to recognize the related revenues earned and expenses incurred during the period.

As you work through this chapter, try to understand how revenues and expenses affect the transaction model and why adjusting entries are required. You should also know how to prepare an income statement and statement of stockholders' equity, compute a company's effective tax rate, and use the return on investment ratio to measure profitability.

READ AND RECALL QUESTIONS

LEARNING OBJECTIVE
After studying this section of the chapter, you should be able to:
1. Understand the time-period assumption and the elements of the income statement.

RETURN TO THE CONCEPTUAL FRAMEWORK

Underlying Assumption of Accounting

What does the time-period assumption recognize? What time periods (shorter than the long life of a company) are used to meet decision makers' needs for periodic information? What are interim reports? What is a natural business year-end?

Elements of the Income Statement

Why are publicly traded companies such as Sbarro required to present three years of income information?

How do revenues result? How are assets and/or liabilities affected when revenues are recorded?

Why are expenses necessary? How are assets and/or liabilities affected when expenses are recorded?

How is a company's effective tax rate computed?

What are gains? What are losses? What are peripheral transactions?

LEARNING OBJECTIVE
After studying this section of the chapter, you should be able to:
2. Understand a typical business operating cycle and the phases in the accounting cycle.

INCOME MEASUREMENT

What are two other terms used to describe a company's operating cycle?

The Operating Cycle

What is the long-term objective for any business? What is the operating cycle? How would you determine the length of time for a company's operating cycle?

Short-Term Debt Financing and the Operating Cycle

Why do businesses need to borrow on a short-term basis? What are the sources of such financing?

LEARNING OBJECTIVE
After studying this section of the chapter, you should be able to:
3. Explain the accrual basis of accounting.

Accrual Basis of Accounting

What is the cash basis of accounting? How is financial performance measured when the cash basis of accounting is used? What types of businesses use the cash basis of accounting? Why isn't the cash basis of accounting considered appropriate?

Which basis of accounting is required by GAAP? When are assets, liabilities, revenues, and expenses recognized when this method is used?

LEARNING OBJECTIVE
After studying this section of the chapter, you should be able to:
4. Apply the revenue and matching principles to determine the timing and amount of revenue and expense recognition.

Timing of Revenues: The Revenue Principle

What three conditions normally must be met for revenue to be recognized (recorded) under the revenue principle?

When would an unearned revenue be recorded? What type of account is unearned revenue? What does the unearned revenue account balance represent? Why is this account known as a deferral? Why does this account need to be adjusted as time passes?

When would a receivable (such as interest, rent or royalties receivable) be recorded? What type of account is a receivable? What does the balance in the receivable account represent? Why is this account known as an accrual?

Determining the Amount of Revenue

What is the requirement of the historical cost principle? How is this principle applied to revenue recognition?

Management's Incentives to Violate the Revenue Principle

What do some managers do when their companies are experiencing financial difficulty? What often happens when such improprieties are discovered?

Timing of Expenses: The Matching Principle

What are the resources that are used to earn revenues called? What does the matching principle require?

Sometimes, the acquisition of goods or services occurs prior to their use and the company ends up owning or controlling something that will be of future benefit (that is, these goods or services can be used at a later date to generate revenues). What are three common types of assets acquired in this manner and what are the expense accounts that are related to each of these assets? Why are these asset accounts also known as deferrals? Why do these asset accounts need to be adjusted as time passes?

When would a payable (such as salaries, interest or property taxes payable) be recorded? What type of account is a payable? What does the balance in the payable account represent? Why is this account known as an accrual?

The Accounting Cycle

What needs to be established before you can measure a company's financial performance and financial position? How might the length of a company's operating cycle differ from that of its accounting cycle?

When are adjusting entries recorded? What types of accounts are adjusted?

Phases in the Accounting Cycle

When does Phase 1 of the accounting cycle take place? What types of transactions are recorded in Phase 1 of the accounting cycle? When does Phase 2 take place? What activities take place in Phase 2?

How are basic accounting concepts impacted when a computerized accounting system is used?

LEARNING OBJECTIVE
After studying this section of the chapter, you should be able to:
5. Apply transaction analysis to examine and record the effects of operating activities on the financial statements.

COMPLETION OF THE TRANSACTION ANALYSIS MODEL

What account is used to accumulate all past revenues and expenses minus any income distributed as dividends to stockholders? Does net income increase or decrease that account balance? When a net loss is reported, what is the effect on that account balance? Does the account balance increase or decrease when dividends are declared?

What is the new transaction analysis model? (Hint: Start with the transaction analysis model that was developed in chapter 2, expand that model to incorporate "dividends declared" and "net income (subtotal)" and then expand it again to incorporate expenses and losses, and revenues and gains. Insert the terms "increase" and "decrease" and "dr" and "cr" under each new heading using the direction rule and debit-credit framework described in chapter 2.) Do revenues normally have debit or credit balances? Do expenses normally have debit or credit balances?

The Feedback Value of Accounting Information

What caused Sbarro's stock price to fall from $50 per share at the end of 1991 to $27 per share by the middle of May 1992?

Transaction Analysis Rules

What is the transaction analysis rule when revenues are earned? Or, in other words, what is used to record the increase in revenues (a debit or credit) and the related increase in an asset or decrease in a liability (a debit or credit)?

What is the transaction analysis rule when expenses are incurred? Or, in other words, what is used to record the increase in expenses (a debit or credit) and the related decrease in an asset or increase in a liability (a debit or credit)?

LEARNING OBJECTIVE
After studying this section of the chapter, you should be able to:
6. Construct a simple income statement and statement of stockholders' equity.

PREPARATION OF THE INCOME STATEMENT AND STATEMENT OF STOCKHOLDERS' EQUITY

If an income statement is prepared before the adjusting entries for accruals and deferrals have been recorded, what is that statement called?

What is a multinational? What additional information is provided in the footnotes to the financial statements of multinationals?

What types of transactions are summarized on the statement of stockholders' equity? (Hint: There are at least four types.)

Financial Analysis

How is return on investment computed? What does it measure?

SELF-TEST QUESTIONS AND EXERCISES

MATCHING

Match each of the key terms listed below with the appropriate textbook definition:

L	1.	Accounting cycle	K	7.	Matching principle
A	2.	Accrual basis accounting	F	8.	Operating cycle
G	3.	Cash basis accounting	I	9.	Revenues
E	4.	Expenses	H	10.	Revenue principle
J	5.	Gains	D	11.	Time-period assumption
B	6.	Losses	C	12.	Timeline

A. Revenues are recorded when earned and expenses when incurred, regardless of when the related cash is received or paid.

B. Decreases in assets or increases in liabilities from peripheral transactions.

C. A visual representation of a series of business activities, listing dates and amounts over time.

D. The long life of a company can be reported in shorter time periods, usually months, quarters, and years.

E. Decreases in assets or increases in liabilities from ongoing operations.

F. The time it takes for a company to purchase goods or services from suppliers, sell goods or services to customers, and collect cash from customers. It is also known as the cash-to-cash cycle or the earnings process.

G. Revenues are recorded when cash is received and expenses are recorded when cash is paid, regardless of when the revenues are earned or expenses are incurred.

H. Revenues are recognized (recorded) when the earnings process is complete or nearly complete, an exchange has taken place, and collection is probable.

I. Increases in assets or settlements of liabilities from ongoing operations.

J. Increases in assets or decreases in liabilities from peripheral transactions.

K. Expenses are recognized (recorded) when incurred in earning revenue.

L. The recordkeeping process used during and at the end of the accounting period that results in the preparation of financial statements.

TRUE-FALSE QUESTIONS

For each of the following statements, enter a T or F in the blank to indicate whether the statement is true or false.

_F_1. Generally accepted accounting principles require a company to report the results of its operations for each calendar year.

_T_2. Publicly traded companies are required to present three years of income information to help users assess trends over time.

_T_3. A company's effective tax rate is computed by dividing its income tax expense by its income before income taxes.

_T_4. Gains and losses from peripheral transactions (that is, not related to the central operations of the company) are combined by most companies and reported in the other income category on the income statement.

_F_5. A company can only receive cash from a customer after it has completed delivery of a product or service to that customer.

_T_6. Many small businesses use the cash basis of accounting.

_F_7. Only publicly held companies must use accrual basis accounting.

_T_8. An exchange transaction has taken place if the customer promises to pay for the service performed by the company.

_T_9. The three criteria for revenue recognition are met by most businesses at the point of delivery of goods or services.

_T_10. Unearned revenue results when a customer pays in advance and the account balance represents the amount of goods or services owed to the customer or the refund due if the customer cancels the order.

_T_11. The resources that are used to earn revenues are called expenses.

_F_12. The time-period principle requires that all of the resources consumed in earning revenues should be recorded in the same period as those revenues.

_T_13. If an employee has earned wages in a one accounting period, but will not be paid until the next period, an adjusting entry will be necessary.

_F_14. Adjusting entries affect only income statement accounts; balance sheet accounts are not affected.

_T_15. Every adjusting entry must have either a credit to a revenue account or a debit to an expense account.

_T_16. There may be several operating cycles within an accounting period or the operating cycle may extend over more than one accounting period.

_T_17. A company's accounting cycle always coincides with its accounting period.

_F_18. The decrease in retained earnings that results is recorded when dividends are paid rather than when dividends are declared.

_F_19. Dividends are reported on the income statement as soon as they are declared.

_F_20. Net income on an accrual basis can never be the same as cash flow from operations.

MULTIPLE CHOICE QUESTIONS

Choose the best answer or response by placing the identifying letter in the space provided.

_e_ 1.   The concept that recognizes the fact that decision makers require periodic information about the financial condition and performance of a business is the

   a.   continuity assumption.
   b.   dual-aspect assumption.
   c.   interim assumption.
   d.   separate-entity assumption.
   e.   time-period assumption.

_d_ 2.   An interim report is a(n)

   a.   annual report.
   b.   estimated set of financial statements prepared in lieu of actually completing the steps in the accounting cycle.
   c.   news release by management summarizing some recent events.
   d.   quarterly report prepared for external users.
   e.   report issued right after year-end, before the auditors have had a chance to complete their work.

_e_3.   Revenues are _____ from ongoing operations.

   a.   increases in cash
   b.   increases in assets
   c.   settlements of liabilities
   d.   contra-expenses
   e.   either b or c

_e_4.   Expenses are _____ from ongoing operations.

   a.   decreases in cash
   b.   decreases in assets
   c.   increases in liabilities
   d.   contra-revenues
   e.   either b or c

_a_ 5. Gains are similar to _____ and losses are similar to _____.

    a. revenues; expenses
    b. expenses; revenues
    c. debits; credits
    d. credits; debits
    e. assets; liabilities

_c_ 6. The time it takes a company to purchase goods or services from suppliers, sell them to customers, and collect cash from customers is

    a. one month.
    b. one year.
    c. the operating cycle.
    d. the accounting cycle.
    e. either c or d.

_c_ 7. The _____ basis of accounting recognizes revenues and expenses when the cash changes hands, whereas the _____ basis of accounting recognizes revenues when earned and expenses when incurred.

    a. proprietorship; corporate
    b. American; international
    c. cash; accrual
    d. conservative; liberal
    e. financial; managerial

_e_ 8. *When* revenues or expenses should be recognized is a _____ issue; *what amounts* should be recognized is a _____ issue.

    a. cost-benefit; materiality
    b. matching; full-disclosure
    c. primary; secondary
    d. time-period; conservatism
    e. timing; measurement

_e_ 9. The earnings process is considered complete when

    a. the company has a written purchase order from the customer.
    b. the company has shipped the goods to its warehouse in the customer's town.
    c. the customer has given the company a deposit on the promised goods or services.
    d. the company has the goods on hand, or has begun the service promised.
    e. the company has delivered, or substantially delivered, the promised goods or services to the customer.

_a_ 10. Under the revenue principle, revenue is recorded as long as the earnings process is substantially complete, there has been payment or a promise to pay, and

    a. collection is reasonably assured.
    b. the check is in the mail.
    c. the company does not permit returns of its product.
    d. the customer is satisfied with the product or service.
    e. the sale has been recorded on the customer's books.

_b_ 11. Assume that you worked 30 hours during the week ending December 31st, but will not be paid until January 7th. Your employer recorded your earned wages as an expense in December, rather than in January. This is an example of

    a. income manipulation.
    b. the matching principle.
    c. the time-period assumption.
    d. the conservatism principle.
    e. the continuity assumption

_b_ 12. Revenues are measured at the cash or cash-equivalent value of the assets received from customers in accordance with the

    a. cash basis.
    b. historical cost principle.
    c. matching principle.
    d. revenue recognition principle.
    e. unit-of-measure assumption.

_b_ 13. Revenues _____ retained earnings, and normally have a _____ balance; expenses _____ retained earnings, and normally have a _____ balance.

    a. increase; debit; decrease; credit
    b. increase; credit; decrease; debit
    c. decrease; debit; increase; credit
    d. decrease; credit; increase; debit
    e. increase; credit; decrease; credit

_d_ 14. An accrual occurs when cash will be received or paid _____ revenues or expenses are recognized; a deferral occurs when cash is received or paid _____ revenues or expenses are recognized.

    a. at the same time; before
    b. at the same time; after
    c. after; after
    d. after; before
    e. before; at the same time

_e_ 15. The return on investment ratio

    a. is computed by dividing average stockholders' equity by average assets.

    b. is computed by dividing net income by total stockholders' equity.

    c. is computed by dividing the markup on a product by its sales price.

    d. measures a company's financial condition.

    e. measures the profitability of a company for investors who expect to earn money on their investment.

_d_ 16. An income statement which is prepared to reflect operating activities before adjusting entries for accruals and/or deferrals have been recorded is called an unadjusted income statement because

    a. total debits will not equal total credits.

    b. the statement of stockholders' equity, balance sheet and statement of cash flows have not yet been prepared.

    c. dividends have not been taken into account.

    d. it does not reflect generally accepted accounting principles based on accrual accounting.

    e. the related revenue and expense accounts are up-to-date but the asset and liability accounts are not.

EXERCISES

Record your answers to each part of these exercises in the space provided. Show your work.

1. The following economic events relate to corporation which operates as a law firm. Indicate whether or not the events would result in recording a revenue on the company's income statement. If a revenue would be recorded, indicate an appropriate account title and amount. Then, indicate the other accounts affected.

Event	Does an Revenue Result?	Revenue Account Title	Amount	Other Accounts Affected
The newly formed corporation issues stock for cash of $50,000.				
A customer makes a payment of $2,500 on account for legal services that were performed last year.				
A client pays a retainer of $15,000 for legal work to be performed during the next twelve months.				
The law firm completes legal work relating to a real estate transaction and is paid $5,500 when the papers are signed.				
A new client calls to request assistance in filing the documents for a patent; a fee of $3,000 is negotiated, and the parties agree that the work will commence next month.				

At the end of the period, the lawyers determine that $26,000 of legal work has not yet been billed to clients.				
The law firm borrows $10,000 from a local bank.				

2. The following economic events relate to a corporation which operates a clothing store. Indicate whether or not the events would result in recording an expense on the company's income statement. If an expense would be recorded, indicate an appropriate account title and amount. Then, indicate the other accounts affected.

Event	Does an Expense Result?	Expense Account Title	Amount	Other Accounts Affected
The company acquires new equipment on account for $155,000.				
Wages earned by employees of $33,000 are paid in cash.				
An advance payment of $12,000 is made for next year's rent.				
A payment of $375 was made on account to a consulting firm for services received and recorded last year.				
A shipment of 200 three-piece suits arrives; the suits were purchased on account for a total of $18,000.				
During the period, the company estimates that it used $125 of electricity and natural gas; the bills have not yet been received.				
A dividend of $15,000 is declared and paid.				

3. Complete the follow table by indicating the amount and effect of each transaction (+ or -) on the accounting equation.

Transaction	Assets	Liabilities	Stockholders' Equity
A. Issued stock for $25,000 of cash.			
B. Borrowed $50,000 from local bank in exchange for a promissory note due in one year.			

C. Signed a lease and made a payment of $4,500 to the landlord comprised of the current month's rent of $1,500 and the required $3,000 security deposit.			
D. Purchased equipment on account for $35,000.			
E. Purchased supplies for $6,500 on account and used them immediately while performing services for customers.			
F. Performed services and received cash of $57,000.			
G. Performed services on account for $28,000.			
H. Received a payment of $24,000 for services to be performed in the future.			
I. Collected $14,000 from customers on account.			
J. Paid employees cash of $11,000.			
K. Made a $35,000 payment on account for equipment that was purchased above.			
L. Made a payment of $6,500 on account for the supplies purchased above.			
M. Purchased supplies on account for $10,700.			
N. Received bills for the current month from telephone and electricity companies totaling $3,800; payments will be made next month.			
Ending balances			

4. Prepare journal entries for the transactions set forth in the prior exercise.

   A.

   B.

   C.

D.

E.

F.

G.

H.

I.

J.

K.

L.

M.

N.

5. Carl's Catering just completed its first year of operations. During the year, customer payments in the amount of $64,000 were received at the time the catering services were performed. Another $35,000 of catering services were performed on account for customers; payments amounting to $6,000 have been received from those customers. On the last day of the year, a local company paid Carl $3,000 for catering services to be performed in 30 days. Employee wages totaled $25,000 and were paid in cash. The food, beverages, and supplies that were used to perform the catering services were paid for in cash and amounted to $26,000. Unpaid bills for truck rentals during the year in the amount of $1,000 were on hand at the end of the year. On the last day of the year, Carl paid $12,000 in advance for rent on some office space. What was the net income for Carl's Catering on a cash basis? What was the net income on an accrual basis?

6. Lisa and Charlie operate a yacht maintenance service which they incorporated as Reliable Yacht Repair, Inc. On May 1, 19B, the business had the following accounts and balances, in alphabetical order. (Note that these are the April 30, 19B balances in the related exercise that you completed in chapter 2.) All accounts have normal balances (debit or credit).

Accounts payable	$ 850
Cash (in bank account)	1,400
Computer	4,000
Contributed capital	7,800
Inflatable launch	5,500
Maintenance supplies	930
Notes payable	1,000
Retained earnings	2,180

A. Using the transaction analysis process outlined in the text [(1) identify the accounts affected, (2) classify each account as an asset (A), liability (L) or stockholders' equity (SE), (3) determine the amount and direction of the effect (increase (+) or decrease (-) on each A, L and/or SE) and (4) determine that the accounting equation remains in balance], perform transaction analysis for each of the transactions entered into by Reliable Yacht Repair during May 19B.

Transaction	Assets	=	Liabilities	+ Stockholders' Equity
1) Lisa and Charlie remove the winter cover from a yacht, and perform maintenance to prepare it for the season. They mail a bill for $800 to the owner of the yacht.				

2)	The owner of another yacht presents Lisa with a check for $200 as an advance payment to paint his boat. He will send a check for the other $800 when the job is complete.	
3)	Charlie stops by the marina and pays $50 to buy supplies (that he uses later that day to refinish the trim on another boat). Charlie also buys $125 of paint on credit that he will use later to paint the boat in (2) above.	
4)	The owner of the boat in (3) above pays Charlie $150 for refinishing the trim.	
5)	Lisa opens the mail and finds a telephone bill for $75 and a bill in the amount of $300 for insurance coverage for the three month period beginning June 1st. The phone bill is not due for another 30 days, so she sets it aside. She pays the insurance bill.	

B. Prepare journal entries for each of the transactions.

1)

2)

3)

4)

5)

C. Set up T-accounts for the company, enter the beginning balances in the T-accounts, and then post your entries to the T-accounts. After posting your entries, review the activity in the company's T-accounts and note any observations.

D. Prepare an unadjusted income statement for Reliable Yacht Repair, Inc. for the month of May 19B.

7. Pixar had total stockholders' equity of $142,907,000 at December 31, 1995 and $170,804,000 at December 31, 1996. Net income of $25,319,000 was reported for the year ended December 31, 1996. What was Pixar's return on investment (ROI)?

SOLUTIONS TO SELF-TEST QUESTIONS AND EXERCISES

MATCHING

1.	L	4.	E	7.	K	10.	H
2.	A	5.	J	8.	F	11.	D
3.	G	6.	B	9.	I	12.	C

TRUE-FALSE QUESTIONS

1. F - The annual accounting period does not have to conform to the calendar year.

2. T

3. T

4. T

5. F - A company can receive cash before, at the same time as, or after it has completed delivery of a product or service to a customer.

6. T

7. F - Any company that prepares its financial statements in accordance with generally accepted accounting principles is required to use the accrual basis of accounting.

8. T

9. T

10. T

11. T

12. F - The matching principle requires that all of the resources consumed in earning revenues should be recorded in the same period as those revenues.

13. T

14. F - Each adjusting entry affects a balance sheet account and an income statement account.

15. T

16. T

17. T

18. F - Dividends are recorded when declared, and, as a result, decrease retained earnings when declared.

19. F - Dividends are reported on the statement of stockholders' equity; not on the income statement.

20. F - Net income on an accrual basis *could be* the same as cash flow from operations if the company was not required to make any adjusting entries; that is, if it always received cash at the time revenues were earned and paid cash at the time expenses were incurred.

MULTIPLE CHOICE QUESTIONS

1.	e	5.	a	9.	e	13.	b
2.	d	6.	c	10.	a	14.	d
3.	e	7.	c	11.	b	15.	e
4.	e	8.	e	12.	b	16.	d

EXERCISES

1.

Event	Does an Revenue Result?	Revenue Account Title	Amount	Other Accounts Affected
The newly formed corporation issues stock for cash of $50,000.	No			
A customer makes a payment of $2,500 on account for legal services that were performed last year.	No			
A client pays a retainer of $15,000 for legal work to be performed during the next twelve months.	No			

The law firm completes legal work relating to a real estate transaction and is paid $5,500 when the papers are signed.	Yes	Legal service revenue	$5,500	Cash
A new client calls to request assistance in filing the documents for a patent; a fee of $3,000 is negotiated, and the parties agree that the work will commence next month.	No			
At the end of the period, the lawyers determine that $26,000 of legal work has not yet been billed to clients.	Yes	Legal service revenue	$26,000	Accounts receivable
The law firm borrows $10,000 from a local bank.	No			

2.

Event	Does an Expense Result?	Expense Account Title	Amount	Other Accounts Affected
The company acquires new equipment on account for $155,000.	No			
Wages earned by employees of $33,000 are paid in cash.	Yes	Wage expense	$33,000	Cash
An advance payment of $12,000 is made for next year's rent.	No			
A payment of $375 was made on account to a consulting firm for services received and recorded last year.	No			
A shipment of 200 three-piece suits arrives; the suits were purchased on account for a total of $18,000.	No			
During the period, the company estimates that it used $125 of electricity and natural gas; the bills have not yet been received.	Yes	Utility expense	$125	Accounts payable
A dividend of $15,000 is declared and paid.	No			

3.

Transaction	Assets	Liabilities	Stockholders' Equity
A. Issued stock for $25,000 of cash.	+ 25,000		+ 25,000
B. Borrowed $50,000 from local bank in exchange for a promissory note due in one year.	+ 50,000	+ 50,000	

C. Signed a lease and made a payment of $4,500 to the landlord comprised of the current month's rent of $1,500 and the required $3,000 security deposit.	+ 3,000 - 4,500		- 1,500
D. Purchased equipment on account for $35,000.	+ 35,000	+ 35,000	
E. Purchased supplies for $6,500 on account and used them immediately while performing services for customers.		+ 6,500	- 6,500
F. Performed services and received cash of $57,000.	+ 57,000		+ 57,000
G. Performed services on account for $28,000.	+ 28,000		+ 28,000
H. Received a payment of $24,000 for services to be performed in the future.	+ 24,000	+ 24,000	
I. Collected $14,000 from customers on account.	+ 14,000 - 14,000		
J. Paid employees cash of $11,000.	- 11,000		- 11,000
K. Made a $35,000 payment on account for equipment that was purchased above.	- 35,000	- 35,000	
L. Made a payment of $6,500 on account for the supplies purchased above.	- 6,500	- 6,500	
M. Purchased supplies on account for $10,700.	+ 10,700	+ 10,700	
N. Received bills for the current month from telephone and electricity companies totaling $3,800; payments will be made next month.		+ 3,800	- 3,800
Ending balances	$175,700	$88,500	$87,200

4.

A.	Cash	25,000	
	Contributed capital		25,000
B.	Cash	50,000	
	Note payable		50,000
C.	Security deposit (or prepaid expense)	3,000	
	Rent expense	1,500	
	Cash		4,500
D.	Equipment	35,000	
	Accounts payable		35,000
E.	Supplies expense	6,500	
	Accounts payable		6,500

F.	Cash	57,000	
	Legal service revenue		57,000
G.	Accounts receivable	28,000	
	Legal service revenue		28,000
H.	Cash	24,000	
	Unearned revenue		24,000
I.	Cash	14,000	
	Accounts receivable		14,000
J.	Wage expense	11,000	
	Cash		11,000
K.	Accounts payable	35,000	
	Cash		35,000
L.	Accounts payable	6,500	
	Cash		6,500
M.	Supplies	10,700	
	Accounts payable		10,700
N.	Utility expense	3,800	
	Accounts payable		3,800

5.

Cash basis net income can be computed as follows:

Cash Receipts		
Catering service revenue ($64,000 + $6,000 + $3,000)		$73,000
Cash Payments		
Employee wage expense	$25,000	
Cost of food, beverage and supplies	26,000	
Rent expense	12,000	
Total cash payments		63,000
Cash basis net income		$10,000

Accrual basis net income can be computed as follows:

Revenues		
Catering service revenue ($64,000 + $35,000)		$99,000
Expenses		
Employee wage expense	$25,000	
Cost of food, beverage and supplies	26,000	
Truck rental expense	1,000	
Total expenses		52,000
Accrual basis net income		$47,000

6A.

	Transaction	Assets =	Liabilities +	Stockholders' Equity
1)	Lisa and Charlie remove the winter cover from a yacht, and perform maintenance to prepare it for the season. They mail a bill for $800 to the owner of the yacht.	Accounts receivable + 800		Maintenance revenue + 800
2)	The owner of another yacht presents Lisa with a check for $200 as an advance payment to paint his boat. He will send a check for the other $800 when the job is complete.	Cash + 200	Unearned revenue + 200	
3)	Charlie stops by the marina and pays $50 to buy supplies (that he uses later that day to refinish the trim on another boat). Charlie also buys $125 of paint on credit that he will use later to paint the boat in (2) above.	Maintenance supplies + 125 Cash - 50	Accounts payable + 125	Maintenance supplies expense - 50
4)	The owner of the boat in (3) above pays Charlie $150 for refinishing the trim.	Cash + 150		Painting revenue + 150
5)	Lisa opens the mail and finds a telephone bill for $75 and a bill in the amount of $300 for insurance coverage for the three month period beginning June 1st. The phone bill is not due for another 30 days, so she sets it aside. She pays the insurance bill.	Prepaid expense + 300 Cash - 300	Accounts payable + 75	Utilities expense - 75

6B.

1)	Accounts receivable	800	
	Maintenance revenue		800
2)	Cash	200	
	Unearned revenue		200
3)	Maintenance supplies expense	50	
	Cash		50
	Maintenance supplies (or paint)	125	
	Accounts payable		125
4)	Cash	150	
	Refinishing revenue		150

5)	Utilities expense	75	
	Accounts payable		75
	Prepaid expenses	300	
	Cash		300

6C. (T-accounts reordered in ledger order.)

Cash

5/1	1,400		
(2)	200	(2)	50
(4)	150	(5)	300
5/31	1,400		

Accounts Receivable

5/1	0	
(1)	800	
5/31	800	

Maintenance Supplies

5/1	930	
(3)	125	
5/31	1,055	

Prepaid Expenses

5/1	0	
(5)	300	
5/31	300	

Inflatable Launch

5/1	5,500	
5/31	5,500	

Computer

5/1	4,000	
5/31	4,000	

Accounts Payable

	5/1	850
	(3)	125
	(5)	75
	5/31	1,050

Unearned Revenue

	5/1	0
	(2)	200
	5/31	200

Note Payable		
	5/1	1,000
	5/31	1,000

Contributed Capital		
	5/1	7,800
	5/31	7,800

Retained Earnings		
	5/1	2,180
	5/31	2,180

Maintenance Revenue		
	5/1	0
	(1)	800
	5/31	800

Refinishing Revenue		
	5/1	0
	(4)	150
	5/31	150

Maintenance Supplies Expense		
5/1	0	
(3)	50	
5/31	50	

Utilities Expense		
5/1	0	
(3)	75	
5/31	75	

As of May 1, 19B, the company owed $850 to a vendor and $1,000 on a promissory note (due in four monthly installments). No payments have been made even though the company has cash on hand. These amounts appear to be past due and, as such, may adversely affect the company's credit rating.

Further, the company seems to have a large amount lot of maintenance supplies on hand. The $930 of supplies on hand on May 1st apparently were not used during May.

6D.

Reliable Yacht Repair, Inc.
Unadjusted Income Statement
for the month ended May 31, 19B

Revenues		
Maintenance revenue	$800	
Refinishing revenue	150	
Total revenues		$950
Expenses		
Maintenance supplies expense	$50	
Utilities expense	75	
Total expenses		125
Net income		$825

7.

ROI = Net Income divided by Average Stockholder's Equity

ROI = $25,319,000 / [($142,907,000 + $170,804,000) / 2]

ROI = $25,319,000 / $156,855,500

ROI = 16.1%

IDEAS FOR YOUR STUDY TEAM

1. Rewrite each of the definitions of the key terms that appear at the end of the chapter using your own words. Imagine that you are trying to explain each key term to a friend who has not taken any accounting classes. Then, get together with the other members of your study team and compare your definitions.

Accounting cycle

Accrual basis accounting

Cash basis accounting

Expenses

Gains

Losses

Matching principles

Operating cycle

Revenues

Revenue principle

Time-period assumption

Timeline

2. Make a list of companies or industries which might have exceptionally long operating cycles with the members of your study team. For each, estimate the length of its operating cycle. Is there a limit on the length of an operating cycle? How do you think that these companies might recognize revenue? How would these companies apply the matching principle to recognize expenses?

3. Get together with the other members of your study team and choose a well-known company. Then, on an individual basis, make a list of ten transactions that this company might enter into. (Make sure you include a variety of revenue and expense transactions.) Next, exchange transactions with another member of your study team. Prepare journal entries for the other person's transactions. Finally, get back together with the other members of your study team. Review the journal entries recorded for each set of transactions. Make sure you come to a consensus on how to record each transaction.

CHAPTER 4
THE ADJUSTMENT PROCESS AND FINANCIAL STATEMENTS

CHAPTER FOCUS SUGGESTIONS

In chapter 3, you learned that cash does not always change hands at the same time a revenue is earned or an expense is incurred. Cash may change hands before the revenue is earned or expense is incurred. This situation is referred to as a deferral. When this happens, the related revenue or expense must be deferred, and adjusting entries must be used as time passes to record the related revenue as it is earned or expense as it is incurred. On the other hand, the revenue may be earned or the expense may be incurred before the cash changes hands. This situation is referred to as an accrual. When this happens, the related revenue or expense must be accrued or recorded using adjusting entries.

Chapter 4 covers the adjustment process that is used to record these adjusting entries. As you analyze transactions which require adjustments, note that every adjusting entry must include either a credit to a revenue account or debit to an expense account. This rule makes sense if you understand the purpose of adjusting entries. The adjustment process ensures that all revenues earned during the period and all expenses incurred to generate those revenues are recorded.

Financial statements are usually prepared after the adjusting entries have been recorded. You will need to know how the financial statements relate to each other. This chapter concludes the coverage of the accounting cycle with the closing process. The revenue and expense accounts are closed (that is, reduced to a zero balance) by transferring their balances to the retained earnings account. Try to understand the closing process in terms of the transaction analysis model.

READ AND RECALL QUESTIONS

BUSINESS BACKGROUND

What might happen to the asset, liability, revenue and expense accounts when the end of the accounting period falls at a point other than the end of the operating cycle? What must be done?

What are accruals? What are deferrals?

Why would balance sheet valuation and income measurement be incomplete if the adjustment process is not performed? What are the primary inputs in determining end-of-period adjustments to revenues and expenses?

LEARNING OBJECTIVE

After studying this section of the chapter, you should be able to:

1. Explain the purpose of a trial balance.

THE TRIAL BALANCE

What is the first step normally taken at the end of the accounting period? What is a trial balance and what does it reflect? Why are the debit and credit columns of the trial balance totaled?

Assume that various errors were made during Phase 1 of the accounting cycle. What types of errors would not be detected by the preparation of a trial balance? (Hint: There are four types.)

What types of errors will detected by the preparation of a trial balance? (Hint: There are four types.)

As discussed above, a variety of errors may occur when a manual accounting system is used. A computerized accounting system may reduce the number of errors because of error checking functions that are built in. (For example, the system might not accept journal entries which do not balance.) Even so, what types of errors probably would not be prevented by an automated system?

Why do the individual account balances for long-lived assets remain at original cost? What is a contra account? What does it represent? What contra account relates to equipment? What is the usual balance of that contra account?

What is the difference between an asset's acquisition cost and its accumulated depreciation called? (Hint: There are at least three terms that describe this difference.)

ADJUSTING ENTRIES

When are adjusting entries recorded? Why are adjusting entries necessary?

What are the two types of internal transactions that require adjustment? What are deferrals? What are accruals?

Deferrals

When the company pays for its insurance coverage before the insurance coverage is used to generate revenues, what account is used to keep track of the prepayment? What type of account is it? What does the balance in that account represent at any point in time? Why does this account balance need to be adjusted as time passes? What other account is involved in the adjusting entry?

When the company receives cash from a customer in advance (that is, before the related service is performed), what account is used to keep track of the prepayment? What type of account is it? What does the balance in that account represent at any point in time? Why does this account balance need to be adjusted as time passes? What other account is involved in the adjusting entry?

> Remember that a deferral results when cash is received from a customer before the related revenue is earned. The amount is initially recorded in a liability account when the company receives the prepayment because the company owes something to its customer. (Debit cash and credit the liability.) As time passes, an adjusting entry is used to record the revenue as it is earned and reduce the liability to the customer. (Debit the liability and credit revenue.)
>
> On the other hand, a deferral also results when cash is paid to a vendor, supplier or other entity before the related expense is incurred. The amount is initially recorded in an asset account when the company makes the payment because the company will realize a benefit in the future. (Debit the asset and credit cash.) As time passes, an adjusting entry is used to record the expense as it is incurred and reduce the asset which has been used up. (Debit the expense and credit the asset.)

An Optional Recordkeeping Efficiency

To simplify recordkeeping, some companies record payments or receipts as expenses or revenues on the cash transaction date. When would this method result in proper balance sheet valuation and income measurement? When would this method necessitate one or more adjustments?

Accruals

How do accruals differ from deferrals? When do accruals occur? What is an accrued revenue? What is an accrued expense?

When the company's payday does not coincide with the end of its accounting period, an adjusting entry must be recorded at the end of the accounting period to accrue the wage expense. What account is used to keep track of the amount owed to the company's employees? What type of account is it? What does the balance in that account represent at any point in time? What other account is involved in the adjusting entry?

The routine entry made every payday includes a debit to wages expense and a credit to cash. How is the routine entry to record a payroll affected when an adjusting entry was made at the end of the previous accounting period?

Assume that the company loaned money to an employee in exchange for a note which includes interest at a given interest rate. What is the formula for calculating the amount of interest that is owed to the company at any point in time?

If the maturity date of the note does not coincide with the end of its accounting period, an adjusting entry must be recorded at the end of the accounting period to accrue the interest earned. What account is used to keep track of the amount of interest owed to the company? What type of account is it? What does the balance in that account represent at any point in time? What other account is involved in the adjusting entry?

The routine entry made to record the receipt of cash at the maturity date of the note includes a debit to cash and credits to notes receivable and interest income. How is this routine entry affected when an adjusting entry to accrue interest revenue was made at the end of the previous accounting period?

Remember that an accrual results when a revenue is earned before the cash is received. Depending on the company's accounting system, a routine journal entry to recognize this revenue may not have been recorded. If so, an adjusting entry must be used to record the revenue earned and the amount due from the customer. (Debit a receivable and credit revenue.) Later, when cash is received, the receivable is reduced. (Debit cash and credit receivable.)

On the other hand, an accrual also results when an expense is incurred (that is, a resource obtained is used to generate revenues) before the cash is paid. Again, depending on the company's accounting system, a routine journal entry to recognize this expense may not have been recorded. If so, an adjusting entry must be used to record the expense incurred and the liability to the vendor, supplier or other entity. (Debit the expense and credit a liability.) Later, when cash is paid, the liability is reduced. (Debit the liability and credit cash.)

Accruals and Deferrals: The Keys to Financial Reporting Strategy

Why are earnings reported by firms that make relatively pessimistic estimates often said to be of "higher quality?"

ADJUSTING ENTRIES ILLUSTRATED

Deferrals

Why does Sbarro's inventory need to be analyzed and adjusted at the end of the accounting period? What accounts are adjusted? What is the effect on each component of the accounting equation?

Why do Sbarro's prepaid expenses need to be analyzed and adjusted at the end of the accounting period? What accounts are adjusted? What is the effect on each component of the accounting equation?

What is depreciation? What is amortization? What does the accounting process of depreciation and amortization involve?

How is depreciation computed under the straight-line method? What is residual value? What types of assets typically have a residual value?

What accounts are adjusted when depreciation is recorded? What is the effect on each component of the accounting equation?

Accruals

What accounts are adjusted when interest revenue is accrued by Sbarro? What is the effect on each component of the accounting equation?

What accounts are adjusted when franchise related revenue is accrued by Sbarro? What is the effect on each component of the accounting equation?

What accounts are adjusted when a utility bill relating to the current period is received by Sbarro? What is the effect on each component of the accounting equation?

What accounts are adjusted when Sbarro owes interest that has not yet been recorded on a promissory note at the end of the accounting period? What is the effect on each component of the accounting equation?

What accounts are adjusted when Sbarro accrues its state, federal and foreign income taxes at the end of the accounting period? What is the effect on each component of the accounting equation?

End-of-Period Adjustments and Auditing

What is the most complex step in the annual recordkeeping process? Why does this step receive a great deal of attention from the company's auditors?

LEARNING OBJECTIVE
After studying this section of the chapter, you should be able to:
3. Present a complete set of financial statements: Income statement, statement of stockholders' equity, balance sheet, and statement of cash flows.

FINANCIAL STATEMENT PREPARATION

What is the income statement equation?

What is the retained earnings equation? How is the amount of ending contributed capital computed on the statement of stockholders' equity?

What is the balance sheet equation? What is the equation for the statement of cash flows?

Income Statement

How is earnings per share computed? Where can EPS disclosures be found? (Hint: EPS may be disclosed in two different places in the annual report.)

Statement of Stockholders' Equity

What amount(s) from the income statement is (are) carried forward to the statement of stockholders' equity?

Balance Sheet

What amount(s) from the statement of stockholders' equity is (are) carried forward to the balance sheet? How is the contra-asset account, accumulated depreciation, shown on the balance sheet?

Statement of Cash Flows

What amount(s) from the balance sheet is (are) carried forward to the statement of cash flows?

Cash Flow from Operations, Net Income, and Financial Analysis

How do some analysts interpret the ratio of cash flow from operations to reported net income? If the ratio is high, what might the analysts suspect?

Incentives, Accruals and Ethics

When actual financial performance lags behind expectations, what might managers and owners be tempted to do? Why? What do most SEC enforcement actions relate to?

LEARNING OBJECTIVE
After studying this section of the chapter, you should be able to:
4. Explain the closing process.

THE CLOSING PROCESS

Which types of accounts are considered to be permanent (or real) accounts? What happens to the balances in these accounts at the end of the accounting period?

Which types of accounts are considered to be temporary (or nominal) accounts? What happens to the balances in these accounts at the end of the accounting period?

What are the two purposes of closing entries? When are closing entries dated?

What accounts are closed? How are the accounts with credit balances closed? How are the accounts with debit balances closed? What is the other account affected by these closing entries?

What is the name of the trial balance that is prepared after the closing entries have been recorded? What types of accounts appear on this trial balance? What financial statement does this trial balance correspond to?

SELF-TEST QUESTIONS AND EXERCISES

MATCHING

Match each of the key terms listed below with the appropriate textbook definition:

C 1. Accruals
F 2. Adjusting entries
D 3. Book value
J 4. Closing entries
G 5. Contra account
K 6. Deferrals

E 7. Income summary
A 8. Permanent accounts
B 9. Post-closing trial balance
I 10. Temporary accounts
H 11. Trial balance

A. The balance sheet accounts that carry their ending balances into the next accounting period and are not closed at the end of the period.

B. Should be prepared as the last step in the accounting cycle to check that debits equal credits and all temporary accounts have been closed.

C. Revenues that have been earned and expenses that have been incurred by the end of the current accounting period but that will not be collected or paid until a future accounting period.

D. The difference between an asset's acquisition cost and accumulated depreciation, its related contra account. Also known as net book value or carrying value.

E. A temporary account used only during the closing process to facilitate the closing of revenues and expenses; it is closed to Retained Earnings.

F. End-of-period entries necessary to measure income properly, correct errors, and provide for adequate valuation of balance sheet accounts.

G. An account that is an offset to, or deduction of, the primary account.

H. A listing of all accounts with their balances to provide a check on the equality of the debits and credits.

I. Income statement accounts that are closed at the end of the accounting period.

J. Made at the end of the accounting period to transfer net income or loss to retained earnings and to establish a zero balance in each of the temporary accounts.

K. Previously recorded assets, liabilities, revenues, or expenses that need to be adjusted at the end of the period to reflect earned revenues or incurred expenses.

TRUE-FALSE QUESTIONS

For each of the following statements, enter a T or F in the blank to indicate whether the statement is true or false.

_F_ 1. A trial balance is considered one of the most useful financial statements because it provides detailed information to external users.

_F_ 2. A trial balance is prepared to give an accountant assurance that all the work done up to the point of adjusting entries was done correctly.

_F_ 3. Depreciation is recorded to reflect declines in the market values of long-lived assets.

_F_ 4. The cost of a long-lived asset less the accumulated depreciation on that asset is the net market value of the asset.

_T_ 5. The net book value, or carrying value, of an asset does not represent the current market value of the asset.

_T_ 6. Nearly all asset and liability accounts need to be analyzed and adjusted at year-end.

_T_ 7. When a payment is made before an expense is recognized, the asset recorded is known as a deferral.

_T_ 8. Previously recorded assets, liabilities, revenues, or expenses that need to be adjusted at the end of the period to properly recognized revenue or expenses are referred to as deferrals.

_F_ 9. An accrual results when a company earns revenue after cash has been exchanged.

_T_ 10. When an accrual exists, either another entity owes something to the company or the company owes something to another entity.

_T_ 11. The difference between an accrual adjusting entry and a deferral adjusting entry is in the timing of the cash payment or receipt that gives rise to that entry.

_T_ 12. Since adjusting entries often involve estimates, and often judgment on the part of the preparer, they can give rise to "income manipulation."

_F_ 13. The flow of information from one statement to the next dictates that the balance sheet should be the first statement prepared.

_T_ 14. The net cash flows that result from operating activities is usually not equivalent to the amount of net income reported by the company on the income statement.

_T_ 15. Temporary or nominal accounts are those used to accumulate data from the current accounting period only.

_T_ 16. Closing entries reduce the balances of income statement accounts to zero and transfer their balances to the retained earnings account.

MULTIPLE CHOICE QUESTIONS

Choose the best answer or response by placing the identifying letter in the space provided.

d 1. A trial balance is prepared to provide assurance that:

    a. journal entries were prepared correctly.
    b. the correct accounts have been debited and credited.
    c. all accounts have been updated.
    d. the total of the debit account balances equals the total of the credit account balances.
    e. all of the above.

e 2. A trial balance will help to uncover many types of errors including:

    a. the use of wrong accounts in journal entries.
    b. the use of wrong but equal amounts in journal entries.
    c. posting correct journal entries to the wrong accounts.
    d. posting wrong but equal amounts from correct journal entries to the correct accounts.
    e. none of the above.

e 3. A contra-asset is an account that is

    a. really a liability which is directly related to a primary asset account.
    b. an incorrectly entered asset account balance.
    c. an offset to an asset account.
    d. a reduction of the primary asset account.
    e. c and d.

e 4. The book value of a long-lived asset

    a. is not meant to represent its market value.
    b. is equal to the difference between an asset's acquisition cost and its accumulated depreciation.
    c. is also referred to as its net book value or carrying value.
    d. results from a cost allocation process.
    e. all of the above.

a 5. An example of a deferral would be

    a. the payment of a premium on an insurance policy before the coverage period.
    b. interest owed on a loan.
    c. interest earned but not yet collected on a loan made to a franchisee.
    d. wages earned by employees but not yet paid.
    e. all of the above.

d 6. An example of an accrual would be

    a. rent collected in advance of occupancy from a tenant.
    b. an insurance premium paid in advance of the start of coverage.
    c. a customer deposit for services to be provided in the future.
    d. interest owed on a promissory note.
    e. none of the above.

_C_ 7. Depreciation for each accounting period is computed using the straight-line method by

    a. dividing the cost of the asset by its useful life.
    b. dividing the residual value of the asset by its cost.
    c. dividing the difference between the cost of the asset and its residual value by its useful life.
    d. dividing the cost of the asset by two.
    e. any of the above.

_b_ 8. The difference between the cost of a long-lived asset and its related accumulated depreciation is its

    a. market value.
    b. net book value.
    c. current cost.
    d. selling price.
    e. salvage value.

_C_ 9. When preparing financial statements, it is best to start with the:

    a. balance sheet.
    b. statement of cash flows.
    c. income statement.
    d. statement of stockholders' equity.
    e. any of the above.

_a_ 10. SEC enforcement sanctions most often relate to:

    a. accrual of revenues and receivables that should be deferred to future periods.
    b. bonuses that have been paid to managers.
    c. deferral of expenses which have been incurred to future periods.
    d. overstatements of the book values of long-lived assets.
    e. unexpected increases in the book value of the company's stock.

_e_ 11. Accounts are closed by transferring their balances to:

    a. the temporary accounts.
    b. the permanent accounts.
    c. the balance sheet accounts.
    d. contributed capital.
    e. retained earnings.

_C_ 12. Accounts that are closed include the:

    a. assets accounts.
    b. liabilities accounts.
    c. revenue and expense accounts.
    d. all stockholders' equity accounts.
    e. all of the above.

EXERCISES

Record your answers to each part of these exercises in the space provided. Show your work.

1. You may recall that Lisa and Charlie operate a yacht maintenance service which they incorporated as Reliable Yacht Repair, Inc. They recently talked to their banker about obtaining a loan. The banker sounded interested, but wants to see last month's income statement. She reminded them that the bank only accepts financial statements that are prepared in accordance with GAAP. Lisa and Charlie ask you for advice. Charlie prepared the following trial balance shown below on May 31, 19B. He put the company's accounts in alphabetical order and tells you that all of the company's accounts have normal balances (debit or credit).

Accounts payable L	$1,050
Accounts receivable A	800
Cash (in bank account) A	1,400
Computer A	4,000
Contributed capital SE	7,800
Inflatable launch A	5,500
Maintenance revenue SE R	800
Maintenance supplies A	1,055
Maintenance supplies expense SE = E	50
Notes payable L	1,000
Prepaid expenses A	300
Refinishing revenue R	150
Retained earnings SE	2,180
Unearned revenue L	200
Utilities expense E	75

Prepare an unadjusted trial balance for Reliable Yacht Repair, Inc. as of May 31, 19B.

Cash	1400	
A R	800	
Prepaid Exp	300	
M. Supplies	1055	
Computer	4000	
In f Launch	5500	
A P		1050
N P		1000
Unearned Rev		200
Contributed Cap		7800
RE		2180
M. Rev		800
Ref Rev		150
M. Supp Exp	50	
Utilities Exp	75	
	13,180	13,180

116

2. Review the unadjusted trial balance you prepared in Exercise 1, identify the accounts that might require adjustment at May 31, 19B, and describe what information you would need to determine the nature and amount of the adjusting entry for each of the accounts identified.

Maint Supplies — month end inventory

Computer
Inflatable Launch } depreciation

Int incurred on note

Any unearned rev earned yet — see if goods or
services were delivered or generated

3. Prepare adjusting entries for the following situations. Assume that you are adjusting the related accounts as of the end of the year, September 30, 19B, and that no adjustments have been made since the dates given below.

A. The company had $4,000 of office supplies on hand on October 1, 19A, purchased $6,300 of supplies during the year, and had $1,200 of supplies were on hand on September 30, 19B.

4000
6300
──────
10300
- 1200
──────
9100

(AE)

Office Supplies Exp   9100
        office Supplies   9100

B. On December 1, 19A, a three-year insurance premium of $27,000 was paid for coverage beginning on that date. The payment was recorded in the prepaid insurance account.

9000/yr

(DE)

750
9000
84
60
60

Insurance Exp   750
        Prepaid Ins   750

C. A delivery truck was purchased for $33,000 on January 1, 19A. The truck's residual value is estimated at $3,000 at the end of its useful life of 5 years and will be depreciated using the straight-line basis.

Sept

33
-3
──────
30000
6000/yr

6000 × 9/12 (3/4)

4500
8000

4/ 16

(AE)

Depreciation Exp   4500
        Accum Dep, Truck   4500

(handwritten margin notes top-left) 2 mos
3000/m
×2
6000   DR

D. The company rents some of its unused factory space to a small manufacturer. The lease required an advance payment of $18,000 for six month's rent. The advance payment received from the tenant was recorded as unearned revenue upon receipt on August 1, 19B.

(handwritten)
Unearned Rev   6000
    Rev   6000

(handwritten margin notes)
37,500/10K
65,00
$32,500
/30
15,25
$ 75000
5

E. Employees work five days per week and are paid $75,000 every other Friday. The last payday during the company's fiscal year was Friday, September 26, 19B. The employees continued to work through September 30, 19B, but they will not be paid until Friday, October 10, 19B.

(handwritten)
2 days
15000 ×2   AE
Wages Exp   30000
    Wages Pay   30000

F. The Accounting Department sends bills to customers every Friday and records the revenue earned at that time. The last bills were sent on Friday, September 26, 19B. Services performed on September 29 and 30, 19B, amounted to $29,000. This amount has not been recorded.

(handwritten)
AR
Accts Rec   29000
    Rev   29000

4. Assume that the accountant neglected to analyze the company's accounts and did not prepare any adjusting entries at the end of the year. For each overlooked adjusting entry, first complete the "current year" columns by indicating the effect of the error on the company's assets (A), liabilities (L) and stockholders' equity (SHE) at the end of the year and its net income (NI) for the year. Indicate whether the effect of the error was to overstate (write "over") or understate (write "under") or have no effect (leave blank) on each of the financial statement totals. Then, do the same for the "next year" columns. Assume that the company recorded only "routine" entries during the next year; no one discovered or recorded the current year adjustments.

Transaction	Current Year				Next Year			
	A	L	SHE	NI	A	L	SHE	NI
The current year's depreciation on the building, furniture, equipment, delivery vehicles and equipment was not recorded.								
A customer payment made in advance for three months of services during the last month of the year was properly recorded; but no adjustment was made at year-end..								

118

	Current Year				Next Year			
Transaction	A	L	SHE	NI	A	L	SHE	NI
The premium paid on a three-month insurance policy during the last month of the current year was properly recorded; no adjustment was made at year-end.								
The entry to record employee wages during the last few days of the year was not recorded; the employees were paid during the next year.								

5. For purposes of computing its earnings per share, Pixar had weighted average shares outstanding of 46,989,000 during 1996 and 40,350,000 during 1995. Total shareholders' (stockholders') equity was $170,804,000 and $142,907,000 at December 31, 1996 and 1995, respectively. Net income amounted to $$25,319,000 during 1995 and $1,627,000 during 1994. What were the amounts of the company's earnings per share for 1995 and 1994?

6. Assume that Charlie (once again) prepared a trial balance in alphabetical order for Reliance Yacht Repair, Inc. on September 30, 19B, the end of the company's fiscal year.

Accounts payable	$1,500
Accounts receivable	6,000
Accumulated depreciation	2,000
Cash (in bank account)	6,900
Computer	4,000
Contributed capital	7,800
Inflatable launch	5,500
Insurance expense	500
Interest expense	80
Maintenance revenue	7,500
Maintenance supplies	1,500
Maintenance supplies expense	2,500
Notes payable	2,500
Prepaid expenses	500
Retained earnings	2,180
Refinishing revenue	3,500
Unearned revenue	2,000
Utilities expense	1,500

A. Prepare closing entries for the company.

B. Post the entries to the retained earnings account.

C. Prepare a post-closing trial balance.

SOLUTIONS TO SELF-TEST QUESTIONS AND EXERCISES

MATCHING

1.	C	4.	J	7.	E	10.	I
2.	F	5.	G	8.	A	11.	H
3.	D	6.	K	9.	B		

TRUE-FALSE QUESTIONS

1. F - A trial balance is not a financial statement that is provided to external users; it is simply a tool used by accountants.

2. F - Certain errors (that is, those which do not affect the equality of debits and credits) will not be detected by the preparation of a trial balance.

3. F - Depreciation is a cost allocation process; the amount of depreciation recorded does not represent the decline in the market value of the asset.

4. F - Cost less accumulated depreciation is referred to as the book value, net book value or carrying value of the asset; it does not represent the market value of the asset.

5. T

6. T

7. T

8. T

9. F - A deferral results when a company earns revenue after cash has been exchanged. An accrual results when a company earns revenue before cash has been exchanged.

10. T

11. T

12. T

13. F - The income statement should be prepared first.

14. T

15. T

16. T

MULTIPLE CHOICE QUESTIONS

1.	d	4.	e	7.	c	10.	a
2.	e	5.	a	8.	b	11.	e
3.	e	6.	d	9.	c	12.	c

EXERCISES

1.

Reliable Yacht Repair, Inc.
Unadjusted Trial Balance
at May 31, 19B

Cash (in bank account)	$ 1,400	
Accounts receivable	800	
Maintenance supplies	1,055	
Prepaid expenses	300	
Computer	4,000	
Inflatable launch	5,500	
Accounts payable		$ 1,050
Unearned revenue		200
Notes payable		1,000
Contributed capital		7,800
Retained earnings		2,180
Maintenance revenue		800
Refinishing revenue		150
Maintenance supplies expense	50	
Utilities expense	75	
Totals	**$13,180**	**$13,180**

2. Accounts which might require adjustment and information needed:

- Accounts receivable and maintenance and/or refinishing revenue - Amount of any maintenance and refinishing services that have been performed but not billed or recorded.

- Accumulated depreciation and depreciation expense -Estimated residual values and lives of the computer and inflatable launch.

- Maintenance supplies and maintenance supplies expense - Supplies on hand at year-end.

- Prepaid expenses and related expense account(s) - Date of prepayment and length of time until prepayment expires.

- Accounts payable and related expense account(s) - Nature and amount of any unpaid bills and estimates of any unbilled amounts that have not been recorded at year-end.

- Interest payable and expense - Date of note(s), principal amount(s), and interest rate(s).

- Unearned revenue and maintenance and/or refinishing revenue - Amount and type of work performed to date for customer(s) who paid in advance.

- Dividends payable and retained earnings - Amount of any dividends declared, but unpaid at year-end.

122

3.

A. Supplies expense 9,100
      Supplies 9,100
    ($4,000 + $6,300 - $1,200)

B. Insurance expense 7,500
      Prepaid insurance 7,500
    ($27,000 / 36 x 10)

C. Depreciation expense 4,500
      Accumulated depreciation 4,500
    (($33,000 - $3,000) / 60 x 9)

D. Unearned revenue ~~3,000~~ 6000
      Rental revenue 6000 ~~3,000~~
    ($18,000 / 6 x 2)

E. Wage expense 30,000
      Wages payable 30,000
    ($75,000 / 5 x 2)

F. Accounts receivable 29,000
      Service revenue 29,000

4.

Transaction	Current Year				Next Year			
	A	**L**	**SHE**	**NI**	**A**	**L**	**SHE**	**NI**
The current year's depreciation on the building, furniture, equipment, delivery vehicles and equipment was not recorded.	Over		Over	Over	Over		Over	
A customer payment made in advance for three months of services during the last month of the year was properly recorded; but no adjustment was made at year-end..		Over	Under	Under		Over	Under	
The premium paid on a three-month insurance policy during the last month of the current year was properly recorded; no adjustment was made at year-end.	Over		Over	Over	Over		Over	

The entry to record employee wages during the last few days of the year was not recorded; the employees were paid during the next year.		Under	Over	Over				Under

5. EPS = Net income divided by weighted average shares outstanding
1996 EPS = \$25,319,000 / 46,989,000 = \$.54 per share
1995 EPS = \$1,627,000 / 40,350,000 = \$.04 per share

6A.

1)
Maintenance revenue	7,500	
Refinishing revenue	3,500	
Retained earnings		11,000

2)
Retained earnings	4,580	
Insurance expense		500
Interest expense		80
Maintenance supplies expense		2,500
Utilities expense		1,500

6B.

Retained earnings

		10/1	2,180
		(1)	11,000
(2)	4,580		
		9/30	8,600

6C.

Reliance Yacht Repair, Inc.
Post-Closing Trial Balance
at September 30, 19B

Cash (in bank account)	\$ 6,900	
Accounts receivable	6,000	
Maintenance supplies	1,500	
Prepaid expenses	500	
Computer	4,000	
Inflatable launch	5,500	
Accumulated depreciation		\$ 2,000
Accounts payable		1,500
Unearned revenue		2,000
Notes payable		2,500
Contributed capital		7,800
Retained earnings		8,600
Totals	\$24,400	\$24,400

IDEAS FOR YOUR STUDY TEAM

1. Rewrite each of the definitions of the key terms that appear at the end of the chapter using your own words. Imagine that you are trying to explain each key term to a friend who has not taken any accounting classes. Then, get together with the other members of your study team and compare your definitions.

Accruals

Adjusting entries

Book value

Closing entries

Contra account

Deferrals

Permanent accounts

Post-closing trial balance

Temporary accounts

Trial balance

2. Adjustments can be categorized in the following manner:

- **Deferred expenses** - Pay cash now, record expense later
- **Deferred revenues** - Receive cash now, record revenues later
- **Accrued expenses** - Record expense now, pay cash later
- **Accrued revenues** - Record revenue now, receive cash later

Get together with the other members of your study team. Each person should select a well-known company from a different industry (such as fast food, airlines, publishing, manufacturing, etc.). Individually, think of two or three transactions that your company might enter into which fall into each of the four adjustment categories listed above. Then, get back together with the other members of your study team and compare your transactions. Were all of the transactions correctly categorized?

3. Get together with the other members of your study team and talk about the closing process. One or more of the members should explain why the temporary accounts are closed at the end of the accounting period. Do the benefits of closing these accounts justify the cost of going through the closing process? What would happen if these accounts weren't closed? Then, one of more members should explain why the permanent accounts are not closed. Is the decision not to close these accounts also a cost-benefit decision?

CHAPTER 5
THE COMMUNICATION OF ACCOUNTING INFORMATION

CHAPTER FOCUS SUGGESTIONS

The conceptual framework of accounting guides the discussion of the communication of financial information in Chapter 5. You should be familiar with the various people involved in the accounting communication process, their roles and the standards that provide guidance to these people. You will need to understand the principles and constraints that guide management and the FASB in deciding what financial information should be reported. You should also be familiar with the different financial statement and disclosure formats that are in use. Finally, you will need to know how to compute and interpret the current ratio and the gross profit percentage.

READ AND RECALL QUESTIONS

BUSINESS BACKGROUND

What is a manufacturer? What is a merchandiser? Is it possible for Callaway to be both a manufacturer and merchandiser of golf-related equipment?

Who are Callaway's four customer groups? Callaway values integrity in the communication of financial results. What benefits does the company realize from this emphasis on integrity?

LEARNING OBJECTIVE
After studying this section of the chapter, you should be able to:
1. Recognize the people involved in the accounting communication process (managers, auditors, information intermediaries, government regulators, and users), their roles in the process, and the guidance they receive from legal and professional standards.

PLAYERS IN THE ACCOUNTING COMMUNICATION PROCESS

Managers (CEO, CFO, and Accounting Staff)

Which two officers of the company are primarily responsible for the information in the financial statements and related disclosures? What do they sign? What does the accounting staff do?

Auditors

When the CPA firm signs an unqualified opinion, what responsibility does the CPA firm assume? By having its financial statements audited, Callaway reduces the risk to the private investors and financial institutions that the company's condition and results of operations were not as represented in the financial statements. What benefits does Callaway realize?

Information Intermediaries: Analysts and Information Services

How do sophisticated financial analysts analyze the information that they gather? What predictions do they make? What decisions do they make based on these predictions?

Where do financial analysts work? What is normally included in the reports that they write? What is market efficiency? Analysts, brokers, and investment bankers earn profits by charging commissions of securities transactions. As a result, what attribute should savvy investors adopt when using investment advice?

What are some of the electronic information services available? (List at least six types.)

Government Regulators

What types of firms are required to file reports with the SEC? What functions does the SEC perform when these forms are filed?

Users: Institutional and Private Investors, Creditors, and Others

What is an institutional investor? What is a private (or retail) investor? How do private investors differ from institutional investors?

Conflicting Interests of Managers, Stockholders, and Creditors

Why are the interests of managers, stockholders, and creditors often in conflict? How are these differing interests kept in check?

How do customers, suppliers and competitors use financial information about a company?

LEARNING OBJECTIVE
After studying this section of the chapter, you should be able to:
2. Understand the principles and constraints that guide management and the FASB in deciding what financial information should be reported.

GUIDING PRINCIPLES FOR COMMUNICATING USEFUL INFORMATION: THE REMAINING PARTS OF THE CONCEPTUAL FRAMEWORK

Qualitative Characteristics of Financial Information

What are the two primary qualitative characteristics that useful information should possess?

What is relevant information? What is reliable information?

What are the two secondary qualitative characteristics that useful information should possess?

What is meant by comparable information? What is meant by consistent information?

Full-Disclosure Principle

What is the full-disclosure principle? What does this principle require?

Materiality Constraint

How do accountants decide if an item is material or immaterial?

Cost-Benefit Constraint

What is recognized by the cost-benefit constraint? What costs should be considered?

How can an accountant justify the expensing of pencil sharpeners that are acquired for use in the business?

Conservatism Constraint

What is required by the conservatism constraint? What does this constraint produce?

Industry Peculiarities

How do long-standing and accepted accounting and reporting practices in various industries affect the financial statements issued by companies in those industries?

LEARNING OBJECTIVE
After studying this section of the chapter, you should be able to:
3. Analyze the different financial statement and disclosure formats used by companies in practice.

A CLOSER LOOK AT FINANCIAL STATEMENT FORMATS

A Classified Balance Sheet

What is meant when "consolidated" is included in the title of a financial statement?

What are two other names given to the balance sheet? What is the report format? What is the account format?

How does a classified balance sheet differ from one that is not classified? How are assets ordered on a classified balance sheet? How are liabilities ordered?

What is a current asset? What are long-term investments?

What are operational assets? What are two other terms used to describe operational assets? What is depreciation? What is book value (or carrying value)? How is book value computed?

What are intangible assets? What are deferred charges?

What are current liabilities? What are long-term liabilities?

What does stockholders' equity represent? What are the two sources of stockholders' equity?

What is par value? What does par value establish? When a corporation issues stock at net market value, what amount is reported as common stock? What account is used to keep track of the difference between the issuance price and the par value of the stock issued? What other names are used for this account? What information about the company's stock is disclosed on the face of the balance sheet?

Liquidity, Current Ratio, and Debt Contracts

What is working capital and how is it computed? How is the current ratio computed and what does it measure? What does a current ratio of 2 mean? Why would the lending agreement that Callaway has with its bank require the company to maintain a minimum specified current ratio?

Classified Income Statements

What are the five major sections found on some income statements? Do all income statements have all five sections?

Continuing Operations

What are the three common formats used to present the results of continuing operations? Which is the simplest format used to present the results of continuing operations? How is net income computed using this format?

What is the difference between the single-step and two multiple-step approaches? What is the primary difference between the two multi-step approaches? What line item and subtotal do nearly all companies separately report regardless of the format used to present the results of continuing operations?

What is cost of goods sold? What is gross margin or gross profit? How is it computed? How is the gross profit percentage computed and what is measured by this ratio?

What are operating expenses? What are selling expenses? What are general and administrative expenses?

What are nonoperating (other) items?

What is another name for the subtotal "income before income taxes?" How is this subtotal computed?

Discontinued Operations

What are discontinued operations? What are the reporting requirements if a company plans to dispose of a major segment of its business? Why is this information useful to users of the financial statements?

Extraordinary Items

What are extraordinary items? What are the related reporting requirements? Why is this information useful to users of the financial statements?

Cumulative Effects of Changes in Accounting Methods

What is the "cumulative effects of a change in accounting method?" Why do companies change accounting methods? (Hint: There are two reasons.) What are the related reporting requirements? Why is this information useful to users of the financial statements?

Earnings per Share

How is a company's earnings per share computed?

A Note on Taxes

What is intraperiod tax allocation?

Statement of Cash Flows Classifications

What are the three classifications of cash flows on the statement of cash flows?

Focus on Cash Flows

Why is the amount of net income reported usually different than the amount of cash flows from operations? What information is provided when the indirect method is used to prepare the cash flows from operations section of the statement of cash flows?

Notes to Financial Statements

What are the three types of notes (footnotes) to the financial statements? What does the description of significant accounting policies tell the user?

Alternative Accounting Methods and GAAP

When more than one acceptable accounting method exists, what does GAAP permit?

What are some examples of the types of information provided by the second category of notes to the financial statements? What are some examples of the types of information provided by the third category of notes?

THE DISCLOSURE PROCESS

Press Releases

Why do companies use press releases? What information does the stock market react to?

Annual Reports

What do the annual reports of privately held companies typically include?

What are the two sections of the annual reports of public companies? What types of information is included in the nonfinancial section? What are the principal components of the financial section?

What information is set forth in the Management Discussion and Analysis section of the annual report of public companies?

Quarterly Reports

How do quarterly reports differ from annual reports?

SEC Reports - 10-K, 10-Q, 8-K

What reports must be filed with the SEC by public companies? How does a From 10-K differ from an annual report? What information about its international sales strategy did Callaway set forth in its Form 10-K?

What is a Form 10-Q? What is a Form 8-K?

SELF-TEST QUESTIONS AND EXERCISES

MATCHING

Match each of the key terms listed below with the appropriate textbook definition:

H   1.   Comparable information
P   2.   Conservatism
B   3.   Consistent information
I   4.   Cost-benefit constraint
O   5.   Cumulative effects of changes
        in accounting methods
A   6.   Current assets
K   7.   Current liabilities
S   8.   Discontinued operations
R   9.   Earnings forecasts
C   10.   Extraordinary items
Q   11.   Form 8-K
D   12.   Form 10-K
T   13.   Form 10-Q

J   14.   Full-disclosure principle
E   15.   Gross margin (gross profit)
F   16.   Income before income taxes
U   17.   Income from operations
X   18.   Institutional investors
W   19.   Lenders (creditors)
Y   20.   Material amounts
G   21.   Par value
Z   22.   Press release
L   23.   Private investors
V   24.   Relevant information
M   25.   Reliable information
N   26.   Unqualified audit opinion
        (clean audit opinion)

A.   Assets that will be turned into cash or expire (be used up) within the longer of one year or the operating cycle.

B.   Information that can be compared over time.

C.   Gains and losses that are both unusual in nature and infrequent in occurrence; they are reported net of tax on the income statement.

D.   The annual report that publicly traded companies must file with the SEC.

E.   Net sales less cost of goods sold.

F.   Revenues less all expenses except income tax expense. Also known as pretax earnings.

G.   A legal amount per share established by the board of directors; it establishes the minimum amount a stockholder must contribute and has no relationship to the market price of the stock.

H.   Information that can be compared across businesses.

I.   The benefits of accounting for and reporting information should outweigh the costs.

J.   The requirement to disclose all relevant economic information of the business.

K.   Obligations to be paid with current assets normally within one year.

L.   Investors who purchase shares in companies.

M.   Information that is accurate, unbiased, and verifiable.

N.   Auditors' statement that the financial statements are fair presentations in all material respects in conformity with GAAP.

O.   Amount reflected on the income statement for adjustments made to the balance sheet accounts when applying different accounting principles.

P.   Care should be taken not to overstate assets and revenues or understate liabilities and expenses.

Q. The report used by publicly held companies to disclose any material event not previously reported that is important to investors.

R. Predictions of earnings for future accounting periods.

S. Results from the disposal of a major segment of the business; reported net of income tax effects.

T. The quarterly report that publicly traded companies must file with the SEC.

U. Net sales less cost of goods sold and other operating expenses.

V. Information that can influence a decision; it is timely and has predictive and/or feedback value.

W. Suppliers and financial institutions that lend money to companies.

X. Managers of pension, mutual, endowment, and other funds that invest on the behalf of others.

Y. Amounts large enough to influence a user's decision.

Z. A written public news announcement that is normally distributed to major news services.

TRUE-FALSE QUESTIONS

For each of the following statements, enter a T or F in the blank to indicate whether the statement is true or false.

F 1. The primary responsibility for the information presented in a company's financial statements lies with the company's auditors.

F 2. Only public companies go to the expense of having audited financial statements prepared.

T 3. Institutional investors usually employ their own analysts; private investors often rely on the advice of information intermediaries or turn their money over to institutional investors.

T 4. Information may be relevant but not reliable.

T 5. Immaterial amounts do not have to conform to GAAP or be separately reported because such amounts would not influence users' decisions.

T 6. Conservative accountants tend to choose accounting methods which understate assets and revenues and overstate liabilities and expenses.

F 7. The full-disclosure constraint recognizes that the cost of providing information should not exceed the benefit of having the information available.

T 8. Companies in the same industry often use the same accounting policies in their published reports.

F 9. Operational assets, like most other assets, are usually held for resale or investment and will eventually be turned into cash.

F 10. Intangible assets have no tangible substance and, as such, are not reported on the balance sheet.

F 11. Deferred taxes represent tax payments to be made in the future.

T 12. Capital in excess of par is also referred to as additional paid-in capital, contributed capital in excess of par, or paid-in capital.

_I_ 13. The current ratio measures the cushion of working capital that is maintained.

?   _T_ 14. There is no difference in the individual revenue, expense, gain, and loss items that are reported using each of the three different formats available to present the results of continuing operations.

_F_ 15. Gross profit is calculated by subtracting the cost of providing services to customers from the revenues earned by providing those services.

_F_ 16. Nonoperating (other) items include selling, general and administrative expenses.

_F_ 17. The results of all segments of the business that were disposed of ~~prior~~ to the beginning of the accounting period covered by the income statement must be separately reported, net of tax, on the face of the income statement. *during*

_F_ 18. An example of an extraordinary item would be a dangerous leak in a furnace requiring a extraordinarily expensive repair of the furnace.

_T_ 19. GAAP often permits more than one accounting method for use in the computation of the amount reported for selected line items on the financial statements.

_T_ 20. A change in accounting principles results in an inconsistent application of accounting methods; as such, footnote disclosure is necessary.

MULTIPLE CHOICE QUESTIONS

Choose the best answer or response by placing the identifying letter in the space provided.

_d_ 1. The primary responsibility for the information reported by a company rests with

    a. the company's auditors.
    b. accountants who prepared the information.
    c. SEC.
    d. company's management.
    e. the Board of Directors.

_e_ 2. Many privately owned companies have their financial statements audited because

    a. it is required by the SEC.
    b. they will eventually be public companies.
    c. the audit opinion lends credibility to the information presented.
    d. lenders and private investors often require this.
    e. both (c) and (d).

_a_ 3. The government regulatory agency that sets and enforces reporting standards for public companies is the

    a. SEC.
    b. Congress.
    c. FASB.
    d. Senate.
    e. AICPA.

_e_ 4. To be useful, information must be:

    a. relevant.
    b. reliable.
    c. comparable.
    d. consistent.
    e. all of the above.

_c_ 5. Relevant information is information

    a. that people want to know.
    b. about current activities only.
    c. capable of influencing decisions.
    d. that management feels is necessary to disclose.
    e. approved for release by the Board of Directors.

_b_ 6. Accurate, unbiased and verifiable information is information that is

    a. audited
    b. reliable
    c. relevant
    d. public
    e. consistent

_d_ 7. Similar accounting methods must be applied by businesses in order for their respective financial information to be

    a. publishable.
    b. reliable.
    c. relevant.
    d. comparable.
    e. cost beneficial.

_c_ 8. Consistent information is information that

    a. can be compared across businesses.
    b. is capable of influencing decisions.
    c. can be compared over time within a company.
    d. is accurate, unbiased, and verifiable.
    e. never changes.

_d_ 9. The _____ constraint requires that care should be taken to avoid overstating revenues and assets.

    a. materiality
    b. cost-benefit
    c. relevancy
    d. conservatism
    e. full disclosure

a 10. The cost to produce and report financial information must not exceed

    a. the benefit gained from the disclosure.
    b. a certain percentage of net income.
    c. the company's revenues.
    d. an amount set by the FASB.
    e. none of the above; all information must be reported.

b 11. The current ratio compares

    a. cash to current liabilities.
    b. current assets to current liabilities.
    c. current assets to noncurrent assets.
    d. current assets to current liabilities and equity.
    e. current assets to total assets.

a 12. Operational assets include

    a. property, plant and equipment.
    b. inventory.
    c. intangible assets.
    d. both (a) and (c).
    e. all of the above.

b 13. The operational asset that does not have any related accumulated depreciation is:

    a. buildings.
    b. land.
    c. equipment.
    d. furniture and fixtures.
    e. tools.

a 14. Net book value or carrying value:

    a. is computed by subtracting accumulated depreciation from the initial cost of the operational asset.
    b. measures the current market value of the operational asset.
    c. represents the cost that has been apportioned to expense.
    d. represents the historical cost of the company's fixed assets.
    e. All of the above.

d 15. The par value of stock is

    a. what the first person who bought the shares paid for them.
    b. an arbitrary number set by the company meaning nothing to accountants.
    c. the approximate amount the company expects to realize for newly issued stock.
    d. a legal term, setting a value below which the stock cannot be sold.
    e. equal to contributed capital.

_e_ 16. Gross profit, or gross margin, is

    a. the same as net income.
    b. equal to income before taxes.
    c. another word for revenues
    d. equal to income before extraordinary items.
    e. sales less cost of goods sold.

_a_ 17. Selling, general and administrative expenses are

    a. operating expenses
    b. part of the gross profit calculation.
    c. non-operating items.
    d. extraordinary items.
    e. not included in a single-step income statement.

_b_ 18. Information relating to a company's sales to customers in Europe would most likely

    a. not be found in the annual report.
    b. be disclosed in a footnote to the financial statements.
    c. be reported on the income statement.
    d. be discussed only in the management discussion and analysis section of the annual report.
    e. be reported on the balance sheet.

_c_ 19. Unexpected earnings are defined as

    a. net income earned when the company thought it was going to have a loss.
    b. being able to obtain a higher selling price than expected for merchandise.
    c. the difference between analysts' expectations of earnings and actual earnings.
    d. sales to a new market sector.
    e. earnings discovered by outside accountants during the annual audit.

EXERCISES

Record your answers to each part of these exercises in the space provided. Show your work.

1. You were introduced to Pixar, a public company, in the third exercise in chapter 2 of this Study Guide. Presented below is a listing of the financial statement items and amounts adapted from a recent Pixar income statement and balance sheet. (Assume the year is 19B.) Except as noted below, these items have normal debit and credit balances and are reported in thousands of dollars. Average shares outstanding were 46,989,000 during 19B.

Accounts payable	$ 1,060	
Accrued liabilities	5,262	
Accumulated deficit *(See note in chapter 2.)*	15,407	(debit)
Animation services revenues	3,947	
Capitalized film production costs *(current asset)*	1,372	
Capitalized film production costs, net of current portion	1,578	
Cash and cash equivalents	44,648	
Common stock	187,308	
Cost of revenues *(Similar to cost of goods sold.)*	4,703	
Film revenues	18,847	
General and administrative expenses	5,577	
Income tax expense	1,906	
Other components of stockholders' equity *(See note below table.)*	1,097	(debit)
Other assets	1,588	
Other income, net	8,031	
Other receivables	5,390	
Patent licensing revenues	9,127	
Prepaid expenses and other current assets	982	
Property and equipment, net	4,655	
Research and development expenses	6,985	
Sales and marketing expenses	1,768	
Short-term investments	116,321	
Software revenues	6,306	
Trade accounts receivable, net	929	
Unearned revenue	337	

Note: At this point, do not be concerned with these "other components." Simply include this line under stockholders' equity. The components are covered in an advanced accounting course.

A. Prepare in good form a multiple-step income statement (showing both gross profit and operating income) for the year ended December 31, 19B Last year, Pixar's gross margin percentage was 80.3%. Compute the current year's percentage and interpret its meaning.

B. Prepare in good form a classified balance sheet as of December 31, 19B. Last year, Pixar's current ratio was 14.72. Compute this year's current ratio and interpret its meaning.

2. Presented below are selected items listed on a recent balance sheet of Arlington Construction as of June 30, 19A, the end of its fiscal year.

Current assets	$ 350,000	Current liabilities	$700,000
Total assets	1,300,000	Total liabilities	950,000

A. Compute the company's working capital and its current ratio at the end of 19A.

B. Listed below are selected transactions from the first quarter of 19B. Describe the effect (increase, decrease or none) of each transaction as indicated. Each transaction is independent.

Transaction	Current Assets	Current Liabilities	Working Capital	Current Ratio
Collection of cash from customers on account in the amount of $150,000.				
Payment of cash to vendors on account in the amount of $300,000.				
Receipt of proceeds of $100,000 from long-term note payable.				
Payment of $100,000 on long-term note payable.				

3. Presented below are selected items listed on a recent balance sheet of McIntyre, Inc. as of December 31, 19A, the end of its year.

Current assets	$ 700,000	Current liabilities	$350,000
Total assets	1,800,000	Total liabilities	850,000

A. Compute the company's working capital and its current ratio at the end of 19A.

B. Listed below are selected transactions from the first quarter of 19B. Describe the effect (increase, decrease or none) of each transaction as indicated. Each transaction is independent.

Transaction	Current Assets	Current Liabilities	Working Capital	Current Ratio
Collection of cash from customers on account in the amount of $75,000.				
Payment of cash to vendors on account in the amount of $150,000.				
Receipt of proceeds of $200,000 from long-term note payable.				

Payment of $200,000 on long-term note payable.				

4. Presented below are selected subtotals (in millions) from Innovative Software Development Companies income statement for 19B.

Total revenues	$40,000
Cost of revenues	20,000
Income from operations	10,000

Listed below are hypothetical additional transactions that you should assume took place during the year. Complete the following table, indicating the effect (increase, decrease or none) of each additional transaction on the items and ratios indicated. Consider each transaction independently.

Transaction	Gross Profit	Gross Profit Percentage	Income from Operations
Revenues earned on account amounted to $200; the related cost of revenues amounted to $100.			
Revenues earned on account amounted to $300; the related cost of revenues amounted to $100.			
Revenues earned on account amounted to $200; the related cost of revenues amounted to $150.			
Additional research and development expenses amounted to $400.			

5. Determine the missing amounts in each of the following independent cases.

	Case A	Case B	Case C	Case D
Administrative expenses	$ 25,000	$ 90,000	$?	$?
Cost of goods sold	50,000	?	55,000	125,000
Gross margin	?	300,000	100,000	?
Income before income taxes	?	100,000	?	?
Income tax expense	15,000	?	?	10,000
Net income	?	70,000	35,000	?
Operating expenses	?	?	50,000	100,000
Sales revenue	125,000	600,000	?	250,000
Selling expenses	10,000	?	15,000	35,000

6. Enterprise Security, Inc. issued 1,000,000 shares of its $.25 par value stock for $1,250,000. Prepare the journal entry required to record the stock issuance.

SOLUTIONS TO SELF-TEST QUESTIONS AND EXERCISES

MATCHING

1. H	7. K	12. D	17. U	22. Z
2. P	8. S	13. T	18. X	23. L
3. B	9. R	14. J	19. W	24. V
4. I	10. C	15. E	20. Y	25. M
5. O	11. Q	16. F	21. G	26. N
6. A				

TRUE-FALSE QUESTIONS

1. F – The primary responsibility for the information presented in a company's financial statements lies with management as represented by the highest officer in the company and the highest officer associated with the financial and accounting side of the business.

2. F – While publicly-traded companies are required by the SEC to have their financial statements audited by CPAs, many privately owned companies also have their financial statements audited.

3. T

4. T

5. T

6. T

7. F – The cost-benefit constraint recognizes that the cost of providing information should not exceed the benefit of having the information available. The full-disclosure principle requires a business to clearly report all required relevant information about the economic affairs of the business in its financial statements.

8. T

9. F Operational asset include tangible assets that are acquired for use in operating the business rather than for resale as inventory items or held as investments.

10. F – Internally developed intangible assets often are not reported on the balance sheet of a company because there is no identifiable transaction (not because there is no tangible substance to these assets). However, intangible assets that are material and purchased from others are reported on the balance sheet.

11. F – Depending on the circumstances, deferred taxes can represent the amount of income taxes that will most likely be paid *or saved* in the future.

12. T

13. T

14. T

15. F – Gross profit is reported by merchandisers and manufacturers and is the difference between net sales and cost of goods sold.

16.　F – Nonoperating (other) items include income, expenses, gains, and losses which are not considered as resulting from the central operations of the business but are not unusual or infrequent in nature. Operating expenses include selling, general and administrative expenses.

17.　F - The results of all segments of the business that were disposed of *during* the accounting period covered by the income statement must be separately reported, net of tax, on the face of the income statement.

18.　Repairs to operational assets are no unusual in nature or infrequent in occurrence; as such, repairs are not reported as extraordinary items.

19.　T

20.　T

MULTIPLE CHOICE QUESTIONS

1. d	5. c	9. d	13. b	17. a
2. e	6. b	10. a	14. a	18. b
3. a	7. d	11. b	15. d	19. c
4. e	8. c	12. a	16. e	

EXERCISES

1.

Transaction	Gross Profit	Gross Profit Percentage	Income from Operations
Revenues earned on account amounted to $200; the related cost of revenues amounted to $100.	Increase	None	Increase
Revenues earned on account amounted to $300; the related cost of revenues amounted to $100.	Increase	Increase	Increase
Revenues earned on account amounted to $200; the related cost of revenues amounted to $150.	Increase	Decrease	Increase
Additional research and development expenses amounted to $400.	None	None	Decrease

2A.

Pixar
Income Statement
for the year ended December 31, 19B
(in thousands)

Revenues:		
Software	$ 6,306	
Animation	3,947	
Film	18,847	
Patent licensing	9,127	
Total revenues		$38,227
Cost of revenues		4,703
Gross margin		33,524
Operating expenses::		
Research and development	$ 6,985	
Sales and marketing	1,768	
General and administrative	5,577	
Total operating expenses		14,330
Income from operations		19,194
Other income, net		8,031
Income before income taxes		27,225
Income tax expense		1,906
Net income		$25,319
Earnings per share		$ 0.54

Gross margin percentage = gross margin / total revenues = $33,524 / $38,227 = 87.7%

If you assume that Pixar's products sell for $100 per unit, Pixar is spending $12.30 to produce its product and its markup or gross profit on each unit sold is $87.70. The company's gross margin percentage improved between 19A and 19B (that is, it increased from 80.3% to 87.7%). This resulted from increases in sales of higher margin products.

2B.

Pixar
Balance Sheet
December 31, 19B
(in thousands)

Assets

Current assets

Cash and cash equivalents	$ 44,648	
Short-term investments	116,321	
Trade accounts receivable, net	929	
Other receivables	5,390	
Prepaid expenses and other current assets	982	
Capitalized film production costs	1,372	
Total current assets		$169,642
Property, plant and equipment, net		4,655
Capitalized film production costs, net of current portion		1,578
Other assets		1,588
Total assets		$177,463

Liabilities

Current liabilities

Accounts payable	$ 1,060	
Accrued liabilities	5,262	
Unearned revenue	337	
Total current liabilities		$ 6,659

Stockholders' equity

Common stock		187,308
Other components of stockholders' equity		(1,097)
Accumulated deficit		(15,407)
Total stockholders' equity		170,804
Total liabilities and stockholders' equity		$177,463

Current ratio = current assets / current liabilities = $169,642 / $6,659 = 25.48

Pixar's current ratio means it has $25.48 of current assets for every $1 of current liabilities. The company's current ratio improved from the end of 19A to the end of 19B (that is, it increased from 14.72 to 25.48) indicating a higher degree of liquidity in 19B.

3A. Working capital = Current assets - current liabilities = \$350,000 - \$700,000 = (\$350,000)
Current ratio = Current assets / Current liabilities = \$350,000 / \$700,000 = .5

3B.

Transaction	Current Assets	Current Liabilities	Working Capital	Current Ratio
Collection of cash from customers on account in the amount of \$150,000.	None	None	None	None
Payment of cash to vendors on account in the amount of \$300,000.	Decrease	Decrease	None	Decrease
Receipt of proceeds of \$100,000 from long-term note payable.	Increase	None	Increase	Increase
Payment of \$100,000 on long-term note payable.	Decrease	None	Decrease	Decrease

4A. Working capital = Current assets - current liabilities = \$700,000 - \$350,000 = \$350,000
Current ratio = Current assets / Current liabilities = \$700,000 / \$350,000 = 2.0

4B.

Transaction	Current Assets	Current Liabilities	Working Capital	Current Ratio
Collection of cash from customers on account in the amount of \$75,000.	None	None	None	None
Payment of cash to vendors on account in the amount of \$150,000.	Decrease	Decrease	None	Increase
Receipt of proceeds of \$200,000 from long-term note payable.	Increase	None	Increase	Increase
Payment of \$200,000 on long-term note payable.	Decrease	None	Decrease	Decrease

5. Unknown amounts can most easily be determined by reorganizing this table in the form of a multi-step income statement as shown below.

	Case A	Case B	Case C	Case D
Sales revenue	\$125,000	\$600,000	\$155,000	\$250,000
Cost of goods sold	50,000	**300,000**	55,000	125,000
Gross margin	**75,000**	300,000	100,000	**125,000**
Administrative expenses	25,000	90,000	**35,000**	65,000
Selling expenses	10,000	**110,000**	15,000	35,000
Operating expenses	**35,000**	**200,000**	50,000	100,000
Income before income taxes	40,000	100,000	**50,000**	25,000
Income tax expense	15,000	**30,000**	15,000	10,000
Net income	**\$ 25,000**	\$ 70,000	\$ 35,000	**\$ 15,000**

6. Cash   1,250,000
     Common stock (\$0.25 per share x 1,000,000 shares)   250,000
     Paid-in capital (\$1,250,000 - \$250,000   1,000,000

155

IDEAS FOR YOUR STUDY TEAM

1. Rewrite each of the definitions of the key terms that appear at the end of the chapter using your own words. Imagine that you are trying to explain each key term to a friend who has not taken any accounting classes. Then, get together with the other members of your study team and compare your definitions.

Comparable information

Conservatism

Consistent information

Cost-benefit constraint

Cumulative effects of changes in accounting methods

Current assets

Current liabilities

Discontinued operations

Earnings forecasts

Extraordinary items

Form 8-K

Form 10-K

Form 10-Q

Full-disclosure principle

Gross margin (gross profit)

Income before income taxes (pretax earnings)

Income from operations (operating income)

Institutional investors

Lenders (creditors)

Material amounts

Par value

Press release

Private investors

Relevant information

Reliable information

Unqualified audit opinion (clean audit opinion)

2. Each member of the study group should obtain the web addresses of one or more companies and visit the web sites. Then, get together and compare and contrast the nature and extent of financial information that is presented on the web sites. What recommendations would your study team make to the companies chosen?

3. Arrange a group tour of your school's learning resource team for the members of your study team. Determine which types of electronic information services are available and how you might use these services.

4. Each member of your study team should locate at least one article that covers quarterly earnings information released by a public company. Then, get together and discuss the articles. Did the article convey positive or negative information? How did the writer of the article react to the information? How did the "market" respond?

CHAPTER 6

REPORTING AND INTERPRETING SALES REVENUE, RECEIVABLES, AND CASH

CHAPTER FOCUS SUGGESTIONS

This chapter begins an in-depth discussion of various items reported on the financial statements. Initially, emphasis is placed on income statement transactions that involve revenue. Cash sales, credit card sales, sales on account, sales discounts, trade discounts and sales returns are addressed, as are certain related selling expenses.

Next, the measurement and reporting issues that arise when the collection of accounts receivable is uncertain are addressed. You will need to be familiar with the allowance method and how bad debt expense and write-offs of accounts receivable are recorded. You should be able to estimate bad debt expense using both the percentage of credit sales and the aging of accounts receivable methods. You will also need to know how to compute and interpret the receivables turnover ratio.

Finally, issues relating to the reporting, control, and safeguarding of cash are addressed. You should be familiar with the concept of internal control and understand the importance of separation of duties. You will need to know how to prepare a bank reconciliation.

READ AND RECALL QUESTIONS

BUSINESS BACKGROUND

How is gross profit calculated when a multi-step format is used to prepare an income statement?

What is the primary source of operating cash for most organizations? What is the primary use of cash?

What is one of the causes of business failure? How can business failure be avoided?

Why do lenders, shareholders and analysts carefully monitor a company's cash, accounts receivable and inventories?

ACCOUNTING FOR SALES REVENUE

When should revenues be recorded? What are the three criteria for recording revenue?

Generally, when do wholesalers and merchandisers record revenue? When do service providers record revenue?

If goods are shipped "F.O.B. shipping point," when does title pass? When does title pass when goods are shipped "F.O.B. destination?" Why do most companies recognize revenue at shipment regardless of whether title passes at shipment or delivery? When is it appropriate to use this common practice?

LEARNING OBJECTIVE
After studying this section of the chapter, you should be able to:
2. Analyze the impact of cash sales, credit card sales, credit sales (and sales discounts), and sales returns on the amounts reported as net sales and selling expenses.

Cash Sales

What entry is recorded when a sale of merchandise is made to a customer for cash?

Credit Card Sales

Why do merchandisers accept credit cards? (Hint: There are at least four reasons.)

Assuming that the credit card receipts are deposited in the company's bank account and the credit card company charges a fee for its services, what entry is recorded when a sale is made to a customer who uses a credit card? How are credit card discounts reported on the income statement? (Hint: There are two methods.)

Credit Sales

What entry is recorded when a credit sale is made to a business on open account? What is a credit sale on open account?

161

Credit Sales and Sales Discounts

What does "n/30" mean? What does "10, EOM" mean? Why do companies grant sales discounts to customers? What does "2/10, n/30" mean?

Customers usually take advantage of sales discounts because the savings are substantial. What formula would you use to compute the annual interest rate that relates to various discount terms?

Most companies record sales discounts using the gross method. That is, the sales revenue is recorded without deducting the sales discount. Assuming that a customer then pays within the discount period, what entry is recorded? What entry is recorded when the customer makes the payment after the discount period has expired?

How are sales discounts reported on the income statement? (Hint: There are two methods.)

What is a trade discount? How do trade discounts affect the recording of sales revenue?

Sales Returns and Allowances

Why do customers return merchandise? What entry is recorded when a customer returns merchandise?

Reporting Net Sales

Assume that customers have returned merchandise and the company treats credit card discounts and sales discounts as contra revenue accounts. How should the amount of net sales be computed?

Contra Revenues and Evaluating Gross Profit

Some companies record sales discounts and credit card discounts as contra revenues. Others treat them as selling expenses. Which method will result in a higher gross profit percentage? (Recall that gross profit percentage is calculated by dividing gross profit by net sales.)

Assume that you are a financial analyst. What information should you obtain before making A comparison of Timberland's gross profit percentage with gross profit percentages reported by other companies?

REPORTING AND INTERPRETING RECEIVABLES

Receivables Defined

What is a note receivable? What do the terms "principal" and "interest" mean?

When should a receivable be classified as a trade receivable? As a nontrade receivable?

When should a receivable be classified as current? As noncurrent?

Evaluating the Efficiency of Credit Granting and Collection Activities

How is the receivables turnover ratio computed? What does the receivables turnover ratio measure? Assume that you are a financial analyst and want to interpret the meaning of Timberland's 1995 receivables turnover ratio. What should you use as a basis of comparison?

Timberland's receivables turnover ratios for 1993, 1994, and 1995 were 5.70, 5.75, and 5.84, respectively. How would you interpret this information?

What factors could cause a company's receivables turnover ratio to decrease over time?

Accounting for Bad Debts

Businesses that sell to customers on open account do so with the understanding that certain customers will not pay. Uncollectible accounts receivable may be thought of as "bad debts." Even though most companies take steps to limit the amount of bad debts, an extremely low rate of bad debts may not be a favorable sign. Why?

What is bad debt expense? To be in conformity with the matching principle, when should bad debt expense be recorded?

The allowance method measures and records bad debt expense in accordance with the matching principle. Why must an estimate be used to record bad debt expense under the allowance method? What are the two steps taken when the allowance method is used?

Recording Bad Debt Expense Estimates

When is bad debt expense recorded? What entry is used to record bad debt expense? Why is the allowance for doubtful accounts credited instead of accounts receivable when bad debt expense is recorded? How is bad debt expense reported on the income statement?

What type of account is the allowance for doubtful accounts? How is it reported on the balance sheet?

What is the normal balance of the allowance for doubtful accounts? What does this balance represent?

How is the net book value of accounts receivable computed?

Writing Off Specific Accounts Determined to be Uncollectible

When should a specific customer's account receivable be written off?

What entry is recorded when a customer's account is written off? How does the write-off of a customer's account receivable affect the company's balance sheet? How does it affect the income statement?

Actual Write-offs Compared with Estimates

The amount of uncollectible accounts actually written off usually does not equal the estimate of bad debt expense that was recorded. How is this situation resolved?

Reporting Accounts Receivable and Bad Debts

An adjusting entry to used to record bad debt expense and increase the allowance for doubtful accounts at the end of the accounting period. How does this adjusting entry affect the balance sheet and income statement?

A write-off is recorded by decreasing both accounts receivable and the allowance for doubtful accounts. How does this entry affect the balance sheet? How does it affect the income statement?

Judging the Accuracy of Bad Debt Estimates

Assume that you are a financial analyst. Would you be able to judge the reasonableness of a company's allowance for doubtful accounts?

Methods for Estimating Bad Debts

An estimate is used in the adjusting entry to record bad debt expense at the end of the accounting period. What are the two methods that can be used to estimate the amount of bad debts?

Percentage of Credit Sales

Why is the percentage of credit sales method also known as the income statement method? How is the average percentage of credit sales that results in bad debts calculated? How is bad debt expense calculated using the percentage of credit sales method?

Aging of Accounts Receivable

Why is the aging of accounts receivable method also known as the balance sheet method? When a company uses the aging method, what information must be gathered and analyzed to determine the amount of estimated uncollectible accounts?

When the aging method is used, why do you need to consider the balance in the allowance account in order to determine the amount of bad debt expense to be used in the adjusting entry?

Not only is the percentage of credit sales method easier for the company to use, it is easier for you to use. The company simply considers the losses from bad debts and total credit sales to come up with an average loss rate. You simply multiply the average loss rate times this year's credit sales to arrive at the amount of bad debt expense for the adjusting entry.

On the other hand, the aging of accounts receivable method is harder for the company to use, and it's more work for you. The company must age all of its accounts receivable and then determine probable loss rates for each of the aging categories before it can estimate its uncollectible accounts. You must multiply each category total by its respective loss rate and then sum the category totals to arrive at the estimate of uncollectible accounts. The final total represents what you want the allowance account balance to be *after* you post your adjusting entry. As a result, you need to compare the balance in the allowance account with your estimate of uncollectible accounts; the difference between these two amounts is the amount that is used in the adjusting entry.

Sales versus Collections - The Marketing/Financial Management Conflict

What does the bad debt expense as a percentage of sales ratio measure? How is it computed?

Timberland's bad debt expense as a percentage of sales increased from .27% in 1993 to .56% in 1995. What factors might have caused this sharp increase?

What two steps did Inc. Magazine recommend to minimize bad debts?

FOCUS ON CASH FLOWS

When the indirect method is used to prepare the cash flow statement, why does the change in accounts receivable during the year have to be considered when adjustments are made to reconcile net income to net cash provided by operating activities?

Should an increase in accounts receivable be added to or subtracted from net income when the indirect method is used? How should a decrease in accounts receivable be handled?

LEARNING OBJECTIVE
After studying this section of the chapter, you should be able to:
4. Report, control, and safeguard cash.

REPORTING AND SAFEGUARDING CASH

Cash and Cash Equivalents Defined

What are cash equivalents?

In addition to protecting the company's cash from theft, fraud or loss through carelessness, what other steps should be taken to ensure effective cash management?

Internal Control of Cash

What does the term "internal control' encompass?

Which duties should be separated to achieve effective internal control of cash?

How does a separation of duties deter theft?

Ethics and the Need for Internal Control

Why should companies implement formal codes of ethics?

Reconciliation of the Cash Accounts and the Bank Statements

Why wouldn't the balance shown on the bank statement agree with the balance in the cash account? What is a bank reconciliation?

What are outstanding checks? How can outstanding checks be identified?

What are deposits in transit? How can deposits in transit be identified?

What is a NSF check? What entry should be made when the bank returns a check marked NSF?

When a bank reconciliation is prepared, what items are added to the cash balance per books? What items are subtracted from the cash balance per books?

What items are added to the cash balance per the bank statement? What items are subtracted from the cash balance per bank statement?

Think of the adjustments to the cash balance per bank statement as items that the bank doesn't know about yet. Add or subtract each item based on what the bank will do when it processes the item. No entries are required for the items reflected as adjustments to the cash balance per bank statement; the related entries have already been recorded.

Think of the adjustments to the cash balance per books as the items that the company doesn't know about until the bank statement is received. Except for errors (which must be individually analyzed), add or subtract each item based on what the bank did. A journal entry is required for each item reflected as an adjustment to the cash balance per books.

CHAPTER SUPPLEMENT A

Determine whether or not you are responsible for this supplement.

Delayed Revenue Recognition: Installment Method

What three criteria should be met before revenue is recognized (that is, recorded)?

If there is a great deal of uncertainty concerning the collectibility of the sales price, when should the revenue be recognized? What method should be used?

173

Exceptions to the Revenue Recognition Criteria: Long-Term Construction Contracts

If the completed contract method was used, when would revenue resulting from long-term construction contracts be recorded? How might this method effect the company's financial statements?

Under the percentage-of-completion method, how would you calculate the amount of revenue that should be recorded during a given year?

Exceptions to the Revenue Recognition Criteria: Service Contracts

What method is used to record revenue when a company provides services over more than one accounting period?

Revenue Recognition and Financial Statement Analysis

If you were a financial analyst, how could you determine which revenue recognition method is being used by a company?

SELF-TEST QUESTIONS AND EXERCISES

MATCHING

Match each of the key terms listed below with the appropriate textbook definition:

J 1. Accounts receivable
N 2. Aging of accounting receivable method
A 3. Allowance for doubtful accounts
R 4. Allowance method
E 5. Bad debt expense
B 6. Bank reconciliation
O 7. Bank statement
D 8. Cash
K 9. Cash equivalent
P 10. Credit card discount

L 11. Internal controls
C 12. Note receivable
H 13. Percentage of sales method
F 14. Sales (or cash) discount
Q 15. Sales returns and allowances
G 16. Trade discount
Supplement A Terms:
M 17. Completed-contract method
S 18. Installment method
I 19. Percentage-of-completion method

A. Contra asset account containing the estimated uncollectible accounts receivable.

B. Process of verifying the accuracy of both the bank statement and the cash accounts of the business.

C. A written promise that requires another party to pay the business under specified conditions.

D. Money and any instrument that banks will accept for deposit and immediately credit to the depositor's account, such as a check, money order, or bank draft.

E. Expense associated with estimated uncollectible accounts receivable.

F. Cash discount offered to encourage prompt payment of an account receivable.

G. A discount that is deducted from list price to derive the actual sales price.

H. Bases bad debt expense of the historical percentage of credit sales that result in bad debts.

I. Records revenue based on the percentage of work completed during the accounting period.

J. Open accounts owed to the business by trade customers.

K. Short-term investments with original maturities of three months or less that are readily convertible to cash and whose value is unlikely to change.

L. Policies and procedures designed to safeguard the assets of the business and ensure the accuracy of financial records.

M. Recognizes revenue when the completed product is delivered to the customer.

N. Method that bases bad debt expense on an estimate of uncollectible accounts.

O. Monthly report from a bank that shows deposits recorded, checks cleared, other debits and credits, and a running bank balance.

P. Fees charged by the credit card company for services.

Q. A contra revenue account used to record return or of allowances for unsatisfactory goods.

R. Method that bases bad debt expense on an estimate of uncollectible accounts.

S.   Recognizes revenue on the basis of cash collection after delivery of goods.

TRUE-FALSE QUESTIONS

For each of the following statements, enter a T or F in the blank to indicate whether the statement is true or false.

T 1. Careful management of receivables and inventory can be the key to avoiding business failure.

T 2. Many companies recognize revenue at shipment regardless of whether title passes at shipment or delivery because it is easier to keep track of shipments.

F 3. When the customer pays with a credit card, the retailer receives cash when the customer pays the credit card issuer.

F 4. Credit card companies are not expected to absorb losses from fraudulent credit card sales.

T 5. The credit card discounts account may be reported as a contra revenue account or as a selling expense.

F 6. The sales discounts account is a contra revenue account and, as such, has a debit balance.

T 7. Sales revenue should always be recorded net of any trade discount.

T 8. The sales returns and allowances account should be deducted from gross sales revenue on the income statement.

T 9. The alternative methods of reporting customer discounts makes comparisons of gross profit percentages of different companies difficult.

T 10. A decrease in the receivables turnover ratio might mean that a company's credit and cash collection procedures have become less effective.

F 11. Analysts have a negative opinion of bad debts expense because it implies that a company's credit policy is too lenient or its collection efforts are not aggressive enough.

T 12. Bad debt expense should be recorded in the period in which the corresponding sales are made, rather than in the period in which a particular account is actually judged to be uncollectible.

F 13. The allowance for doubtful accounts account should be closed at the end of the accounting period.

T 14. The entry to write-off a customer account balance does not affect the income statement.

T 15. A company using the percentage of credit sales method typically estimates its bad debt expense by multiplying credit sales in the current year by its historical percentage of credit sales that resulted in bad debts.

F 16. When the aging of accounts receivable method is used, the estimate that is computed becomes the amount that is used in the adjusting entry and, as such, is added to the allowance for doubtful accounts account.

T 17. Cash and cash equivalents can be combined as one amount for financial reporting purposes.

T 18. Internal controls are the policies and procedures that the business has implemented to properly account for and safeguard all of its assets and ensure the accuracy of its financial records.

I 19. The separation of duties deters theft.

T 20. All cash receipts should be deposited in a bank on a daily basis.

T 21. The installment method is a very conservative method of revenue recognition that takes into account the uncertainty of collection of the full amount of certain types of sales. *(Supplement A)*

F 22. Title to the goods must pass from the seller to the buyer before the seller is allowed to recognize revenue. *(Supplement A)*

MULTIPLE CHOICE QUESTIONS

Choose the best answer or response by placing the identifying letter in the space provided.

b 1. A company's primary source of cash is

   a. proceeds from short-term lines of credit.
   b. customers as they purchase goods or services and make payments on account.
   c. proceeds from the issuance of new shares of the company's stock.
   d. proceeds from borrowings on long-term debt contracts.
   e. both b and c.

d 2. The revenue principles requires that revenues be recognized when

   a. an exchange has taken place.
   b. the earnings process is nearly complete.
   c. collection from the customer is probable.
   d. all of the above.
   e. any of the above.

e 3. When you return to school in January, you begin to search for decent air fares for Spring break. You find an airline willing to sell you a ticket at less than one-half the usual rate, but you have to buy the ticket now. You purchase the ticket. Assuming the accrual basis of accounting is used by both, you have a(n) _____; the airline has a(n) _____.

   a. asset; revenue
   b. expense; revenue
   c. expense; asset
   d. expense; liability
   e. asset; liability

d 4. Title passes from the seller to the purchaser upon shipment of the goods if

   a. a properly executed purchase order was issued.
   b. the customer paid for the goods in advance of the shipment.
   c. collection is reasonably assured.
   d. the goods are shipped FOB shipping point
   e. the goods are shipped FOB destination point.

C 5. A credit card discount is

    a. the amount off the list price of an item that the merchant allows a credit card customer.

    b. the amount off the pump price that gas stations offer to customers to induce them to pay with cash rather than with credit cards.

    c. the amount the issuing bank charges a retailer as a handling fee for each credit card sale submitted for payment.

    d. an amount paid by the issuing bank to retailers to encourage the use of their credit cards.

    e. the amount saved by a credit card holder who pays credit card bills in full by their due date.

C 6. Sales discounts, also called cash discounts, are often granted to

    a. give favorable terms to high-volume buyers.

    b. encourage customers to buy slow-moving merchandise.

    c. motivate credit customers to pay invoices promptly.

    d. increase the company's chances to collect the receivable and, as a result, minimize bad debts.

    e. increase the company's gross profit percentage.

C 7. A sales transaction which includes a trade discount is normally recorded

    a. at the gross amount, and the trade discount is recorded in an offsetting contra account.

    b. at the gross amount, and the trade discount is recorded in an expense account.

    c. at the net amount, after the trade discount has been deducted.

    d. either a or b.

    e. either b or c.

C 8. The primary difference between accounts receivable and notes receivable is that

    a. accounts receivable are classified as current; whereas notes receivable are classified as long-term.

    b. accounts receivable are classified as trade receivables, whereas notes receivable are classified as nontrade.

    c. a note receivable is a promise in writing, whereas an accounts receivable is created when there is a credit sale on an open account.

    d. all of the above.

    e. none of the above

a 9. The primary reason for establishing an allowance account (rather than writing off uncollectible accounts to bad debt expense) is that the allowance method

    a. conforms to the matching principle.

    b. ensures that overdue accounts receivable are not overlooked.

    c. results in a more accurate reporting of revenues on the income statement.

    d. simplifies the bookkeeping effort.

    e. increases the net realizable value of the company's accounts receivable.

_b_ 10. Upon purchase, a U. S. Treasury bill that matures in two months should be classified as

    a.   cash.
    b.   a cash equivalent.
    c.   a short-term investment.
    d.   a long-term investment.
    e.   any of the above depending on the company's investment philosophy.

_C_ 11. The most important reason to reconcile the company's cash account immediately upon receipt of its monthly bank statement is

    a.   the need to know how much cash is available to pay bills.
    b.   to ensure that errors made by the bank are corrected by the company.
    c.   to ensure that the cash account is being properly accounted for and safeguarded.
    d.   to ensure that collusion has not resulted in theft.
    e.   the requirement to do so under generally accepted accounting principles.

_b_ 12. A credit memo in a bank statement might represent

    a.   a bank service charge.
    b.   a note receivable collected by the bank for the depositor.
    c.   a memo returning a NSF check.
    d.   a cash withdrawal at an automated teller machine (ATM).
    e.   any of the above.

Answer the next six questions by selecting one of the following:

    a.   added to the cash balance per books.
    b.   deducted from the cash balance per books.
    c.   added to the cash balance per bank statement.
    d.   deducted from the cash balance per bank statement.

_d_ 13. When a bank reconciliation is being prepared, the amount of outstanding checks should be

_b_ 14. When a bank reconciliation is being prepared, a check marked NSF returned with the bank statement should be

_b_ 15. When a bank reconciliation is being prepared, bank service charges

_C_ 16. When a bank reconciliation is being prepared, deposits in transit should be

_a_ 17. When a bank reconciliation is being prepared, interest income reflected on the bank statement

_a_ 18. When a bank reconciliation is being prepared, proceeds of customer notes collected by the bank

EXERCISES

Record your answers to each part of these exercises in the space provided. Show your work.

1. Prepare journal entries for each of the following transactions:

   A. Sold two items with a list price of $5,000 each to H. Hunter for cash of $9,500.

   B. Sold goods to J. Lange for $2,000 and billed that amount subject to terms 2/10, n/30.

   C. Sold goods to D. Moore for $6,000 and billed that amount subject to terms 2/10, n/30.

   D. Sold goods to J. Roberts who charged the $5,000 purchase on her VISA card. VISA charges the company a 2% credit card fee.

   E. Accepted a return of one item from H. Hunter.

   F. Collected from J. Lange within the discount period.

   G. Collected from D. Moore after the discount period had expired.

   H. Wrote-off a customer account balance of $35,000.

2. Pixar reported trade accounts receivable with a net realizable value of $929,000 and $784,000 and total assets of $177,463,000 and $153,015,000 at December 31, 1995 and 1994, respectively. Total revenues were $38,227,000 and $12,113,000 and Pixar reported net income of $25,319,000 and $1,627,000 for 1995 and 1994, respectively. Compute Pixar's receivables turnover ratio for 1995. What does this ratio measure?

3. Starseekers, Inc. began the year with $4,800 of accounts receivable and an allowance for doubtful accounts of $546. Starseekers' sales were all on account and amounted to $41,800 during the year. Collections from customers amounted to $40,600 and the company wrote-off customer account balances totaling $500 during the year.

   A. Using T-accounts, determine how much Starseekers' customers owe the company at year-end and the unadjusted balance in its allowance for doubtful accounts account.

   B. The company currently uses the percentage of credit sales method for determining its bad debt expense. Historically, bad debts have approximated 3% of credit sales. Prepare the related adjusting entry and determine the ending balance in the allowance for doubtful accounts account.

   C. Assume instead that the company uses the aging of accounts receivable method. This method resulted in an estimate of uncollectible accounts of $1,105. Prepare the related adjusting entry and determine the ending balance in the allowance for doubtful accounts account.

4. Kochano Company's January bank statement indicated a balance of $10,300. A service charge of $40 and interest of $135 were listed on the statement. A credit memo in the amount of $4,400 for the collection of a note was included on the bank statement; interest on the note was $400. NSF checks received from customers totaling $14,900 were also included. Kochano's cash balance was $24,000 on January 31st. A comparison of checks written before and during January with the paid checks included with the bank statement showed outstanding checks at the end of January of $33,600. A comparison of deposits made with those listed on the bank statement showed that deposits of $33,295 were in transit on January 31st. The comparison also revealed an error made in recording a deposit of a check received from a customer on account. The $1,500 deposit was correctly listed on the bank statement, but was recorded on the company's books at $5,100.

A. Prepare a detailed bank reconciliation for January.

B. Prepare any required journal entries as a result of the reconciliation.

C. What amount of cash should be reported on the balance sheet prepared at the end of January?

5. Compute the annual interest rate implicit in a sales discount when the terms are 1.5/10, n/30. If your bank charges 21% interest, should you borrow the money to take advantage of the discount?

SOLUTIONS TO SELF-TEST QUESTIONS AND EXERCISES

MATCHING

1. J	5. E	9. K	13. H	17. M
2. N	6. B	10. P	14. F	18. S
3. A	7. O	11. L	15. Q	19. I
4. R	8. D	12. C	16. G	

TRUE-FALSE QUESTIONS

1. T

2. T

3. F - The retailer deposits the credit card receipt directly into its bank account on the day of the sale.

4. F - The credit card company absorbs any losses from fraudulent credit card sales as long as the retailer follows the credit card company's verification procedure.

5. T

6. F - The sales discounts account normally has a debit balance; however, it can be reported as a contra revenue account (and be deducted in the computation of net sales) *or* a selling expense.

7. T

8. T

9. T

10. T

11. F - A business that extends credit expects a certain amount of bad debts. Analysts have the same expectation. In fact, an extremely low rate of bad debts might even indicate that the company's credit policy is too tight or restrictive. If this is the case, the company may turn away good customers and experience a loss in sales volume.

12. T

13. F - The allowance for doubtful accounts account is not closed at the end of the accounting period because it is a balance sheet account.

14. T

15. T

16. F - When the aging of accounts receivable method is used, the estimate that is computed actually represents the desired ending balance in the allowance for doubtful accounts account. The amount used in the adjusting entry is the difference between the desired ending balance and the unadjusted balance that exists in that account.

17. T

18. T

19. T

20. T

21. T

22. F - Even though it does not satisfy the second revenue recognition criteria, many companies involved in long-term construction projects use the percentage-of-completion method to account for the revenues earned. Revenues are based on the amount of work done each year.

MULTIPLE CHOICE QUESTIONS

1. b	5. c	9. a	13. d	17. a
2. d	6. c	10. b	14. b	18. a
3. e	7. c	11. c	15. b	
4. d	8. c	12. b	16. c	

EXERCISES

1.

A. Cash	9,500	
Sales		9,500
B. Accounts receivable	2,000	
Sales		2,000
C. Accounts receivable	2,000	
Sales		2,000
D. Cash ($5,000 x 98%)	4,900	
Credit card discounts ($5,000 x 2%)	100	
Sales		5,000
E. Sales returns and allowances ($9,500 x ½)	4,750	
Cash *(Use accounts receivable if customer has not yet paid bill.)*		4,750
F. Cash ($2,000 x 98%)	1,960	
Sales discounts ($2,000 x 2%)	40	
Accounts receivable		2,000
G. Cash	6,000	
Accounts receivable		6,000
H. Allowance for doubtful accounts	35,000	
Accounts receivable		35,000

2. Total revenues / Average accounts receivable = Receivables turnover ratio
$38,227,000 / [($929,000 + $784,000) / 2] = $38,227,000 / $856,500 = 44.63

Note that total revenues was used above to compute the receivables turnover ratio because the amount of credit sales is not known. This ratio reflects how many times average trade receivables were recorded, collected, and then recorded again during the year.

3A.

Accounts Receivable			
Beginning	4,800		
Sales	41,800	Collections	40,600
		Write-offs	500
Ending	5,500		

Allowance for Doubtful Accounts			
		Beginning	546
Write-offs	500		
		Unadjusted	46

3B.   Bad debt expense ($41,800 x 3%)   1,254
    Allowance for doubtful accounts   1,254

Allowance for Doubtful Accounts		
	Unadjusted	46
	Adjustment	1,254
	Adjusted	1,300

3C.   Bad debt expense ($1,105 - $46)   1,254
    Allowance for doubtful accounts   1,254

Allowance for Doubtful Accounts		
	Unadjusted	46
	Adjustment	1,059
	Adjusted	1,105

4A.

Kochano Company
Bank Reconciliation
For the month ended January 31, 19A

Ending cash balance per books	$24,000	Ending cash balance per bank statement	$10,300
Additions:			
Proceeds of note collected by bank	4,400	Additions:	
Interest	135	Deposits in transit	33,295
	28,535		43,595
Deductions:		Deductions:	
Bank service charges	40	Outstanding checks	33,600
NSF checks	14,900		
Error in recording deposit			
($5,100 - $1,500)	3,600		
Ending correct cash balance	$ 9,995	Ending correct cash balance	$ 9,995

4B.

Cash	4,400	
Note receivable		4,000
Interest income		400
To record note collected by bank		

Cash	135	
Interest income		135
To record interest income paid by bank		

Bank service charge expense	40	
Cash		40
To record service fees charged by bank		

Accounts receivable	14,900	
Cash		14,900
To record NSF checks		

Accounts receivable	3,600	
Cash		3,600
To correct error made in recording a payment received from a customer		

4C. Cash in the amount of $9,995 should be reported on the balance sheet at the end of January.

5. If the bill is paid on the 10th day instead of on the 30th day, it is paid 20 days early.

(Amount Saved / Amount Paid) = (1.5% / 98.5%) = 1.52% Interest Rate for 20 days
Interest Rate for 20 days x (365 days / 20 days) = Annual Interest Rate
1.52% x (365 / 20) = 27.79% Annual Interest Rate

You should borrow from the bank at 21% interest to take advantage of these discount terms.

IDEAS FOR YOUR STUDY TEAM

1. Rewrite each of the definitions of the key terms that appear at the end of the chapter using your own words. Imagine that you are trying to explain each key term to a friend who has not taken any accounting classes. Then, get together with the other members of your study team and compare your definitions.

Accounts receivable

Aging of accounting receivable method

Allowance for doubtful accounts

Allowance method

Bad debt expense

Bank reconciliation

Bank statement

Cash

Cash equivalent

Credit card discount

Internal controls

Note receivable

Percentage of sales method

Sales (or cash) discount

Sales returns and allowances

Trade discount

Supplement A Terms:

Completed-contract method

Installment method

Percentage-of-completion method

2. Assume that your company uses the percentage of credit sales method. During the last five years, write-offs approximated 3% of credit sales. Credit sales during the current year amounted to $3,000,000 and the unadjusted balance in the allowance for doubtful accounts account is $10,000. What adjusting entry would you make to record bad debt expense for the current year? What is the adjusted balance in the allowance for doubtful accounts account?

Get together with the other members of your study team and compare your answers. Then, discuss and consider the following. Early in the current year, a new Credit and Collections Manager was hired. This strategy certainly seemed to be successful; in fact, most of the company's accounts receivable had been collected by year-end. The $80,000 balance in accounts receivable at year-end represents credit sales made to customers during December. What are the implications of this scenario? (Hint: Start by determining the net book value of the company's accounts receivable at year-end. Then, discuss any other implications that come to mind.)

3. Get together with the other members of your study team and discuss why different results were obtained when the aging of receivables and percentage of credit sales methods were used. Which method is "better?" What factors would you consider if you were a small business owner trying to decide between the two methods?

4. Get together with the other members of your study team and discuss the internal controls that you experienced firsthand during the last week or so. Did anyone see a movie? Return some merchandise? Buy fast food? What policies and procedures were in place to safeguard assets and/or ensure the accuracy of financial records? Did you see any evidence of separation of duties?

CHAPTER 7
REPORTING AND INTERPRETING COST OF GOODS SOLD AND INVENTORY

CHAPTER FOCUS SUGGESTIONS

This chapter focuses on transactions related to cost of goods sold and inventory. In conformity with the matching principle, the total cost of the goods sold during the period must be determined and then matched with the sales revenue earned from selling those goods. You will need to be able to determine the amount of inventory on hand and the cost of goods sold using each of the four inventory costing methods: first-in, first-out (FIFO), last-in, first-out (LIFO), weighted-average cost, and specific identification. All four methods are in conformity with GAAP, but produce different results. Given a certain set of assumptions (for example, inflation and increasing inventory quantities) you should be able to determine how the choice of an inventory costing method affects the financial statements. You will also need to be able to determine the impact of inventory errors and apply the lower-of-cost-or-market rule.

You should also become familiar with the two systems used to keep track of inventory. When deciding which system to use, managers must weigh benefits against costs. When a periodic inventory system is used, detailed inventory records are not maintained. Instead, the company counts its inventory to determine how much is on hand and the cost of the goods that have been sold. Information necessary for inventory management is lacking (that is, it is available only periodically), but recordkeeping costs are minimal. When a perpetual inventory system is used, detailed inventory records are maintained and updated as transactions affecting inventory occur. As such, management always (or perpetually) knows how much inventory is on hand and its cost of goods sold. The benefits of the availability of this information for inventory management purposes must be weighed against the higher recordkeeping costs.

READ AND RECALL QUESTIONS

BUSINESS BACKGROUND

What two other terms are used to describe cost of goods sold? How is gross profit computed?

What are the two primary goals of inventory management? What three roles does the accounting system play in the inventory management process?

What is a manufacturer? What is a wholesaler? What is a retailer? What is a merchandiser?

LEARNING OBJECTIVE

After studying this section of the chapter, you should be able to:

1. Apply the cost principle to identify the amounts that should be included in inventory and the matching principle to determine cost of goods sold for typical retailers, wholesalers, and manufacturers.

NATURE OF INVENTORY AND COST OF GOODS SOLD

Items Included in Inventory

What is inventory? Why is inventory reported as a current asset on a classified balance sheet?

What type of inventory do merchandisers hold? What are the characteristics of this type of inventory? What three types of inventory do manufacturers hold? What are the characteristics of each?

Inventory Cost

What is cash equivalent cost? What costs should be included when raw materials and merchandise are purchased? When should the accumulation of costs of purchases cease? How should any subsequent costs be reported?

Applying the Materiality Constraint in Practice

For practical purposes, how are incidental costs such as inspection and preparation costs reported? How are transportation charges for shipment to the warehouse treated?

Inventory Flows

What account is increased when merchandise is purchased? What account is increased and what account is decreased when the goods are sold?

What are raw materials? What account is increased when raw materials are purchased? What account is increased and what account is decreased when raw materials are used in the manufacturing process?

What is direct labor? What are factory overhead costs? What account are direct labor and factory overhead costs added to when these costs are incurred in the manufacturing process?

What account is increased and what account is decreased when the manufactured goods are completed and ready for sale?

What account is increased and what account is decreased when finished goods are sold?

Modern Manufacturing Techniques and Inventory Costs

Why would Harley-Davidson want to minimize its raw materials and purchased parts inventories? How does the company minimize these inventories?

Nature of Cost of Goods Sold

How does the amount of beginning inventory increase during the accounting period? How is cost of goods available for sale computed? How is cost of goods sold computed?

Gross Profit Comparison

How is gross profit (gross margin) computed? What does gross profit reflect (or measure)? How is the gross profit percentage (gross margin percentage) computed? How would an analyst react if Harley-Davidson's gross profit percentage changed or a major competitor reported a much different gross profit percentage?

Errors in Measuring Ending Inventory

Why does the measurement of ending inventory affect not only the net income of the current accounting period, but also the net income for the next accounting period?

Assume that ending inventory is overstated as a result of a clerical error and the error is not discovered. How does this error affect the current year's cost of goods sold and income before taxes? How does this error affect the following year's beginning inventory, cost of goods sold and income before taxes?

INVENTORY COSTING METHODS

What are the four generally accepted inventory costing methods?

Why are the four inventory costing methods considered alternative allocation methods? How is the cost of goods available for sale computed? What is the cost of goods available for sale allocated to?

How does a company's physical flow of goods affect its choice of inventory costing methods? Why are the inventory-costing methods referred to as cost flow assumptions?

First-In, First-Out Inventory Costing Method

What does FIFO stand for? What does the FIFO method assume? What unit costs does FIFO allocate to cost of goods sold? What unit costs are allocated to ending inventory?

Last-In, First-Out Inventory Costing Method

What does LIFO stand for? What does the LIFO method assume? What unit costs does LIFO allocate to cost of goods sold? What unit costs are allocated to ending inventory?

Weighted-Average Inventory Costing Method

What per unit amount needs to be computed when the weighted-average inventory costing method is used? How is this per unit amount computed? How is ending inventory determined when this method is used? How is cost of goods sold determined?

Specific Identification Inventory Costing Method

What does the company need to keep track of when it uses the specific identification method? How does the company track this information? How can net income be manipulated when this method is used?

Comparison of the Inventory Costing Methods

Which inventory costing method will always produce ending inventory and net income amounts that fall between the amounts produced by two other methods? What are those other methods?

Assuming that inventory quantities are constant or rising, and unit costs are rising, which inventory costing method (ignoring the specific identification method) produces the lowest net income? Which produces the lowest ending inventory? Which produces the highest net income? Which produces the highest ending inventory?

When LIFO is used, which unit costs (older or most recent) are reflected in cost of goods sold? Which unit costs (older or most recent) are reflected in ending inventory?

When FIFO is used, which unit costs (older or most recent) are reflected in cost of goods sold? Which unit costs (older or most recent) are reflected in ending inventory?

What factors affect a particular company's choice of an inventory costing method?

ALTERNATIVE INVENTORY COSTING METHODS IN PRACTICE

Choosing Inventory Costing Methods

What is the "least-latest rule?" What is the LIFO conformity rule?

Which inventory costing method typically is used by U.S. companies facing rising costs of inventory?

LIFO and International Comparisons

What causes comparability problems when analysts attempt to compare companies across international borders? Why doesn't Harley-Davidson use LIFO for its non-U.S. motorcycle inventory?

LIFO and Conflicts between Managers' and Owners' Interests

During periods of rising prices, why do owners prefer the use of LIFO? Why do managers prefer FIFO?

In theory, why doesn't LIFO provide permanent tax savings?Why are many high-technology companies currently using FIFO?

LEARNING OBJECTIVE
After studying this section of the chapter, you should be able to:
5. Analyze financial statements prepared using different inventory costing systems.

Alternative Inventory Costing Methods and Financial Statement Analysis

Why do critics of GAAP dislike the existence of alternative accounting methods? How can knowledgeable users make meaningful comparisons when different inventory costing methods are used?

What is the LIFO Reserve? How can the effects of the difference in cost flow assumptions be computed when the LIFO Reserve is reported? What type of account is the LIFO Reserve? How is it reported on the financial statements?

When costs are rising, why doesn't LIFO always result in a reduction of pretax income and taxes?

What is a LIFO liquidation? What causes a LIFO liquidation?

LIFO and Financial Statement Analysis

How is the inventory turnover ratio computed and what does it measure? What does a higher inventory turnover ratio indicate? What does it mean in terms of efficiency?

LEARNING OBJECTIVE
After studying this section of the chapter, you should be able to:
6. Apply the lower-of-cost-or-market (LCM) rule.

VALUATION AT LOWER OF COST OR MARKET

When the goods remaining in ending inventory can be replaced with identical goods at a lower cost, what unit cost should be used for inventory valuation?

When the goods remaining in ending inventory are damaged, obsolete, or deteriorated, what unit cost should be used for inventory valuation?

What is the lower of cost or market (LCM) rule? What constraint justifies the departure from the cost principle when the lower cost or market rule is followed?

What is a holding loss? When should a holding loss be recognized?

What is a write-down? How does an inventory write-down affect the amounts of cost of goods sold and net income reported in the year of the write-down? How does the inventory write-down affect the amounts of cost of goods sold and net income reported in the following year?

What is a holding gain? When should a holding gain be recognized?

What is net realizable value? When net realizable value drops below cost, what are the effects on the current year's cost of goods sold and net income? What are the effects on the following year's cost of goods sold and net income?

How is the LCM rule applied for tax purposes?

FOCUS ON CASH FLOWS

When net income is reconciled to cash flows from operations, should an increase in inventory be added to or deducted from net income? Should a decrease in inventory be added or deducted?

When net income is reconciled to cash flows from operations, should an increase in accounts payable be added to or deducted from net income? Should a decrease in accounts payable be added or deducted?

LEARNING OBJECTIVE

After studying this section of the chapter, you should be able to:

7. Keep track of inventory quantities and amounts in different circumstances.

KEEPING TRACK OF INVENTORY QUANTITIES AND COSTS

Periodic Inventory System

What is a periodic inventory system? How is ending inventory determined when a periodic inventory system is used? How is cost of goods sold calculated?

In the past, what was the primary reason for using a periodic inventory system? What is the primary disadvantage of a periodic inventory system?

Perpetual Inventory System

What is a perpetual inventory system? What records are maintained when a perpetual inventory system is used?

How is ending inventory determined when a perpetual inventory system is used? Why should a physical count be performed from time to time when a perpetual inventory system is used?

Comparison of Periodic and Perpetual Inventory Systems

When a periodic inventory system is used, what account is used to accumulate purchases? What account is used to accumulate purchases when a perpetual inventory system is used?

Perpetual Inventory Records in Practice

Which inventory costing method is normally used to keep track of the costs of individual items or lots when a perpetual inventory system is in use? Why is this method normally used?

Methods for Estimating Inventory

When a periodic inventory system is used, why is a physical inventory done only once a year? What must be done if managers wish to prepare monthly or quarterly financial statements?

What is the gross margin method? How is cost of goods sold estimated this method is used?

Purchase Returns and Allowances

Why would goods that are purchased be returned to the vendor? (Hint: There are at least three reasons.) Assuming that a periodic inventory system is used, what account is used to accumulate the amount of purchased goods that are returned to the vendor? How is this account reported on the financial statements? What account accumulates purchase returns when a perpetual inventory system is used?

Purchase Discounts

What is a purchase discount? Assuming that a periodic inventory system is used, what account is used to accumulate the amount of purchase discounts? How is this account reported on the financial statements? What account accumulates purchase discounts when a perpetual inventory system is used?

CHAPTER SUPPLEMENT A
Determine whether or not you are responsible for this supplement.

LIFO Liquidation

What causes a LIFO liquidation? How does tax law allow LIFO to be applied with regards to purchases made during an accounting period? As a result, how can a temporary LIFO liquidation be eliminated?

Inventory Management and LIFO Liquidations

How do many firms avoid LIFO liquidations and the accompanying increase in tax expense?

What normally happens to inventory levels when a company switches to a just-in-time inventory system? Why does tax law provide an incentive for U.S. companies *not* to become more efficient?

SELF-TEST QUESTIONS AND EXERCISES

MATCHING

Match each of the key terms listed below with the appropriate textbook definition:

D	1.	Cost of goods sold equation	G	13. Net realizable value
P	2.	Direct labor	F	14. Periodical inventory system
R	3.	Factory overhead	B	15. Perpetual inventory system
T	4.	Finished goods inventory	H	16. Purchase discount
Q	5.	First-in, first-out (FIFO)	W	17. Purchase discounts account
V	6.	Goods available for sale	J	18. Purchase returns and allowances
L	7.	Inventory	U	19. Raw material inventory
O	8.	Last-in, first-out (LIFO)	C	20. Replacement cost
E	9.	LIFO liquidation	K	21. Specific identification method
M	10.	LIFO Reserve	A	22. Weighted-average method
S	11.	Lower of cost or market (LCM)	I	23. Work in process inventory
N	12.	Merchandise inventory		

A. Inventory costing method that uses the weighted-average unit cost of the goods available for sale for both cost of goods sold and ending inventory.

B. A detailed inventory record is maintained recording each purchase and sale during the accounting period.

C. The current purchase price for identical goods.

D. Beginning inventory + purchases – ending inventory = cost of goods sold

E. A sale of a lower-cost inventory item from beginning LIFO inventory.

F. Ending inventory and cost of goods sold are determined at the end of the accounting period based on a physical inventory count.

G. The expected sales price less selling costs (e.g., repair and disposal costs).

H. Cash discount received for prompt payment of an account payable.

I. Goods in the process of being manufactured.

J. A deduction from the cost of purchases associated with unsatisfactory goods.

K. Inventory costing method that identifies the cost of the specific item that was sold.

L. Tangible property that is held for sale in the normal course of business or will be used in producing goods or services for sale.

M. A contra-asset for the excess of FIFO over LIFO inventory.

N. Goods held for resale in the ordinary course of business.

O. Inventory costing method that assumes the most recently acquired units are sold first.

P. The earnings of employees who work directly on the products being manufactured.

Q. Inventory costing method that assumes the oldest units are the first units sold.

R. Manufacturing costs that are not raw material or direct labor costs.

S. Valuation method departing from cost principle that serves to recognize a loss when replacement cost or net realizable value drops below cost.

T. Manufactured goods that are completed and ready for sale.

U. Items acquired for the purpose of processing into finished goods.

V. The sum of beginning inventory and purchases (or transfers to finished goods) for the period.

W. A deduction from the cost of purchases in the calculation of costs of goods sold for discounts taken.

TRUE-FALSE QUESTIONS

For each of the following statements, enter a T or F in the blank to indicate whether the statement is true or false.

T 1. The primary goals of inventory management are to have sufficient quantities of goods on hand to meet customer needs while minimizing the costs of carrying those goods.

F 2. Work in process inventory for a merchandiser consists of items not yet displayed for sale.

T 3. Goods manufactured by a business, completed and ready for sale, are classified as finished goods inventory.

T 4. The company should cease accumulating costs of purchases when raw materials are ready for use.

T 5. If the costs are incidental and not material in amount, the materiality constraint allows a merchandiser to expense transportation charges for shipment to the warehouse instead of inventorying these costs.

F 6. Factory overhead costs include raw materials, direct labor and all other manufacturing costs.

F 7. The cost of goods sold equation states that beginning inventory plus purchases plus ending inventory equals cost of goods sold.

T 8. An error in ending inventory affects not only the net income for that period but also the net income for the next accounting period.

T 9. FIFO allocates the oldest unit costs to cost of goods sold and the most recent unit costs to ending inventory.

T 10. LIFO allocates the most recent unit costs to cost of goods sold and the oldest unit costs to the ending inventory.

_F_11. The weighted-average unit cost is computed by dividing the cost of goods sold by the number of units available for sale.

_T_12. Manipulation of results is impossible when the specific identification method of inventory costing is used.

___13. The inventory costing method that gives the highest ending inventory amount also gives the highest gross margin and income amounts and vice versa.

___14. When unit costs and inventory quantities are rising, FIFO produces a lower inventory valuation than LIFO.

___15. A company's choice of an inventory costing method must at least approximate the physical flow of its inventory (that is, the actual physical flow of a company's inventory determines which method it must use).

___16. The LIFO conformity rule leads many companies to adopt LIFO for both tax and financial reporting purposes.

___17. In theory, the tax savings provided by LIFO are not permanent.

___18. The LIFO Reserve provides the needed information to convert the balances in inventory and cost of goods sold from LIFO to FIFO.

___19. Higher inventory turnover indicates that inventory is turned into cash more quickly.

___20. A holding loss is recognized when the purchase price of an item exceeds the current purchase price for an identical item.

___21. The lower of cost or market rule requires that damaged, deteriorated or obsolete items be assigned a unit cost that represents their current estimated net realizable value.

___22. The primary disadvantage of a periodic inventory system is the lack of inventory information.

___23. Perpetual inventory records are rarely kept on a LIFO basis.

___24. When a periodic inventory system is used, managers who wish to prepare monthly or quarterly financial statements for internal use often estimate the cost of goods sold and ending inventory.

___25. Purchase returns and allowances and purchase discounts are accounted for as deductions from the cost of purchases.

___26. A LIFO liquidation takes place when a LIFO company purchases or manufacturers more inventory than it sells. *(Supplement A)*

MULTIPLE CHOICE QUESTIONS

Choose the best answer or response by placing the identifying letter in the space provided.

_C_1. In a manufacturing company, raw materials are

    a. items purchased as spare parts for their products.
    b. items intended for resale.
    c. items that will be used to manufacture the company's products.
    d. completed products that have not yet been sold.
    e. items ordered but not yet received.

d 2. A merchandiser's inventory consists of

    a. raw materials and finished goods.
    b. raw materials, work in process and finished goods.
    c. finished goods.
    d. merchandise inventory intended for resale.
    e. raw materials.

d 3. A company overstated its ending inventory at the end of year one. Ignoring taxes, if the error went <u>undetected</u>, <u>retained earnings</u> would be _____ at the end of year one and _____ at the end of year two.

    a. overstated by the same amount; understated by the same amount.
    b. overstated by the same amount; overstated by the same amount.
    c. understated by the same amount; overstated by the same amount
    d. overstated by the same amount; unaffected
    e. understated by the same amount; understated by the same amount

d 4. The inventory costing method <u>least</u> likely to be used by a candy store is

    a. LIFO
    b. FIFO
    c. LCM
    d. specific identification
    e. weighted average

C 5. If a company uses LIFO for tax purposes, then for financial reporting purposes

    a. they are free to choose any inventory method they wish.
    b. they must disclose this fact.
    c. they must also use LIFO.
    d. they must use either LIFO or FIFO.
    e. they cannot use LIFO.

C 6. A LIFO liquidation occurs when a company

    a. converts from LIFO to FIFO.
    b. sells off all of its inventory.
    c. sells in one period more inventory than is purchased or manufactured.
    d. goes out of business.
    e. using LIFO experiences a decrease instead of an increase in merchandise cost.

d 7. The lower of cost or market rule (LCM) is applied

    a. when inventory costs less than it can be sold for.
    b. when the market value of a long-lived asset is less than its cost.
    c. when inventory has been held for more than one year.
    d. when the replacement cost or net realizable value of inventory drops below cost.
    e. all of the above.

8. In order to calculate cost of goods sold in a periodic inventory system, it is necessary to

    a. refer to the balance in the merchandise inventory account.
    b. add up sales receipts for the period.
    c. refer to the balance of the cost of goods sold account.
    d. physically count the merchandise inventory that is on hand.
    e. subtract gross profit from sales.

9. A perpetual inventory system differs from a periodic system in that

    a. up-to-date inventory records are maintained.
    b. a uniform base stock of inventory is always kept on hand.
    c. the books of account are closed more often.
    d. a perpetual system regularly takes physical counts of inventory on hand.
    e. a periodic system breaks the year into measurable accounting periods.

10. The purchases account is used

    a. in a perpetual system to record all purchases of inventory for resale.
    b. in a periodic system to record all purchases of inventory for resale.
    c. in both perpetual and periodic inventory systems to record all purchases of inventory for resale.
    d. only by manufacturers.
    e. as a contra account which relates to the inventory account.

EXERCISES

Record your answers to each part of these exercises in the space provided. Show your work.

1. Claremont Sweet Shoppe orders and sells toffees by the pound. On July 1st, Claremont had 500 pounds of toffee on hand which was purchased at $1.00 per pound. Claremont made a number of purchases of toffee during July:

Date of Purchase	Pounds	Cost per Pound	Total Cost
July 5	1,000	$1.10	$1,100
July 9	1,200	1.15	1,380
July 20	1,200	1.20	1,440
July 30	1,500	1.25	1,875

During July, the company sold 3,800 pounds of toffee at $1.45 per pound.

A. Compute the number of pounds of toffee on hand on July 31st, and the cost of goods available for sale for the month of July.

B. Assume that the company uses FIFO. Compute its ending inventory on July 31st, the cost of goods sold during July, and the company's gross profit during July.

C. Assume that the company uses LIFO. Compute its ending inventory on July 31st, the cost of goods sold during July, and the company's gross profit during July.

D. Compute the amount of the company's LIFO Reserve at the end of July. Using an effective income tax rate of 40%, determine the amount of tax savings that the company would realize for the month of July if it adopts LIFO rather than FIFO.

E. Assume that the company uses the weighted-average inventory method. Compute its ending inventory on July 31st, the cost of goods sold during July, and the company's gross profit during July.

F. On July 31st, the current purchase price for toffee dropped to $.99 per pound. Compute the ending inventory amount that should be reported on the balance sheet on July 31st.

2. Nassau Navigational Supplies, Inc. had $104,000, $92,000, and $78,000 of inventory, and accounts payable of $43,000, $38,000, and $29,000 on December 31, 19A, 19B and 19C, respectively. Nassau purchased $815,000 of inventory during 19B and $699,000 of inventory during 19C. Nassau reported net income of $319,000 for 19B and $327,000 for 19C.

A. Compute Nassau's cost of goods sold for the years ended December 31, 19B and 19C.

B. Compute Nassau's inventory turnover ratio for 19B and 19C. What does this ratio measure? Comment on the change, if any, in the ratio between 19B and 19C.

C. Using, only the information provided above, compute Nassau's net cash flows from operating activities for the year ended December 31, 19B and 19C.

D. Assume that Nassau made a computational error which understated its ending inventory by $5,000 at December 31, 19B. Compute the corrected amounts of cost of goods sold and net income for 19B and 19C. Determine the effect on retained earnings at December 31, 19C.

3. Prepare journal entries for each of the following transactions. Assume that the company uses a periodic inventory system and records freight charges in a separate account.

A. Sold merchandise for cash of $125,000.

B. Refunded $12,000 to customers for merchandise returned.

C. Purchased $15,000 of merchandise from Abaco Vending on credit, terms 2/10, n/30.

D. Paid $500 freight bill on merchandise purchased.

E. Paid Abaco Vending before the discount period had expired.

SOLUTIONS TO SELF-TEST QUESTIONS AND EXERCISES

MATCHING

1.	D	6.	V	11.	S	16.	H	21.	K
2.	P	7.	L	12.	N	17.	W	22.	A
3.	R	8.	O	13.	G	18.	J	23.	I
4.	T	9.	E	14.	F	19.	U		
5.	Q	10.	M	15.	B	20.	C		

TRUE-FALSE QUESTIONS

1.   T

2.   F - All goods held for resale in the ordinary course of business by a merchandiser, whether displayed for sale or not, are classified as merchandise inventory. Goods in the process of being manufactured are classified as work-in-process inventory.

3.   T

4.   T

5.   T

6.   F - All manufacturing costs *other than* raw materials and direct labor costs are classified as factory overhead costs.

7.   F - The cost of goods sold equation states that beginning inventory plus purchases *less* ending inventory equals cost of goods sold.

8.   T

9.   T

10.   T

11.   F - The weighted-average unit cost is computed by dividing the cost of goods *available for sale* by the number of units available for sale.

12.   F - The specific identification method may be manipulated when the units are identical; a manager could affect the cost of goods sold and the ending inventory by picking and choosing from among the several available units costs, even though the goods are identical in other respects.

13.   T

14.   F - When unit costs and inventory quantities are rising, FIFO produces a *higher* inventory valuation than LIFO. FIFO uses the most recent unit costs, LIFO uses the oldest unit costs to value ending inventory.

15.   F - A company's choice of an inventory costing method does not need to approximate the physical flow of its inventory.

16.   T

17.   T

18.   T

19. T

20. T

21. F - The lower of cost or market rule requires that a damaged, deteriorated or obsolete item be assigned a unit cost that represents its current estimated net realizable value *only* if the net realizable value of the item is below its cost.

22. T

23. T

24. T

25. T

26. F - A LIFO liquidation takes place when a LIFO company sells more inventory than it purchases or manufacturers.

MULTIPLE CHOICE QUESTIONS

1.	c	3.	d	5.	c	7.	d	9.	a
2.	d	4.	d	6.	c	8.	d	10.	b

EXERCISES

1A.

Beginning inventory		500
Purchases:		
July 5	1,000	
July 9	1,200	
July 20	1,200	
July 30	1,500	4,900
Available for sale		5,400
Less pounds sold		3,800
Ending inventory		1,600

Beginning inventory	(500 @ $1.00)		$ 500
Purchases:			
July 5	(1,000 @ $1.10)	$1,100	
July 9	(1,200 @ $1.15)	1,380	
July 20	(1,200 @ $1.20)	1,440	
July 30	(1,500 @ $1.25)	1,875	5,795
Goods available for sale			$6,295

1B. (Remember that FIFO assumes that the newest units are left in ending inventory.)

Sales	(3,800 @ $1.45)			$5,510
Beginning inventory	(from A above)		$ 500	
Purchases	(from A above)		5,795	
Goods available for sale			6,295	
Less ending inventory:				
from July 30 purchase	(1,500 @ $1.25)	$1,875		
from July 20 purchase	(100 @ $1.20)	120	1,995	
Cost of goods sold				4,300
Gross profit				$1,210

1C. (Remember that LIFO assumes that the oldest units are left in ending inventory.)

Sales	(3,800 @ $1.45)			$5,510
Beginning inventory	(from A above)		$ 500	
Purchases	(from A above)		5,795	
Goods available for sale			6,295	
Less ending inventory:				
from beginning inventory	(500 @ $1.00)	$ 500		
from July 5 purchase	(1,000 @ $1.10)	1,100		
from July 9 purchase	(100 @ $1.15)	115	1,715	
Cost of goods sold				4,580
Gross profit				$ 930

1D.

Ending inventory at FIFO	$1,995
Ending inventory at LIFO	1,715
LIFO Reserve	$ 280

Cost of goods sold (LIFO)	$1,210
Cost of goods sold (FIFO)	930
Difference in pretax income	280
Effective tax rate	x .40
Difference in taxes	$ 112

1E.

Goods available for sale / Number of units available for sale = Weighted average unit cost

$6,295 / 5,400 pounds = $1.1657 per pound (could round to $1.17)

Ending inventory = 1,600 pounds @ $1.1657 per pound = $1,865

Cost of goods sold = 3,800 pounds @ $1.1657 per pound = $4,430

Sales	(3,800 @ $1.45)		$5,510
Beginning inventory	(from A above)	$ 500	
Purchases	(from A above)	5,795	
Goods available for sale		6,295	
Less ending inventory:	(from above)	1,865	
Cost of goods sold	(from above)		4,430
Gross profit			$1,080

1F. Ending inventory = 1,600 pounds @ $.99 per pound = $1,584

2A.

	19B	19C
Beginning inventory	$104,000	$ 92,000
Purchases	815,000	699,000
Goods available for sale	919,000	791,000
Less ending inventory:	92,000	78,000
Cost of goods sold	$827,000	$713,000

2B.

19B

Cost of goods sold / Average inventory = Inventory turnover

$827,000 / [($104,000 + $92,000) / 2] = $827,000 / $98,000 = 8.44

19C

Cost of goods sold / Average inventory = Inventory turnover

$713,000 / [($92,000 + $78,000) / 2] = $713,000 / $85,500 = 8.34

Inventory turnover measures the liquidity (nearness to cash) of the inventory. The lower inventory ratio in 19C indicates that inventory is being turned into cash less quickly. This ratio also measures the efficiency of using inventory. The lower ratio means less efficiency.

2C.

	19B	19C
Cash flows from operating activities:		
Net income	$319,000	$327,000
Plus decrease in inventory	12,000	14,000
Less increase in accounts payable	(5,000)	(9,000)
Net cash flows from operating activities	$326,000	$332,000

2D.

	19B		19C	
	As		As	
	Reported	**Corrected**	**Reported**	**Corrected**
Cost of goods sold	$827,000	$822,000	$713,000	$718,000
Net income	319,000	324,000	327,000	322,000

The error made in the inventory at the end of 19B understated 19B net income by $5,000 and overstated 19C net income by $5,000. Unless repeated, inventory errors are self-correcting over a two year period. As a result, retained earnings at the end of 19C will be correctly reported.

3.

A.	Cash	125,000	
	Sales		125,000
B.	Sales returns and allowances	12,000	
	Cash		12,000
C.	Purchases	15,000	
	Accounts payable		15,000
D.	Freight-in	500	
	Cash		500
E.	Accounts payable	15,000	
	Purchase discounts		300
	Cash		14,700

IDEAS FOR YOUR STUDY TEAM

1. Rewrite each of the definitions of the key terms that appear at the end of the chapter using your own words. Imagine that you are trying to explain each key term to a friend who has not taken any accounting classes. Then, get together with the other members of your study team and compare your definitions.

Cost of goods sold equation

Direct labor

Factory overhead

Finished goods inventory

First-in, first-out (FIFO)

Goods available for sale

Inventory

Last-in, first-out (LIFO)

LIFO liquidation

LIFO Reserve

Lower of cost or market (LCM)

Merchandise inventory

Net realizable value

Periodical inventory system

Perpetual inventory system

Purchase discount

Purchase returns and allowances

Raw material inventory

Replacement cost

Specific identification method

Weighted-average method

Work in process inventory

2. List all of the things that a company can do to affect its gross profit (either as a dollar amount or as a ratio). Then, get together with the other members of your study team, compare your lists, and discuss the following questions. Is the gross profit ratio subject to manipulation? What can users of financial statements do to assure themselves as to the reliability of inventory information?

3. The following table contains alternative ending inventory figures for a company that began business on January 1, 19A. Assume that inventory quantities increased during 19B. Review information provided, answer each of the questions and then get together with the other members of your study team to compare your answers.

	FIFO	LIFO	Weighted Average
December 31, 19A	$ 20	$100	$ 71
December 31, 19B	150	130	142

Were inventory prices rising or falling during 19A? Were inventory prices rising or falling during 19B? How can you tell?

During 19A, which inventory method would produce the highest net income? Which method would produce the lowest net income? During 19B, which inventory method would produce the highest net income? Which method will produce the lowest net income?

Which method would management choose in 19A if tax savings were the primary consideration? Would they still consider this a good choice in 19B?

Which method gives the most realistic balance sheet inventory value? Which method shows the most realistic income statement value? Why?

CHAPTER 8
REPORTING AND INTERPRETING PROPERTY, PLANT, AND EQUIPMENT; NATURAL RESOURCES; AND INTANGIBLES

CHAPTER FOCUS SUGGESTIONS

This chapter focuses on the accounting for noncurrent assets that a business retains for long periods of time for use in the course of normal operations. These assets are not held for sale. Noncurrent assets, also known as operational assets, include both tangible assets (such as property, plant, and equipment, and natural resources) and intangible assets (such as goodwill, trademarks, copyrights, franchises, leaseholds, and leasehold improvements). You will need to know how to determine cost when operational assets are acquired. Cost includes the cash equivalent price plus all reasonable and necessary expenditures made to acquire and prepare the asset for its intended use. Ordinary repair and maintenance costs relating to property, plant, and equipment are classified as revenue expenditures, and immediately expensed. Extraordinary repairs and additions are classified as capital expenditures, and added to the related asset accounts.

An operational asset represents a future service or benefit that is paid for in advance. (Recall the definition of a deferral from chapter 4.) Over its life, an operational asset is used to generate revenues. In conformity with the matching principle the expenses associated with the use of these assets must be matched with, or allocated to the same period as, the revenues generated. The allocation process is called depreciation for property, plant, and equipment, depletion for natural resources, and amortization for intangibles. You should be able to compute depreciation expense using the straight-line, units-of-production, and declining balance methods.

When operational assets are disposed of, the cost of the asset and the related accumulated depreciation, depletion or amortization must be removed from the related accounts. You should know how to compute the gain or loss that will result when the disposal price is different from the book value of the asset.

READ AND RECALL QUESTIONS

LEARNING OBJECTIVE
After studying this section of the chapter, you should be able to:
1. Define, classify, and explain the nature of noncurrent productive assets.

CLASSIFICATION OF OPERATIONAL ASSETS

What are the two types of operational assets? What are the characteristics of each type? How are these assets reported on the balance sheet?

After studying this section of the chapter, you should be able to:
2. Apply the cost principle to measure the acquisition of property, plant, and equipment.

MEASURING AND RECORDING ACQUISITION COST

What does "capitalized" mean? What three types of costs should be capitalized when an operational asset is acquired? What two types of costs sometimes associated with the acquisition of an operational asset should not be capitalized? How should these costs be reported?

What types of costs are capitalized when land is purchased? Is land subject to depreciation?

Various Acquisition Methods

For Noncash Consideration (including Equity)

How is the cash-equivalent cost measured when noncash consideration is part of the transaction to purchase an operational asset? (Address situations in which the market value of the noncash consideration is known, and those in which the market value cannot be determined.)

By Construction

What types of costs are capitalized when a company constructs an asset for its own use? What is capitalized interest? What is the amount of capitalized interest based on?

As a Basket Purchase of Assets

What is a basket purchase? Why must the purchase price be apportioned between the assets acquired? What is the most logical basis to allocate the purchase price to the various assets acquired?

LEARNING OBJECTIVE

After studying this section of the chapter, you should be able to:

3. Understand the financial statement impact of management's decisions regarding ordinary and extraordinary repairs, various cost allocation methods, and changes in estimates, as assets are held and used over time.

USING PROPERTY, PLANT, AND EQUIPMENT AFTER ACQUISITION

Repairs, Maintenance, and Additions

What are capital expenditures? How are capital expenditures recorded? What are revenue expenditures? How are revenue expenditures recorded? Why do auditors closely review the items reported as capital and revenue expenditures?

What are ordinary repairs and maintenance? How are ordinary repairs and maintenance reported? What are extraordinary repairs? How are extraordinary repairs reported?

What are additions? How are additions reported?

What is depreciation? How is the amount of depreciation recorded each period reported? How is the amount of depreciation accumulated since the acquisition date of the operational asset reported?

What is book value? What other term is used to describe book value? What does book value represent? What doesn't it represent?

Financial Analysis

How is the fixed asset turnover ratio computed and what does it measure? Delta Air Lines' fixed asset turnover has been increasing in recent years. What does this trend suggest?

Depreciation Concepts

What three amounts are needed to compute depreciation expense? Which of the amounts are estimates?

Book Value as an Approximation of Remaining Life

What can be approximated when book value is compared to original cost?

What is residual value? What other term is used to describe residual value? How do disposal costs affect residual value?

What is represented by estimated useful life? How does the continuity assumption affect the determination of estimated useful life?

Differences in Estimated Useful Lives within a Single Industry

Why would companies in a single industry, such as the airline industry, use different estimated useful lives for the same operational assets, such as aircraft? What factors affect this estimate?

Alternative Depreciation Methods

What are the three most common depreciation methods?

Straight-Line Method

Which depreciation method is used by more companies that all other methods combined? What is the formula for computing straight-line depreciation?

Units-of-Production Method

What is the formula for computing units-of-production depreciation? Why is depreciation expense considered to be a variable expense when the units-of-production method is used?

Accelerated Depreciation – Declining Balance Method

What is meant by "accelerated" depreciation? What are two reasons for the use of accelerated depreciation?

How is the declining balance (DB) rate found? What is the double declining rate?

What is the formula for computing double-declining balance depreciation? How and when does residual value affect the calculation of depreciation expense when this method is used?

What types of companies would use the declining-balance method of depreciation?

Impact of Alternative Depreciation Methods

If one company uses accelerated depreciation and another uses straight-line, which company would you expect to report lower depreciation expense and, as a result, higher net income? (Hint: The answer is not as obvious as it seems.)

Managers' Selection Among Accounting Alternatives

Which depreciation method is easy to use and explain? Which depreciation method reports lower depreciation expense and, as a result, higher net income compared to other methods during the early years of the life of an asset? As such, which depreciation method do most managers prefer?

Depreciation and Federal Income Tax

Why does Delta Air Lines maintain two sets of accounting records? Why is it legal to do so? What is the "least and the latest" rule?

What depreciation method is used for tax purposes by most companies? Why isn't this method acceptable under GAAP? What principle is violated by this method?

Depreciation Methods in Other Countries

Many other countries permit the revaluation of property, plant, and equipment to current cost as of the balance sheet date. What is the primary argument in favor of revaluation? Revaluation is not permitted by GAAP. What is the primary argument against revaluation?

Changes in Depreciation Estimates

If an asset's cost has been increased, or the estimates of its useful life and/or residual value change, what should be done? What is a "change in estimate?"

When does GAAP allow changes in accounting estimates and deprecation methods? What does the consistency principle require? Why did Delta change the estimated life of its flight equipment and the estimated residual value of its flight equipment in 1993?

Increased Profitability Due to an Accounting Adjustment?
Reading the Footnotes

Why do analysts pay close attention to changes in accounting estimates?

LEARNING OBJECTIVE
After studying this section of the chapter, you should be able to:
4. Explain the impact of cost allocation methods on cash flows.

FOCUS ON DEPRECIATION AND CASH FLOWS

Why is depreciation expense a noncash expense? Should depreciation expense be added back to or deducted from net income to compute cash flows from operations?

How can depreciation result in a reduction of cash outflows for the company?

LEARNING OBJECTIVE
After studying this section of the chapter, you should be able to:
5. Analyze the disposal of property, plant, and equipment.

DISPOSAL OF OPERATIONAL ASSETS

Why might a business voluntarily decide not to hold an operational asset for its entire life? What could cause a business to involuntarily dispose of an operational asset?

What two entries must be made when as a result of the disposal of an operational asset?

Why might a gain or loss occur upon the disposal of an operational asset? How is the gain or loss on disposal computed?

Taking a Different Strategy to Success

Why does Singapore Airlines report significantly higher depreciation expense when compared to the rest of the airline industry? What happens when Singapore Airlines sells its aircraft? What is management able to accomplish by using its strategy for managing the company's operational productivity?

LEARNING OBJECTIVE
After studying this section of the chapter, you should be able to:
6. Understand the measurement and reporting of natural resources and intangible assets.

NATURAL RESOURCES

What are natural resources? Why are natural resources called "wasting assets?"

Acquisition and Cost Allocation

What is depletion? How is a depletion rate computed? How is depletion expense computed?

INTANGIBLE ASSETS

Acquisition and Cost Allocation

If an intangible asset is developed internally, how is the cost of development recorded? Should research and development costs be capitalized or expensed? Should the amount spent to purchase a patent be capitalized or expensed?

What method is usually used to amortize intangible assets? What life should be used to compute the annual amortization expense? How does residual value affect amortization expense?

Examples of Intangible Assets

What is goodwill? What factors result in goodwill? What is "internally generated" goodwill? Is internally generated goodwill reported in the financial statements?

What is another term used to describe goodwill for accounting purposes? How is goodwill computed when one company purchases another?

232

What method is usually used to amortize goodwill? What life should be used to compute the annual amortization expense? What is the maximum period allowed for amortization?

What is a patent? How is cost measured when a patent is purchased?

GAAP requires the immediate expensing of research and development costs. As such, what costs can be recorded as an intangible asset when a patent is developed internally?

What is a trademark? Should the costs of developing a trademark be recorded as an asset or an expense?

What is a copyright?

What is a franchise?

What is a leasehold? What are leasehold improvements?

LEARNING OBJECTIVE
After studying this section of the chapter, you should be able to:
7. Explain the effect of asset impairment on the financial statements.

IMPAIRED ASSETS

What is impairment? When does impairment occur? When should an impairment loss be recognized?

Fierce Pressure to Report Smooth, Ever Higher Earnings

How do companies use long-lived assets to meet or beat earnings estimates? (Hint: There are at least three ways.)

SELF-TEST QUESTIONS AND EXERCISES

MATCHING

Match each of the key terms listed below with the appropriate textbook definition:

K   1.   Accelerated depreciation
D   2.   Acquisition cost
R   3.   Additions
X   4.   Amortization
M   5.   Basket purchase
A   6.   Book (or carrying) value
H   7.   Capital expenditures
L   8.   Capitalized interest
J   9.   Copyright
Z   10.   Declining-balance (DB)
               depreciation
Q   11.   Depletion
AA   12.   Depreciation
B   13.   Estimated useful life
C   14.   Extraordinary repairs
P   15.   Franchise

G   16.   Goodwill (cost in excess of net
               assets acquired)
O   17.   Intangible assets
BB   18.   Leaseholds
N   19.   Natural resources
U   20.   Operational assets (long-lived
               assets)
W   21.   Ordinary repairs and maintenance
F   22.   Patent
T   23.   Residual (or salvage) value
E   24.   Revenue expenditures
V   25.   Straight-line (SL) depreciation
I   26.   Tangible assets
Y   27.   Trademark
S   28.   Units-of-production depreciation

A.   Acquisition cost of an operational asset less accumulated depreciation, depletion, or amortization.

B.   Expected service life of an operational asset to the present owner.

C.   Major, high-cost, long-term repairs that increase the economic usefulness of the asset; increase an asset account (or decrease accumulated depreciation); a capital expenditure.

D.   Net cash equivalent amount paid or to be paid for the asset.

E.   Expenditures that provide benefits during the current accounting period only, recorded as expenses.

F.   An exclusive right granted by the federal government for an invention; the owner as the right to use, manufacture, and sell the subject of the patent.

G.   For accounting purposes, the excess of the purchase price of a business over the market value of the business' assets and liabilities.

H.   Expenditures that provide future benefits, recorded as increases in asset accounts, not as expenses.

I.   Operational assets (or fixed assets) that have physical substance.

J.   An exclusive legal right to use a special name, image, or slogan.

K.   Methods that result in higher depreciation expense in the early years of an operational asset's life and lower expense in the later years.

L.   Interest expenditures included in the cost of a self-constructed asset.

M.   Acquisition of two or more assets in a single transaction for a single lump sum.

N. Mineral deposits, timber tracts, oil, and gas.

O. Operational assets that have special rights but not physical substance.

P. A contractual right to sell certain products or services, use certain trademarks, or perform activities in a geographical region.

Q. Systematic and rational allocation of the cost of a natural resource over the period of exploitation.

R. Extensions to, or enlargements of, existing assets; increase the cost of the existing asset; a capital expenditure.

S. Method that allocates the cost of an operational asset over its useful life based on its periodic output related to its total estimated output.

T. Estimated amount to be recovered, less disposal costs, at the end of the company's estimated useful life of an operational asset.

U. Tangible and intangible assets owned by a business and used in its operations.

V. Depreciation method that allocates the cost of an operational asset in equal periodic amounts over its useful life.

W. Expenditures for the normal operating upkeep of operational assets; increase an expense for ordinary repairs.

X. Systematic and rational allocation of the acquisition cost of an intangible asset over its useful life.

Y. Exclusive right to publish, use, and sell a literary, musical, or artistic work.

Z. The method that allocates the cost of an operational asset over its useful life based on a multiple (often two times) the straight-line rate.

AA. Systematic and rational allocation of the cost of property, plant, and equipment (but not land) over their useful lives.

BB. Rights granted to a lessee under a lease contract.

TRUE-FALSE QUESTIONS

For each of the following statements, enter a T or F in the blank to indicate whether the statement is true or false.

___1. The cost of an asset includes all reasonable and necessary costs to acquire the asset, place it in its operational setting, and prepare it for its intended use.

___2. If the market value of the noncash consideration that is included in the purchase of an operational asset cannot be determined, the cash-equivalent cost of the asset should be limited to the cash paid.

___3. Interest on self-constructed assets should only be capitalized when funds are borrowed directly to support the construction.

___4. When several operational assets are acquired in a basket purchase, the purchase price should be divided by the number of assets acquired to determine the acquisition cost of each individual asset acquired.

___5. Revenue expenditures are expenditures that provide benefits during the current accounting period only.

___6. If material, repair and maintenance expenditures should be added to the related asset account.

___7. The decision as to whether an expenditure is a capital expenditure or a revenue expenditure can be based on the materiality of the amount involved.

___8. Depreciation expense is an estimate.

___9. Fixed asset turnover is computed by dividing average fixed assets (net) by sales or operating revenues.

___10. The useful life estimated for a piece of equipment should be based on the number of years that the equipment would be expected to last under normal use by an average user of the equipment.

___11. More companies use the declining balance accelerated depreciation method for financial reporting purposes than all other methods combined.

___12. The declining balance rate is found by computing the straight-line rate, ignoring residual value, and then multiplying that rate by a selected acceleration rate which may not exceed 200%.

___13. The declining balance method is used by companies in industries that expect fairly rapid obsolescence of equipment.

___14. The consistency principle requires that accounting information reported in the financial statements should be comparable across accounting periods, and, as such, changes in estimates of useful life and residual value are not allowed under GAAP.

___15. The depreciation conformity rule requires companies to use the same depreciation method for financial reporting and tax return purposes.

___16. A company wishing to improve its cash flow should use the straight-line method rather than an accelerated method of depreciation for financial reporting purposes.

___17. A loss on disposal occurs when the book value of the operational asset is less than the resources received.

___18. The acquisition cost of natural resources (or wasting assets) must be reported as a revenue expenditure because these assets are depleted.

___19. Amortization, depletion and depreciation are cost allocation processes.

___20. Goodwill is only reported if it arises in connection with the purchase of another company.

MULTIPLE CHOICE QUESTIONS

Choose the best answer or response by placing the identifying letter in the space provided.

D 1. _____ assets have physical substance, whereas _____ assets have no physical substance, but rather grant rights to their owner.

    a. Operational; long-lived
    b. Tangible; intangible
    c. Operational; non-operating
    d. Intangible; tangible
    e. Tangible; natural resources

_e_ 2. The acquisition cost of an operational asset may include

    a. the market value of any noncash consideration given.
    b. incidental costs, such as title fees, sales commissions, legal fees, etc.
    c. renovation and repair costs incurred prior to use.
    d. capitalized interest.
    e. all of the above.

_d_ 3. When a basket purchase takes place

    a. the assets are recorded as a single asset, at the purchase cost.
    b. the assets are recorded individually at their market values.
    c. the assets are recorded as a single asset at the total of their market values.
    d. each individual asset is recorded separately, at an apportioned cost based on the relative market values of all the assets purchased.
    e. each individual asset is recorded separately, with the cost evenly divided between them.

_a_ 4. The primary purpose of depreciation is to

    a. allocate the cost of an asset over its useful life in conformity with the matching principle.
    b. determine the market value of an asset at any point of its life.
    c. delay as long as possible the payment of taxes by charging expense against income.
    d. approximate the total cost of using an asset.
    e. decrease the value of an asset in conformity with the conservatism principle.

_c_ 5. Residual value is

    a. the difference at any point in time between net book value and market value.
    b. the excess of cost over accumulated depreciation.
    c. the part of the acquisition cost of an asset expected to be recovered when the asset is disposed of at the end of its usefulness to the current owner.
    d. the part of an asset not yet depreciated at any point in time.
    e. the scrap value of the asset.

_b_ 6. Accelerated depreciation methods include the sum-of-the-years' digits method and the

    a. straight-line method.
    b. declining-balance method.
    c. units-of-production method.
    d. depletion method.
    e. annuity method.

_a_ 7. For tax purposes, Delta Air Lines probably uses the _____ to compute depreciation.

    a. Modified Accelerated Cost Recovery System
    b. straight-line method
    c. sum-of-the-years' digits
    d. 200% declining balance
    e. units of service

_b_ 8. If a company completely rebuilds a motor on a piece of equipment during its useful life, and the rebuilt motor extends the useful life of the equipment and increases the residual value, this expenditure would be classified as a

   a. capital expenditure and capitalized as a separate asset.
   b. capital expenditure and capitalized as part of the cost of the equipment.
   c. revenue expenditure and capitalized as part of the cost of the equipment.
   d. revenue expenditure and expensed in the period in which it was spent.
   e. capital expenditure and expensed in the period in which it was spent.

_e_ 9. Depletion is the term used to describe the periodic cost allocation process over the life of

   a. an intangible asset.
   b. land.
   c. a building.
   d. supplies.
   e. a natural resource.

_d_ 10. All of the following are intangible assets except

   a. a copyright.
   b. a McDonald's franchise.
   c. goodwill.
   d. an offshore oil well.
   e. a leasehold on a large office building.

EXERCISES

Record your answers to each part of these exercises in the space provided. Show your work.

1. On January 1, 19A, Coopers Industries bought a parcel of land and a building for use in its operations by paying the seller $100,000 in cash, signing a five year, 12% note payable in the amount of $100,000, and issuing 3,000 shares of Coopers Industries $1 par value common stock ($100 per share market value). In connection with the purchase of the land and building, Coopers incurred legal fees of $19,000, a real estate agent sales commission of $25,000, surveying fees of $1,000, and an appraisal fee of $5,000 in connection with the purchase, and prepaid its 19A insurance premium on the property of in the amount of $12,500. (All of these amounts were paid in cash.) The land was appraised at $240,000 and the building at $360,000. The building has an estimated useful life of 30 years and an estimated residual value of $37,000.

A. Compute the total acquisition cost relating to this basket purchase.

B. Apportion the total acquisition cost to the land, and building.

C. Prepare the journal entry for the acquisition.

D. Prepare the journal entry to record depreciation expense for 19A.

2. On January 1, 19A, Trueblood, Inc. purchased a piece of machinery for use in operations. The total acquisition cost was $33,000. The machine has an estimated useful life of three years, and a residual value of $3,000. Assume that units produced by the machine will amount to 16,000 during 19A, 23,000 during 19B and 20,000 during 19C.

A. Complete the following table. Show your work in the space below the table.

Method	Depreciation Expense			Book Value at End of Year		
	19A	19B	19C	19A	19B	19C
Straight-line						
Units of production						
Double declining balance						

B. On January 1, 19B, the machine was rebuilt at a cost of $7,000. After the rebuild, the total estimated life was increased to five years (instead of three) and the residual value to $6,000 (from $3,000). Assume that the company chose the straight-line method for depreciation. Compute the annual depreciation expense after the change in estimates.

C. On December 31, 19E, the machine was sold for $7,500. Compute the book value on that date, and then prepare the journal entry for the sale.

3. Pixar reported property and equipment, net, of $4,655,000 and $1,552,000 on its balance sheet at December 31, 1996 and 1995, respectively. Revenues earned from software, animation, film and patent licensing amounted to $38,227,000 and $12,113,000 for the years ended December 31, 1996 and 1995, respectively.

A. Compute Pixar's 1996 fixed asset turnover ratio.

B. What does the fixed asset turnover ratio measure? How might an analyst interpret an increasing ratio? Does a declining ratio always indicate a negative trend?

4. On January 1, 19A, Morris Minerals paid $300,000 for a mineral deposit in Morris, Illinois. During February of that year, Morris spent $45,000 to prepare the deposit for exploitation. It was estimated that 690,000 total cubic yards could be extracted economically. During 19A, 69,000 yards were extracted. During January 19B, another $10,000 was spend for additional development work. At this time, the estimated remaining recovery was increased to 920,000 cubic yards. During 19B, another 70,000 cubic yards were extracted.

A. Compute the acquisition cost of the deposit after the February 19A preparation costs. Compute the depletion expense for 19A.

B. Compute the acquisition cost of the deposit after the January 19B development costs. Compute the depletion expense for 19B.

5. On January 1, 1C, Drafke Companies paid $15,000 to Beltran Industries for a patent. Beltran had registered the patent with the U. S. Patent Office two years earlier on January 1, 19A. Prepare journal entries for Drafke's purchase of the patent, and the amortization expense for 19C.

SOLUTIONS TO SELF-TEST QUESTIONS AND EXERCISES

MATCHING

1.	K	6.	A	11.	Q	16.	G	21.	W	26.	I
2.	D	7.	H	12.	AA	17.	O	22.	F	27.	Y
3.	R	8.	L	13.	B	18.	BB	23.	T	28.	S
4.	X	9.	J	14.	C	19.	N	24.	E		
5.	M	10.	Z	15.	P	20.	U	25.	V		

TRUE-FALSE QUESTIONS

1. T

2. F - If the market value of the noncash consideration given cannot be determined, the current market value of the asset purchased should be used for measurement purposes.

3. F - Interest on self-constructed assets should be capitalized *even* in cases where funds were not borrowed directly to support the construction.

4. F - When several operational assets are acquired in a basket purchase, the purchase price must be apportioned between each of the assets acquired on a rational basis; relative market value of the several assets on the date of acquisition is the most logical basis on which to allocate the single lump sum.

5. T

6. F - Ordinary repairs and maintenance are recorded as an expense in the period in which incurred; extraordinary repairs are added to the related asset account.

7. T

8. T

9. F - Fixed asset turnover is computed by dividing sales (or operating revenues) by average fixed assets (net).

10. F - Estimated useful life represents the useful economic life to the present owner rather than the total economic life to all potential users.

11. F - More companies use straight-line depreciation for financial reporting purposes than all other methods combined.

12. T

13. T

14. F - The consistency principles places a significant *constraint* on changing depreciation estimates unless the effect is to improve the measurement of depreciation expense and net income; however, GAAP does permit changes in estimates of useful life and residual value when it is clear that either estimate should be revised to a material degree.

15. F - Some of the depreciation methods used for financial reporting purposes are not acceptable for federal income tax reporting and vice versa; most corporations use the Modified Accelerated Cost Recovery System (which is not permitted under GAAP) for calculating depreciation expense for tax purposes.

16. F - The depreciation expense recorded for financial reporting purposes is a noncash expense which does not directly affect cash flows.

17. F - A loss on disposal occurs when the book value of the operational asset is *greater than* the resources received.

18. F - When a natural resource is acquired or developed, it is recorded in conformity with the cost principle, and, as the natural resource is used up, its acquisition cost is apportioned among the various periods in which the resulting revenues are earned. That is, the cost is recorded in a separate noncurrent asset account and then depletion expense is recorded over the economic life of the natural resource.

19. T

20. T

MULTIPLE CHOICE QUESTIONS

1. b	3. d	5. c	7. a	9. e
2. e	4. a	6. b	8. b	10. d

EXERCISES

1A.

Purchase price:		
Cash		$100,000
Noncash consideration:		
Note payable	$100,000	
Common stock (3,000 shares @ $100.share)	300,000	400,000
Incidental costs paid by purchaser:		
Legal fees	$ 19,000	
Commission	25,000	
Surveying fees	1,000	
Appraisal fee	5,000	50,000
Total acquisition cost		$550,000

1B.

Land

[$240,000 / ($240,000 + $360,000)] x $550,000 = $220,000

Building

[$360,000 / ($240,000 + $360,000)] x $550,000 = $330,000

1C.

Building	330,000	
Land	220,000	
Cash ($100,000 + $50,000)		150,000
Note payable		100,000
Common stock (3,000 shares @ $1/share)		3,000
Contributed capital in excess of par		
(3,000 shares @ $99/share)		297,000
Prepaid insurance	12,500	
Cash		12,500

1D.

Depreciation expense		
($220,000 - $37,000)/30)	6,100	
Accumulated depreciation		6,100

2A.

	Depreciation Expense			Book Value at End of Year		
Method	**19A**	**19B**	**19C**	**19A**	**19B**	**19C**
Straight-line	$10,000 (1)	$10,000 (1)	$10,000 (1)	$23,000	$13,000	$3,000
Units of production	8,000 (2)	11,500 (3)	10,500 (4)	25,000	13,500	3,000
Double declining balance	22,000 (5)	7,333 (6)	667 (7)	11,000	3,667	3,000

(1)   ($33,000 - $3,000) / 3 = $10,000

(2) $16,000 / ($16,000 + $23, 000 + $21,000) x ($33,000 - $3,000) = $8,000

(3) $23,000 / ($16,000 + $23, 000 + $21,000) x ($33,000 - $3,000) = $11,500

(4) $21,000 / ($16,000 + $23, 000 + $21,000) x ($33,000 - $3,000) = $10,500

(5)   ($33,000 - $0) x 2/3 = $22,000

(6)   ($33,000 - $22,000) x 2/3 = $7,333

(7)   ($33,000 - $22,000 - $7,333) x 2/3 = $2,445; however, recording this amount of depreciation expense in 19C would cause the book value to drop below the residual value, so record only $667 ($3,667 - $3,000) of depreciation expense.

2B.

Acquisition cost	$ 33,000
Less accumulated depreciation at December 31, 19A	(10,000)
Add extraordinary repair (considered to be an addition)	7,000
Book value at January 1, 19B	30,000
Less residual value	(6,000)
Undepreciated balance	24,000
Divided by remaining useful life (5 years - 1 year)	4
Revised amount of annual depreciation	$ 6,000

2C.

Acquisition cost		$33,000
Add extraordinary repair		7,000
Balance in machinery account		40,000
Accumulated depreciation:		
19A	$10,000	
19B through 19E ($6,000 x 4)	24,000	34,000
Book value at December 31, 19E		$ 6,000

Cash	7,500	
Accumulated depreciation	34,000	
Machinery		40,000
Gain on sale ($7,500 - $6,000)		1,500

3A.

Sales (or operating revenues) / Average fixed assets (net) = Fixed asset turnover ratio

$38,227,000 / [($4,655,000 + $1,552,000) / 2] = $38,227,000 / $3,103,500 = 12.3

3B.

This ratio measures how efficient the company utilizes it investment in property, plant, and equipment over time. An increasing fixed asset turnover rate suggest improvements in efficiency, and vice versa. However, a declining rate may, instead, indicate a company that is expanding in anticipation of higher sales in the future.

4A.

Purchase price	$300,000
Preparation costs	45,000
Acquisition cost	$345,000

$345,000 x (69,000 / 690,000) = $34,500

4B.

Purchase price	$345,000
Less 19A depletion	(34,500)
Book value at December 31, 19A	310,500
Development costs	10,000
Undepleted balance	$320,500

$320,500 x (70,000 / 920,000) = $34,500

5.

Patent	15,000	
Cash		15,000
Amortization expense [$15,000 / (17 - 2)]	1,000	
Patent		1,000

IDEAS FOR YOUR STUDY TEAM

1. Rewrite each of the definitions of the key terms that appear at the end of the chapter using your own words. Imagine that you are trying to explain each key term to a friend who has not taken any accounting classes. Then, get together with the other members of your study team and compare your definitions.

Accelerated depreciation

Acquisition cost

Additions

Amortization

Basket purchase

Book (or carrying) value

Capital expenditures

Capitalized interest

Copyright

Declining-balance (DB) depreciation

Depletion

Depreciation

Estimated useful life

Extraordinary repairs

Franchise

Goodwill (cost in excess of net assets acquired)

Intangible assets

Leaseholds

Natural resources

Operational assets (long-lived assets)

Ordinary repairs and maintenance

Patent

Residual (or salvage) value

Revenue expenditures

Straight-line (SL) depreciation

Tangible assets

Trademark

Units-of-production depreciation

2. You may recall that residual value is the estimated amount to be recovered less any estimated costs of dismantling, disposal, and sale. The useful life represents the estimated useful economic life to the present owner of the operational asset. Assume that you were the accounting manager for a manufacturer. List the factors that would you consider when you estimate the residual value and useful life of a major piece of machinery recently installed in the factory.

If you wanted to recognize a modest gain upon the ultimate disposal of the machinery at the end of its life, would you tend to understate or overstate the estimate of residual value? Would you tend to understate or overstate the useful life?

Get together with the other members of your study team and compare your answers. Then, discuss the following. Would it be appropriate to intentionally misstate the estimated residual value and useful life in order to recognize a modest gain? Each opinion should be supported by references to the appropriate accounting principle(s) or constraint(s) to support his or her answer.

CHAPTER 9
REPORTING AND INTERPRETING LIABILITIES

CHAPTER FOCUS SUGGESTIONS

The last three chapters addressed the reporting and interpretation of assets. The next three chapters address the other side of the balance sheet. A variety of business and accounting issues arise when managers need to obtain funds to finance the acquisition of assets and the operations of the business. Measurement and reporting issues relating to liabilities are covered in chapters 9 and 10 and issues relating to owners' equity are addressed in chapter 11.

Chapter 9 focuses on the liabilities that are common to most companies: accounts payable; accrued liabilities relating to income taxes and payroll; deferred revenues and service obligations; notes payable; long-term debt; deferred taxes; and accrued retirement benefits. Contingent liabilities are also addressed. You should be familiar with the characteristics and measurement of each type of liability, and able to classify each as current or noncurrent. You will also need to know how to compute the payable turnover ratio, the amount of working capital and the current ratio.

This chapter also introduces present and future value concepts. You will need to be able to distinguish between present value and future value problems. You will also need to know how to compute the present value of a single amount, the present value of an annuity, the future value of a single amount, and the future value of an annuity.

READ AND RECALL QUESTIONS

BUSINESS BACKGROUND

How do businesses finance the acquisition of their assets? (Hint: There are at least two sources.)

Why is debt capital more risky than equity? Given the risk associated with debt, why do most companies include borrowed funds in their capital structure?

LIABILITIES DEFINED AND CLASSIFIED

What are liabilities? How do liabilities arise? How is a liability measured when it is first recorded? When funds are borrowed, should the amount of interest that will be paid in the future be included in the amount of the liability recorded?

What are current liabilities? What are noncurrent liabilities?

Evaluating Liquidity

How is the current ratio computed? How is working capital computed? What do these ratios measure?

Most companies report a current ratio between 1.0 and 2.0. General Mills reported a current ratio of 0.73. Is this a cause for concern? Why or why not?

LEARNING OBJECTIVE
After studying this section of the chapter, you should be able to:
2. Record and report current liabilities.

CURRENT LIABILITIES

Accounts Payable

How are trade accounts payable created? Why isn't it advisable to delay payment to suppliers for as long as possible to conserve cash?

How is the payable turnover ratio computed? What does it measure? What does a high payable turnover ratio mean? What does a low payable turnover ratio mean?

Accrued Liabilities

What is another term for accrued liabilities? When are accrued liabilities recorded? What type of entry is normally used to record accrued liabilities?

Income Taxes Payable

Why did the amount of income taxes payable reported on the General Mills balance sheet differ from the income tax obligation for the year that was reported in the footnotes to its financial statements?

Payroll Liabilities

In addition to accruing salaries that have been earned but unpaid, what other payroll liabilities must be accrued?

Other Payroll Liabilities

In conformity with the matching principle, when should the cost of vacation time be recorded?

Deferred Revenues and Service Obligations

What are deferred revenues? When should revenue be recognized (reported on the income statement)?

What are future service obligations? Why is it difficult to measure these liabilities?

Notes Payable

What is the "time value of money?" What is the formula to calculate interest? In conformity with the matching principle, when should interest expense be recorded?

Current Portion of Long-Term Debt

What is the current portion of long-term debt?

Refinanced Debt: Current or Noncurrent

If a company intends to refinance debt and has the ability to do so, should currently maturing debt that will be refinanced be classified as a current or long-term liability?

Working Capital Management

Why is the management of working capital such an important activity?

LONG-TERM LIABILITIES

How do many companies generate funds to purchase operational assets?

What do some companies do to reduce risk for creditors who are willing to lend money for a long period? How does the company (the borrower) benefit?

How does secured debt differ from unsecured debt?

Long-Term Debt

What is a private placement? What is this type of debt often called?

What are bonds? How are bonds similar to notes?

Borrowing in Foreign Counties

Why do many corporations with foreign operations elect to finance those operations with foreign debt? If a company does not have international operations, why might it elect to borrow in foreign markets?

If a company has foreign debt, what must be done for financial reporting purposes?

LEARNING OBJECTIVE
After studying this section of the chapter, you should be able to:
4. Apply deferred income tax allocation.

OTHER TOPICS

Deferred Taxes

Why is the amount of income before income taxes reported on the income statement normally different from the amount of taxable income computed on the tax return? Should income tax expense be based on income reported on the income statement or on the tax return?

What are deferred tax items? Why do deferred tax items exist? What are temporary differences?

LEARNING OBJECTIVE
After studying this section of the chapter, you should be able to:
5. Explain liabilities for retirement benefits.

Accrued Retirement Benefits

What is a defined contribution retirement program? What is the employer's only obligation under a defined contribution program?

What is a defined benefit retirement program? What amount of pension expense must be accrued each year under a defined benefit retirement program?

Some employers agree to continue to pay for health care costs after employees retire. When should the cost of these benefits be recorded?

LEARNING OBJECTIVE
After studying this section of the chapter, you should be able to:
6. Record and report contingent liabilities.

CONTINGENT LIABILITIES

What is a contingent liability? What two factors must be considered to decide if a transaction causes a recorded or contingent liability?

What are the three types of "probabilities of occurrence?" How is each type defined?

What are the general guidelines for (a) a liability that must be recorded, (b) a liability that does not need to be recorded but must be disclosed, and (c) a liability that does not need to be recorded or disclosed?

Other Obligations

What is an operating lease? What is a capital lease? How does the accounting for an operating lease differ from that of a capital lease?

LEARNING OBJECTIVE
After studying this section of the chapter, you should be able to:
7. Apply the concepts of the future and present values of a single amount.

PRESENT AND FUTURE VALUE CONCEPTS

What is a "present value problem?" What is a "future value problem?"

How does an annuity differ from a single payment?

FUTURE AND PRESENT VALUE OF A SINGLE AMOUNT

To solve a future value problem, what three items need to be known?

Assuming an interest rate of 10%, the future value of $1,000 in three years is $1,331. What does this mean?

Assuming an interest rate of 10%, the present value of $1,000 received three years from now is $751.30. What does this mean?

If the assumed interest rate in a present value problem is increased, will the present value increase or decrease?

FUTURE AND PRESENT VALUES OF AN ANNUITY

What are the three characteristics of an annuity?

260

Assuming an interest rate of 10%, the future value of a deposit of $1,000 each year for three years is $3,310. What does this mean?

Assuming an interest rate of 10%, the present value of three annual payments of $1,000 is $2,486.80. What does this mean?

LEARNING OBJECTIVE
After studying this section of the chapter, you should be able to:
8. Apply present value concepts to liabilities.

ACCOUNTING APPLICATIONS OF FUTURE AND PRESENT VALUES

Question of Ethics – Truth in Advertising

How do many consumers misinterpret seasonal promotions with special financing incentives that are offered by many car companies? (For example, a car dealer may offer 4% interest on car loans when banks are charging 10%.)

Case A

Assume that General Mills purchases a truck and signs a note agreeing to pay $200,000 for a truck in two years, and that the market rate of interest is 12%. Is this a present value or future value problem? Is a single payment or an annuity involved?

The present value of $200,000 at 12% for two years is $159,440. What amount should be recorded in the truck account? What are the two alternatives for recording the note payable?

If an interest rate is not stated in the note, does the company need to record interest expense? Why or why not?

Case B

Assume that General Mills purchases new printing equipment and signs a note agreeing to pay three equal annual installments of $163,686, and that the each installment includes principal plus interest on the unpaid balance of 11%. Is this a present value or future value problem? Is a single payment or an annuity involved?

The present value of three annual payments of $163,686 at 11% is $400,000. What amount should be recorded in the printing equipment account?

Federal Income Tax Concepts

What are five common examples of differences between GAAP and the rules that govern the preparation of the federal income tax returns?

Why should you take a course in federal income taxation?

What is tax evasion? Are tax minimization efforts considered to be tax evasion?

SELF-TEST QUESTIONS AND EXERCISES

MATCHING

Match each of the key terms listed below with the appropriate textbook definition:

H 1. Accrued liabilities
E 2. Annuity
L 3. Contingent liability
M 4. Current liabilities
G 5. Deferred tax items
K 6. Deferred revenues
B 7. Future value

J 8. Liabilities
I 9. Long-term liabilities
A 10. Present value
F 11. Temporary differences
D 12. Time value of money
C 13. Working capital

A. The current value of an amount to be received in the future, a future amount discounted for compound interest.

B. The sum to which an amount will increase as the result of compound interest.

C. The dollar difference between total current assets and total current liabilities.

D. Interest that is associated with the use of money over time.

E. A series of periodic cash receipts or payments that are equal in amount each interest period.

F. Timing differences that cause deferred income taxes, and will reverse, or turn around, in the future.

G. Difference between income tax expense and income tax liability; caused by temporary differences; may be a liability or an asset.

H. Expenses that have been incurred but have not yet been paid at the end of the accounting period.

I. All obligations of the entity that are not classified as current liabilities.

J. Probable future sacrifices of economic benefits that arise from past transactions.

K. Revenues that have been collected but not earned; liabilities until the goods or services are provided.

L. Potential liability that has arisen as the result of a past event; not an effective liability until some future event occurs.

M. Short-term obligations that will be paid within the current operating cycle or one year, whichever is longer.

TRUE-FALSE QUESTIONS

For each of the following statements, enter a T or F in the blank to indicate whether the statement is true or false.

T 1. Current liabilities are likely to be satisfied with current assets.

T 2. Trade accounts payable are generally incurred as a result of the purchase of goods and services in the normal course of business.

F 3. An example of a deferred revenue for a retailer is the sale of furniture on a 90-day financing agreement.

F 4. When long-term debt, or a portion thereof, becomes due within the next year, it is reported as a noncurrent liability on the balance sheet and disclosure is made in a footnote to the financial statements.

T 5. Companies generally use long-term debt to finance long-lived assets, matching the life of the asset to the term of the debt.

F 6. In a defined contribution program, the employer agrees to pay the employee a fixed amount upon the employee's retirement.

F 7. A contingent liability that is material in amount and has at least a remote possibility of occurrence must be disclosed in a footnote to the financial statements.

F 8. In a present value problem, the value in the future of a known cash flow today needs to be determined.

F 9. Since compound interest problems involve more complex interest calculations, the simple interest formula cannot be used to compute interest expense.

F 10. All business entities are required to pay federal income taxes. *(Supplement A)*

MULTIPLE CHOICE QUESTIONS

Choose the best answer or response by placing the identifying letter in the space provided.

C 1. The current ratio is computed by

   a. subtracting current assets from current liabilities.
   b. subtracting current liabilities from current assets.
   c. dividing current assets by current liabilities.
   d. dividing current liabilities by current assets.
   e. dividing current liabilities by noncurrent liabilities.

b 2. Working capital is computed by

   a. subtracting current assets from current liabilities.
   b. subtracting current liabilities from current assets.
   c. dividing current assets by current liabilities.
   d. dividing current liabilities by current assets.
   e. dividing current liabilities by noncurrent liabilities.

C 3. Deferred revenues represent a liability because

   a. no cash has changed hands.
   b. collection is uncertain.
   c. goods or services have been paid for, but not yet provided to the customer.
   d. the company is transferring them to another period for tax reasons.
   e. the customer may someday return items purchased for a refund.

C 4. Interest expense is computed by multiplying

a. the face value of the note by the annual percentage rate
b. the face value of the note by the annual interest rate by the number of days outstanding divided by 365.
c. the face value of the note by the annual interest rate by the number of days outstanding divided by 360.
d. the face value of the note by the annual interest rate divided by 365.
e. the face value of the note by the annual interest rate divided by 360.

a 5. Deferred taxes items

a. are caused by timing differences which will reverse, or turn around, in the future.
b. represent amounts the company will pay at year-end, as opposed to during the year.
c. represent amounts owed to taxing authorities.
d. relate to reported income that will never be taxed for various reasons.
e. equal the difference between taxes accrued at the end of the period (that will be paid during the following accounting period) and amounts paid to taxing authorities during the current accounting period.

6. Reported pension expense for an employee under a defined benefit program is the change in the current cash value of the employee's retirement package. The current cash value changes each year

a. as the employee is closer to receiving benefits.
b. as the retirement benefits increase as a result of higher pay or longer service.
c. if the employee's life expectancy changes.
d. a, b and/or c.
e. only a and/or b.

7. In order to be recorded as a liability on the balance sheet, an item must be

a. reasonably possible and subject to estimate.
b. probable.
c. remote, but subject to estimate.
d. probable, and subject to estimate.
e. all of the above.

e 8. A contingent liability

a. is dependent on another company in order to occur.
b. will result from a future event.
c. cannot be estimated.
d. is only remotely possible.
e. is a potential liability that has arisen because of events or transactions that have already occurred.

_e_ 9. A contingent liability that cannot be reasonably estimated

    a. may be recorded as a balance sheet item or disclosed in a footnote to the financial statements, at the discretion of management.

    b. may be disclosed in a footnote to the financial statements, at the discretion of the management.

    c. need not be disclosed in the footnotes to the financial statements.

    d. must be reported as a liability on the balance sheet.

    e. requires disclosure in a footnote to the financial statements if occurrence is at least reasonably possible.

_d_ 10. An annuity is

    a. a series of annual payments of the same amount.

    b. any group of payments, equally spaced.

    c. any payments to a beneficiary from a fund set aside for that purpose.

    d. a series of consecutive equal payments, equally spaced, with the same implicit interest rate each period.

    e. annual payments of equal amounts at a fixed interest rate.

_C_ 11. The present value of a known future amount

    a. will always be more than the future amount.

    b. will be equal to the future amount.

    c. will always be less than the future amount.

    d. may be greater than or less than the future amount, depending on the interest rate used.

    e. may be greater than or less than the future amount, depending on the amount of time between.

_e_ 12. An example of a future value problem for a single amount is

    a. a defined benefit pension plan.

    b. a savings account to be established to fund $100,000 college tuition in 6 years.

    c. a mortgage.

    d. a Individual Retirement Account.

    e. an inheritance that will be invested in a mutual fund.

EXERCISES

Record your answers to each part of these exercises in the space provided. Show your work.

1. Pixar reported the following information in its 1996 report to stockholders:

	12/31/96	12/31/95
Current assets	$169,642,000	$148,796,000
Current liabilities	6,659,000	10,108,000

Compute Pixar's working capital and current ratios as of December 31, 1996 and 1995, and comment on the company's liquidity.

2. At the end of December 19A, there were two days' wages unpaid and unrecorded because the weekly payroll will not be paid until January 3, 19B. The weekly payroll amounts to $5,000, and wages for the last two days of December amounted to $2,000. In addition, at December 31, 19A, vacation time not yet taken or recorded amounted to $12,000. Prepare the adjusting entries that are required at December 31, 19A.

3. On December 15, 19A, Newco, Inc. paid $6,000 in rent to Property Managers, Inc. for the two month period which began on that date. Property Manager credited the rent in full to Rent Revenue. Prepare the adjusting entry that is required at December 31, 19A.

4. On December 31, 19A, Newco borrowed $100,000 from First National Bank, and signed a 12% note payable due in two years. Interest on the note is due at maturity.

A. Prepare the journal entry to record the borrowing transaction. How should the note be reported on Newco's balance sheet at December 31, 19A? How should it be reported on the balance sheet at December 31, 19B?

B. Prepare the adjusting entry that is required at December 31, 19B, and the entry to record the payment of the note on December 31, 19C.

5. Safety Net, Inc. entered into the following transactions on January 1, 19A. Assume an interest rate of 6%.

- Established Fund A by making a deposit of $150,000.

- Established Fund B by agreeing to make four annual deposits of $10,000 at the end of each year.

- Established Fund C by depositing a single amount that will increase to $250,000 by the end of 19E.

- Established Fund D by depositing a single amount that will provide six equal annual year-end payments of $5,000 to a retired employee beginning on December 31, 19A.

   A. Compute the balance of Fund A at the end of 19C (year 3).

   B. Compute the balance of Fund B at the end of 19D (year 4).

   C. Compute the single amount that must be deposited in Fund C on January 1, 19A.

   D. Compute the single amount that must be deposited in Fund D on January 1, 19A.

6. Assume that Blackhawk Industries computed taxes payable of $1,050,000 based on the amount of taxable income reported on its 19A tax return, and tax expense of $1,080,000 based on its 19A income statement.

    A. Prepare the adjusting entry to record the company's tax obligation for 19A.

    B. Why does a deferred tax item exist? Is it an asset or liability?

    C. Assume that the amount of income tax due for the year is paid on March 15 of the following year. Prepare the entry to record the payment of its 19A income taxes on March 15, 19B.

SOLUTIONS TO SELF-TEST QUESTIONS AND EXERCISES

MATCHING

1.	H	4.	M	7.	B	10.	A	13. C
2.	E	5.	G	8.	J	11.	F	
3.	L	6.	K	9.	I	12.	D	

TRUE-FALSE QUESTIONS

1.   T

2.   T

3.   F - This revenue would not be deferred, since the goods have presumably been delivered, and payment reasonably assured.

4.   F - Long-term debt, or a portion thereof, which is due within the next year must be reported on the balance sheet as a *current* liability.

5.   T

6.   F - In a defined *benefit* program, the employer agrees to pay the employee a fixed amount upon the employee's retirement. In a defined contribution program, the employers only obligation is to make the required annual payment to a fund which invests those contributions; upon retirement, each employee is entitled to a portion of the fund.

7.   F - A contingent liability with only a remote possibility of occurrence does not need to be disclosed in the footnotes to the financial statements.

8.   F - A present value problem requires the calculation of the value *today* of a know future cash flow.

9.   F - The simple interest formula is used for all interest calculations, simple or compound. The rate and time are adjusted in compound interest calculations for compounding more frequently than annually.

10.   F - Sole proprietorships and partnerships are not required to pay federal income taxes, but their owners must report and pay taxes on their personal tax returns. Corporations, as separate legal entities, are required to pay income taxes.

MULTIPLE CHOICE QUESTIONS

1.	c	4.	c	7.	d	10.	d
2.	b	5.	a	8.	e	11.	c
3.	c	6.	d	9.	e	12.	e

EXERCISES

1.

December 31, 1996

Current Assets - Current Liabilities = Working Capital

$169,642,000 - $6,659,000 = $162,983,000

December 31, 1995

$148,796,000 - $10,108,000 = $138,688,000

December 31, 1996

Current Assets / Current Liabilities = Current Ratio

$169,642,000 / $6,659,000 = 25.5

December 31, 1995

$148,796,000 / $10,108,000 = 14.7

Pixar's liquidity increased significantly during 1996. Its working capital increased from $138,688,000 to $162,983,000 and its current ratio increased from 14.7 to 25.5. Its current ratio of 25.5 means that the company has $25.50 of current assets for every $1 of current liabilities. Based on this information, Pixar seems able to meet its short-term obligations.

2.

Wage expense	2,000	
Wages payable		2,000
Wage expense	12,000	
Accrued vacation liability		12,000

3.

Rent revenue ($6,000 x 1.5 / 2)	4,500	
Deferred revenue (or unearned revenue)		4,500

4A.

Cash	100,000	
Note payable		100,000

The note should be classified as a long-term (noncurrent) liability on the balance sheet at December 31, 19A, and as a current liability on the balance sheet at December 31, 19B.

4B.

Interest expense ($100,000 x .12 x 360 / 360)	12,000	
Interest payable		12,000
Note payable	100,000	
Interest payable	12,000	
Interest expense ($100,000 x .12 x 360 / 360)	12,000	
Cash		124,000

5A.

Refer to Table A-1, Future Value of $1.

For i = 6%, n = 3, the value is 1.1910.

The balance at the end of year 3 will be $150,000 x 1.1910 = $178,650.

5B.

Refer to Table A-3, Future Value of Annuity of $1.

For i = 6%, n = 4, the value is 4.3746.

The balance at the end of year 4 will be $10,000 x 4.3746 = $43,746.

5C.

Refer to Table A-2, Present Value of $1.

For i = 6%, n = 5, the value is 0.7473.

The amount that must be deposited on January 1, 19A, is $250,000 x 0.7473 = $186,825.

5D.

Refer to Table A-4, Present Value of Annuity of $1.

For i = 6%, n = 6, the value is 4.9173

The amount that must be deposited on January 1, 19A, is $5,000 x 4.9173 = $24,586.50.

6A.

Tax expense	1,080,000	
Deferred taxes		30,000
Taxes payable		1,050,000

6B.

A deferred tax item exists because of timing differences in reporting revenues and expenses on the company's income statement and tax return. The deferred tax amount is a liability that will be paid in the future.

6C.

Taxes payable	1,050,000	
Cash		1,050,000

IDEAS FOR YOUR STUDY TEAM

1. Rewrite each of the definitions of the key terms that appear at the end of the chapter using your own words. Imagine that you are trying to explain each key term to a friend who has not taken any accounting classes. Then, get together with the other members of your study team and compare your definitions.

Accrued liabilities

Annuity

Contingent liability

Current liabilities

Deferred tax items

Deferred revenues

Future value

Liabilities

Long-term liabilities

Present value

Temporary differences

Time value of money

Working capital

2. There is some controversy about the amount of the liabilities that are recorded for frequent flyer programs. The following paragraph from the "Deferred Revenues and Service Obligations" section of chapter 9 discusses the controversy:

"Notice that the amount of the liability is the incremental cost of providing free travel and not the actual selling price of an air line ticket. Some analysts believe that the true cost of frequent flyer program is the lost revenue associated with giving a ticket to a customer instead of selling it. These analysts believe that the liabilities reported for frequent flyer programs are severely understated. Currently GAAP permits recording these liabilities based on incremental cost because there is no accurate method to estimate the number of travelers who would have bought tickets if they had not earned a free award."

Think about the measurement issues which relate to frequent flyer programs, and then get together with the other members of your study team to discuss the following questions.

What is the cost of providing a frequent flyer program?

What impact, if any, do each of the following have on the measurement of the liability?

• Would the traveler have flown anyway, at full price?

• What would the full price have been? Are prices uniform?

• Did the airplane have empty seats?

• What portion of frequent flyer points granted are redeemed?

Are there any other factors that might be pertinent?

3. Circle the correct choice to complete the following statements about present and future values. Then get together with the other members of your study team, and compare your answers.

The higher the interest rate, the (higher / lower) the present value of a known future amount.

The more often interest is compounded, the (higher / lower) the present value of a known future amount will be.

The more often interest is compounded, the (higher / lower) the future value of a known present cash flow will be.

The present value of an annuity of a given amount will always be (greater / less) than that amount, whereas the present value of a single sum is always (greater / less) than that sum.

As the number of compounding periods increases, present value (increases / decreases) but future value (increases / decreases).

4. Assume that one of the members of your study team works for an employer that has a pension plan. Upon retirement, the pension plan states that each vested (that is, eligible) employee will be paid a yearly amount equal to 60% of their average annual salary for the last five years prior to retirement. Get together with the other members of your study team, and design a "sample" employee by answering the following questions.

How much will the employee be paid when he/she starts working for the company?

At what age will he/she most likely retire? How long will he/she work? (For simplicity, assume that the employee spends his/her entire career with this employer.)

Realistically, what will his/her annual salary be during each of the five years before retirement?

How many years after retirement will he/she collect retirement pay? (Assume that retirement pay ends upon the death of the retiree.)

What is your estimate of the total amount of retirement pay that will be paid to the employee?

Your employer will make annual contributions to the pension plan and then invest those funds. What is a reasonable estimate of the average return on the investment of retirement funds that the employer can expect to receive during the time the employee works for the company?

Considering your answers to all of the above, how would you go about calculating the pension expense that should be recorded during the first year that the employee works for the company?

CHAPTER 10
REPORTING AND INTERPRETING BONDS

CHAPTER FOCUS SUGGESTIONS

This chapter completes the coverage of liabilities. Emphasis is placed on the use of bonds as a primary way of obtaining funds to acquire long-term assets and to expand the company's operations.

Bonds may be sold at par, at a premium, or at a discount. The determining factor is the relationship between the interest rate stated on the bonds and the market rate of interest. If the stated rate equals the market rate, the bonds will be sold at par. If the stated rate is higher than the market rate, the bonds will be sold at a premium. If the stated rate is less than the market rate, the bonds will be sold at a discount. You will need to be able to use the present and future value concepts that you learned in chapter 9 to determine the issuance (sales) price of bonds.

Premiums and discounts on bonds payable represent adjustments to the interest expense relating to the bonds. You will need to know how to amortize premiums and discounts using both the straight-line and effective-interest methods. Issues relating to the payment of the bonds payable (such as the early retirement of bonds that are called or redeemed, and the use of bond sinking funds) are also addressed.

You will need to know how to compute the debt-to-equity and interest coverage ratios.

This chapter also covers investments in bonds issued by other companies. These bonds may be purchased at par, at a premium, or at a discount. You should be familiar with the reporting of investments in a held-to-maturity portfolio.

READ AND RECALL QUESTIONS

LEARNING OBJECTIVE
After studying this section of the chapter, you should be able to:
1. Explain corporations' use of bonds payable.

BUSINESS BACKGROUND

Why would a creditor prefer to lend money by purchasing a bond? Why does the use of bonds allow companies to reduce the cost of borrowing money for long periods of time?

What are the other advantages of using bonds to raise long-term capital? (Hint: There are at least four.)

What is financial leverage?

What are the two primary disadvantages to the issuance of bonds?

Evaluating the Risk Associated with Debt

How is the debt-to-equity ratio computed? What does it measure? Why are companies with large debt-to-equity ratios normally considered to be more risky than less highly leveraged companies?

How is the interest coverage ratio computed? What does it measure?

LEARNING OBJECTIVE
After studying this section of the chapter, you should be able to:
2. Classify bonds payable.

What is a debenture? What is a secured bond?

What are the principal repayment terms of an ordinary or single-payment bond? What are the principal repayment terms of a serial bond?

What are callable bonds? What are redeemable bonds? What are convertible bonds?

What is bond principal? What three other terms are used to describe bond principal?

How are the periodic interest payments on a bond computed?

What is a bond indenture? What types of provisions are set forth in a bond indenture? (Hint: There are at least three provisions and sometimes four.)

What is a prospectus? What is a firm commitment underwriter? What is a best efforts underwriter?

What is a bond certificate? What is included on the face of a bond certificate?

What is a bond trustee? What are the duties of a trustee?

What is senior debt? What is subordinated debt?

What is default risk? How can potential investors obtain information about default risk?

LEARNING OBJECTIVE
After studying this section of the chapter, you should be able to:
3. Record bonds payable and interest expense.

MEASURING BONDS PAYABLE AND INTEREST EXPENSE

What does the principal amount of the bond represent? What other two terms are used to describe the principal amount of a bond?

What is the coupon rate? What other two terms are used to describe the coupon rate? Why do the cash interest payments represent an annuity?

What is the "market interest rate?" What two other terms are used to describe the market interest rate?

What is a bond premium? Why do bonds sell at a premium?

What is a bond discount? Why do bonds sell at a discount?

Bond Information from the Business Press

What is the coupon interest rate? How do changes in the daily prices of bonds affect the financial statement of the company that issued the bonds?

Why would bonds sell at par value? What entry is used to record the interest payments when bonds are sold at par value?

What must be done at the end of the accounting period when bond interest payment dates do not coincide with the last day of a company's fiscal year?

When the effective rate of interest is equal to the stated rate of interest, what is the relationship between the present value of the future cash flows associated with a bond and the bond's par amount? (That is, will the present value be more than, equal to, or less than the par amount?)

What determines the selling price of a bond? (That is, does the par value or the present value of the future cash flows determine the selling price?) Which amount is used to record the initial bond liability?

Bonds Issued at a Discount

Why would bonds sell at a discount? How is the cash issue price of the bonds computed? What interest rate should be used in the computation?

What does a cash price of 88.5 mean?

When a bond is issued at a discount, will the cash received be more than, equal to, or less than the par value of the bonds? What entry is used to record the issuance of bonds at a discount? What amount is credited to the bonds payable account? What account is used to record the difference between the cash received and the par value of the bonds issued? What type of account is it? What is the normal balance of this account?

The balance sheet reports the bonds payable at their book value. How is the book value computed when bonds are sold at a discount?

Measuring and Recording Interest on Bonds Issued at a Discount

What does amortized mean? What happens when the bond discount is amortized?

Straight-Line Amortization

How is the amount of bond discount that is amortized each period determined when the straight-line method is used? What entry is used to record interest payments when bonds have been issued at a discount? Is the amortization of bond discount added to or deducted from the amount of interest paid to the bondholders to compute interest expense for the period?

When bonds that were sold at a discount mature, what is relationship between the maturity amount of the bonds and their book value at maturity?

Zero Coupon Bonds

What are zero coupon bonds? Why is a bond with a zero coupon interest rate called a deep discount bond?

When bonds are issued at a discount, why does the book value of the bonds increase each year?

Bonds Issued at a Premium

Why would bonds sell at a premium? How is the cash issue price of the bonds computed? What interest rate should be used in the computation?

When a bond is issued at a premium, will the cash received be more than, equal to, or less than the par value of the bonds? What entry is used to record the issuance of bonds at a premium? What amount is credited to the bonds payable account? What account is used to record the difference between the cash received and the par value of the bonds issued? What type of account is it? What is the normal balance of this account?

The balance sheet reports the bonds payable at their book value. How is the book value computed when bonds are sold at a premium?

Measuring and Recording Interest on Bonds Issued at a Premium

How is the amount of bond premium that is amortized each period determined when the straight-line method is used? What entry is used to record interest payments when bonds have been issued at a premium? Is the amortization of bond premium added to or deducted from the amount of interest paid to bondholders to compute interest expense for the period?

When bonds that were sold at a premium mature, what is relationship between the maturity amount of the bonds and their book value at maturity?

FOCUS ON CASH FLOWS

How is the sale of bonds reported on the statement of cash flows?

BONDS ISSUED AT VARIABLE INTEREST RATE

What is inflation? What do some bond issuers do to compensate creditors for unexpected inflation?

International Financial Markets

What is the London Interbank Offer Rate (LIBOR)?

LEARNING OBJECTIVE

After studying this section of the chapter, you should be able to:

6. Use the effective-interest method of amortization.

ADDITIONAL TOPICS IN ACCOUNTING FOR BONDS PAYABLE

Effective-Interest Amortization of Bond Discounts and Premiums

What is the only advantage of the straight-line method of amortization of bond discounts and premiums? When does GAAP allow the use of the straight-line method of amortization?

When a bond is sold, what is the "true" interest rate? What is the actual amount borrowed when a bond is sold?

How is interest expense for a bond computed when the effective-interest method is used? What does the difference between interest expense and the amount of cash paid (or accrued) represent?

Understanding Alternative Amortization Methods

How does the materiality constraint affect the choice between the straight-line and effective-interest amortization methods? Which method is preferred conceptually? When may the other method be used?

Bonds Sold between Interest Dates

Bonds that are sold between interest dates sell for their market value plus any interest that has accrued on the bonds since the last interest payment. How is the amount of interest accrued since the last interest payment computed? What entry is used to record the issuance of bonds sold between interest dates?

LEARNING OBJECTIVE
After studying this section of the chapter, you should be able to:
7. Record the early retirement of bonds.

Early Retirement of Debt

Who can decide to call bonds in for early retirement if the bonds have a call feature? What is a call premium? How is a call premium usually computed? What entry is used to record bonds that have been called? How is the loss on bond call computed?

What factors would cause the price of a bond to fall? Why would a company that wants to retire a bond before its maturity date buy the bond in the market?

How is the gain or loss on the early retirement of debt reported in the financial statements?

Bond Sinking Funds

What is a bond sinking fund? What does it assure? How does the bond sinking fund increase in amount? How is a bond sinking fund normally reported in the financial statements? What happens to the balance of the bond sinking fund at the maturity date of the bonds?

LONG-TERM INVESTMENTS IN BONDS

Why would someone invest in bonds? How can a manager use bonds to plan future cash flows with a minimum of risk?

What uncertainty is eliminated if bonds are held to maturity? What is a held-to-maturity portfolio? What criteria must be met to list bonds as held-to-maturity securities?

Why are the bonds in a held-to-maturity portfolio carried at cost instead of at market value?

REPORTING BOND INVESTMENTS HELD TO MATURITY

Bonds Purchased at Par

What entry is used to record the purchase of a bond at par? What entry is used to record the receipt of interest when the bond has been purchased at par?

Bonds Purchased at a Discount

When bonds are purchased at a discount, what amount is debited to the held-to-maturity investment account? Why does the company need to keep track of the bond discount? What entry is used to record the receipt of interest when the bond has been purchased at a discount? What method do most companies use to amortize a bond discount or premium relating to bonds in a held-to-maturity portfolio?

SELF-TEST QUESTIONS AND EXERCISES

MATCHING

Match each of the key terms listed below with the appropriate textbook definition:

H	1.	Bond certificate	S	13.	Financial leverage
Q	2.	Bond discount	V	14.	Held-to-maturity portfolio
R	3.	Bond premium	C	15.	Indenture
P	4.	Bond principal	M	16.	Market interest rate
I	5.	Bond sinking fund	N	17.	Net interest cost
U	6.	Callable bonds	W	18.	Par value
J	7.	Convertible bonds	T	19.	Redeemable bonds
D	8.	Coupon rate	B	20.	Stated rate
G	9.	Debenture	L	21.	Straight-line amortization
K	10.	Effective-interest amortization	F	22.	Trustee
E	11.	Effective-interest rate	O	23.	Yield
A	12.	Face amount			

A. Another name for principal or the principal amount of a bond.

B. The stated rate of interest on bonds.

C. A bond contract that specifies the legal provisions of a bond issue.

D. The rate of cash interest per period specified in the bond contract.

E. Another name for the market rate of interest on a bond when issued; also called the yield rate.

F. An independent party appointed to represent the bondholders.

G. An unsecured bond; no asset are specifically pledged to guarantee repayment.

H. The bond document; each bondholder receives one.

I. A cash fund accumulated for payment of a bond at maturity.

J. Bonds that may be converted to other securities of the issuer (usually common stock).

K. Method that amortizes a bond discount or premium on the basis of the effective-interest rate; theoretically preferred method.

L. Simplified method of amortizing a bond discount or premium that allocates an equal dollar amount to each interest period.

M. Current rate of interest on a debt when incurred; also called yield or effective interest rate.

N. Interest cost, less any income tax savings associated with interest expense.

O. Another name for the market rate of interest on a bond.

P. The amount payable at the maturity of the bond; face amount, on which the periodic cash interest payments are computed.

Q. The difference between selling price and par when a bond is sold for more than par.

R. The difference between selling price and par when a bond is sold for less than par.

S. Use of borrowed funds to increase the rate of return on owners' equity; occurs when the interest rate on debt is lower than the earnings rate on total assets.

T. Bonds that may be turned in for early retirement at the option of the bondholder.

U. Bonds that may be called for early retirement at the option of the issuer.

V. A long-term investment in bonds that management has the ability and intent to hold until maturity.

W. Another name for bond principal or the maturity amount of a bond.

TRUE-FALSE QUESTIONS

For each of the following statements, enter a T or F in the blank to indicate whether the statement is true or false.

___1. One disadvantage of bonds, compared to stock, for financing a company's operations is that dividends on stock are discretionary, whereas bond interest must be paid.

___2. Financial leverage is the ratio of debt to equity financing.

___3. A debenture is another word for any bond.

___4. An independent trustee is appointed in a bond issue to control the money raised and the payment of interest and principal.

___5. When a company issues bonds, it tries to set the coupon rate on the bond slightly higher than the market rate so that the bond can be issued at a premium and they will receive more money.

___6. The par value of a bond is a minimum legal amount below which the bond cannot be issued.

___7. A zero coupon bond is one on which no periodic cash interest payments are made.

___8. Straight-line amortization of discount or premium is simpler, but the effective-interest method is conceptually preferable.

___9. The net liability of a bond at any point in time is the present value of the future cash flows from the bond, discounted at the market interest rate on the date of issue of the bond.

___10. The sum of the cash interest payments less the premium on the bond payable on the date of issue is the total interest expense on the bond.

___11. A call premium, stated as a percentage of par value, is often included in the bond indenture in the event that bonds are retired before their maturity date.

___12. A bond sinking fund is always established as part of the bond indenture to provide for the retirement of the bonds at maturity.

___13. Investors classify bonds as held-to-maturity securities, because they have a definite maturity date.

MULTIPLE CHOICE QUESTIONS

Choose the best answer or response by placing the identifying letter in the space provided.

b 1. The capital structure of a company is

    a. its property, plant and equipment.
    b. the mixture of debt and equity used to finance its operations.
    c. the composition of its stockholders' equity.
    d. the different types of debt the company has outstanding.
    e. its management plan.

b 2. A significant advantage for the holders of bonds, as opposed to other debt, is

    a. their freedom from risk.
    b. their liquidity.
    c. their low cost.
    d. their high interest rate.
    e. their convertibility.

c 3. When a bond is issued at a discount,

    a. the company did not receive as much money as it needed.
    b. the market rate was lower than the coupon rate.
    c. the market rate was higher than the stated rate.
    d. the company was not able to sell the bonds as easily as they'd anticipated.
    e. fewer bonds were sold than were offered.

b 4. When bonds are issued at a premium, interest expense

    a. will be equal to cash interest paid each compounding period.
    b. will be less than the cash interest paid each compounding period.
    c. will be equal to the amount of premium amortized each period.
    d. will be more than cash interest paid each compounding period.
    e. will be calculated based on the face value of the bond.

c 5. The effective interest method of amortizing discount or premium

    a. yields a consistent amount of interest, but a different interest rate, each period.
    b. is not materially different in most cases from the straight-line method.
    c. yields a consistent interest rate, but a different amount of interest expense, each period.
    d. divides the discount or premium into equal amounts for each year of the bond's life.
    e. calculates interest expense based on the net liability and the coupon interest rate.

e 6. Blazing Lasers Co. retired $400,000 face value of bonds on June 30, 1995, when the discount on bonds payable account had a balance of $32,495. They paid $360,000 to retire the bonds. Blazing Lasers would report a _____ on its income statement.

    a. gain of $72,475.
    b. loss of $40,000
    c. gain of $40,000.
    d. loss of $7,505.
    e. a gain of $7,505.

294

Use the following information to answer the last eight questions. Scuppers Boat Works Inc. issued 200 bonds to finance expansion into a new line of designs. The bonds had a total principal of $200,000. They would pay interest semiannually at a rate of 9% per annum and will be paid off in five years. On the day the bonds were issued, January 15, 1995, similar securities were yielding a rate of 10% per annum. Scuppers' underwriter, Reedham and Ouip, purchased the entire issue to resell them to individual investors. Scuppers retained the right to buy back the bonds from the bondholders in two years at a price of $102. The bondholders may at any time trade in their bonds for common stock of Scuppers, Inc. at a rate of 50 shares of stock for each bond.

_a_ 7. The par value of the bond issue is

    a. $200,000.
    b. $18,000.
    c. $20,000.
    d. $102,000.
    e. $192,275.

_c_ 8. The stated rate of interest on the bonds is __9__%; bondholders will be paid $_____ every _____.

$200,000 \times 4.5\%$

    a. 9%; $18,000; year.
    b. 9%; $18,000; six months.
    c. 9%; $9,000; six months.
    d. 10%; $10,000; six months.
    e. 10%; $20,000; year.

_c_ 9. When Scuppers decided to issue the bonds, they would have executed a bond contract, or _____, which spelled out the terms of the bond, and any privileges and covenants.

    a. certificate
    b. debenture
    c. indenture
    d. trustee
    e. commitment

_d_ 10. Since Reedham and Ouip has agreed to buy the bonds from Scuppers, Reedham and Ouip would be called a(n)

    a. indenture.
    b. trustee.
    c. investment banker.
    d. firm commitment underwriter.
    e. best efforts underwriter.

_e_ 11. The provision that allows Scuppers to retire the bonds before maturity makes these _____ bonds.

    a. debenture
    b. subordinated
    c. convertible
    d. redeemable
    e. callable

_a_ 12. Should Scuppers decide to redeem the bonds after two years have gone by, each individual bond will be bought back for

    a. $1,020.
    b. $102.
    c. $1,000.
    d. $1,002.
    e. $981.

_e_ 13. The privilege of trading the bonds for common stock is called a _____ feature.

    a. capitalized
    b. retirement
    c. callable
    d. redeemable
    e. convertible

_c_ 14. The 10% rate for similar securities on the date of issue is known as the

    a. stated rate.
    b. par rate.
    c. market rate.
    d. coupon rate.
    e. contract rate.

EXERCISES

Record your answers to each part of these exercises in the space provided. Show your work.

1. On January 1, 19A, First Canadian, Inc. plans to issue $500,000, five year, 8% bonds that will mature on December 31, 19E. Interest is payable semiannually each June 30 and December 31.

   A. Assuming that the market (yield) rate is also 8%, prepare the journal entry to record the issuance of the bonds. Compute the amount of interest that will be paid on a semiannual interest to the bondholders.

   Then, prepare the journal entries to record the payment of interest on June 30, 19A, and December 31, 19A.

   B. Assuming that the market (yield) rate is 6%, compute the issue (sale) price on January 1, 19A, and prepare the journal entry to record the issuance of the bonds.

Then, assuming that First Canadian uses the straight-line method for amortization purposes, prepare the journal entries to record the payment of interest on June 30, 19A, and December 31, 19A. Finally, compute the book value of the bonds on December 31, 19A.

C. Using the information provided in part B above, and assuming instead that First Canadian uses the effective-interest method for amortization purposes, prepare the journal entries to record the payment of interest on June 30, 19A, and December 31, 19A. Then, compute the book value of the bonds on December 31, 19A.

D. Assuming that the market (yield) rate is 10%, compute the issue (sale) price on January 1, 19A, and prepare the journal entry to record the issuance of the bonds.

Then, assuming that First Canadian uses the straight-line method for amortization purposes, prepare the journal entries to record the payment of interest on June 30, 19A, and December 31, 19A. Finally, compute the book value of the bonds on December 31, 19A.

E. Using the information provided in part D above, and assuming instead that First Canadian uses the effective-interest method for amortization purposes, prepare the journal entries to record the payment of interest on June 30, 19A, and December 31, 19A. Then, compute the book value of the bonds on December 31, 19A.

2. Norwegian Industries issued $1,000,000, ten year, 10% bonds at par value. Interest is payable semiannually each June 30 and December 31. All of the bonds will be sold on April 1, 19A. The company's fiscal year ends on September 30.

   A. Prepare the journal entry to record the issuance of the bonds on April 1, 19A.

   B. Prepare the journal entry to record the payment of interest on June 30, 19A.

   C. Prepare the adjusting entry required at September 30, 19A.

   D. Prepare the journal entry to record the payment of interest on December 31, 19A.

3. Summit Companies reported total liabilities of $400,000 and $351,000, and stockholders' equity of $4,000,000 and $3,900,000 at December 31, 19B and 19A, respectively. Interest expense amounted to $82,000 during 19B and $97,000 during 19A, and income before interest and taxes was $256,000 during 19B and $212,000 in 19A.

A. Compute Summit's debt-to-equity ratios as of December 31, for 19B and 19A, and comment on the change noted, if any.

B. Compute Summit's interest coverage ratios for 19B and 19A, and comment on the change noted, if any.

4. On January 1, 19A, the Aurora Star paid $388,000 for a 7% bond with a maturity value of $400,000. The bond will mature in five years (on December, 31, 19E). Management intends to hold the bond until maturity. Interest is paid semiannually on June 30 and December 31. Prepare the journal entries to record the purchase of the bond on January 1, 19A, and the receipt of interest on June 30, 19A.

SOLUTIONS TO SELF-TEST QUESTIONS AND EXERCISES

MATCHING

1.	H	5.	I	9.	G	13.	S	17.	N	21.	L
2.	R	6.	U	10.	K	14.	V	18.	W	22.	F
3.	Q	7.	J	11.	E	15.	C	19.	T	23.	O
4.	P	8.	D	12.	A	16.	M	20.	B		

TRUE-FALSE QUESTIONS

1. T

2. F - Financial leverage is the ability of a company to invest borrowed money at a rate of return higher than their borrowing rate, thus increasing return to stockholders.

3. F - A debenture is an unsecured bond. Some bonds are secured by specific assets, and, as such, are not considered debentures.

4. F - An independent trustee is appointed to monitor the interests of the bondholders.

5. F - Companies try to select a coupon rate that will approximate the market rate that is expected to be in effect on the date of issuance.

6. F - The par value is the face value of the bond; the bond might be issued at par, at a premium (above par), or at a discount (below par) depending on the relationship between the coupon rate and the market rate on the date of issuance.

7. T

8. T

9. T

10. T

11. T

12. F - A bond sinking fund may or may not be required by the bond contract.

13. F - Bonds are the only security that *can* be classified as held-to-maturity securities, but bonds can only be classified as held-to-maturity if the company has both the ability and the intent to hold them to maturity.

MULTIPLE CHOICE QUESTIONS

1.	b	4.	b	7.	a	10.	d	13.	e
2.	b	5.	c	8.	c	11.	e	14.	c
3.	c	6.	e	9.	c	12.	a		

EXERCISES

1A.

Cash	500,000	
Bonds payable		500,000

Semiannual interest payment = $500,000 x .08 x 6/12 = $20,000

Interest expense	20,000	
Cash		20,000

Interest expense	20,000	
Cash		20,000

1B.

Present Value of Principal
Refer to Table A-2, For i = 3%, n = 10, the value is 0.7441
Present value of principal is $500,000 x 0.7441 $372,050
Present Value of Interest
Refer to Table A-4, For i = 3%, n = 10, the value is 8.5302
Present value of interest payments are $20,000 x 8.5302   170,604
Present Value of Principal and Interest $542,654

Cash	542,654	
Bonds payable		500,000
Premium on bonds payable		42,654

Interest expense ($20,000 - $4,265)	15,735	
Premium on bonds payable ($42,654 / 10)	4,265	
Cash		20,000

Interest expense ($20,000 - $4,265)	15,735	
Premium on bonds payable ($42,654 / 10)	4,265	
Cash		20,000

Bonds payable			$500,000
Premium on bonds payable		$42,654	
Less amortization during 19A:			
June 30	$(4,265)		
December 31	(4,265)	(8,530)	34,124
Book value at end of 19A			$534,124

303

1C.

Interest expense		16,280	
($542,654 x .06 x 6 / 12)			
Premium on bonds payable		3,720	
($20,000 - $16,280)			
Cash			20,000

Interest expense		16,168	
[($542,654 - $3,720) x .06 x 6 / 12]			
Premium on bonds payable		3,832	
($20,000 - $16,168)			
Cash			20,000

Bonds payable			$500,000
Premium on bonds payable		$42,654	
Less amortization during 19A:			
June 30	$(3,720)		
December 31	(3,832)	(7,552)	35,102
Book value at end of 19A			$535,102

1D.

Present Value of Principal
Refer to Table A-2, For i = 5%, n = 10, the value is 0.6319
Present value of principal is $500,000 x 0.6319 — $315,950
Present Value of Interest
Refer to Table A-4, For i = 5%, n = 10, the value is 7.7217
Present value of interest payments are $20,000 x 7.7217 — 154,434
Present Value of Principal and Interest — $470,384

Cash	470,384	
Discount on bonds payable	29,616	
Bond payable		500,000

Interest expense ($20,000 + $2,962)	22,962	
Discount on bonds payable ($29,616 / 10)		2,962
Cash		20,000

Interest expense ($20,000 - $2,962)	22,962	
Discount on bonds payable ($29,616 / 10)		2,962
Cash		20,000

Bonds payable			$500,000
Less discount on bonds payable		$(29,616)	
Less amortization during 19A:			
June 30	$2,962		
December 31	2,962	5,924	(23,692)
Book value at December 31, 19A			$476,308

1E.

Interest expense	23,519	
($470,384 x .10 x 6 / 12)		
Discount on bonds payable		3,519
($23,519 - $20,000)		
Cash		20,000

Interest expense	23,695	
[($470,384 + $3,519) x .10 x 6 / 12]		
Discount on bonds payable		3,695
($23,695 - $20,000)		
Cash		20,000

Bonds payable			$500,000
Less discount on bonds payable		$(29,616)	
Less amortization during 19A:			
June 30	$3,519		
December 31	3,695	7,214	(22,402)
Book value at December 31, 19A			$477,598

2A.

Cash	1,025,000	
Bonds payable		1,000,000
Interest payable		25,000
($1,000,000 x .10 x 3 / 12)		

2B.

Interest expense ($1,000,000 x .10 x 3 / 12)	25,000	
Interest payable (from above)	25,000	
Cash ($1,000,000 x .10 x 6 / 12)		50,000

2C.

Interest expense ($1,000,000 x .10 x 3 / 12)	25,000	
Interest payable		25,000
($1,000,000 x .10 x 3 / 12)		

2D.

Interest expense ($1,000,000 x .10 x 3 / 12)	25,000	
Interest payable (from above)	25,000	
Cash ($1,000,000 x .10 x 6 / 12)		50,000

3A.

19B

Total Debt / Total Equity = Debt-to-Equity Ratio

$400,000 / $4,000,000 = .10

19A

$351,000 / $3,900,000 = .09

Summit's debt-to-equity ratio increased slightly during 19B. Summit is therefor more highly leveraged, and, as a result, is more risky.

3B.

19B

Income before interest and taxes / Interest expense = Interest coverage ratio

$256,000 / $82,000 = 3.1

19A

$212,000 / $97,000 = 5.3

Summit's interest coverage ratio decreased during 19B. Summit is generating less income compared to obligatory payments to creditors. This suggests a higher risk of defaulting on required interest payments.

4.

Held-to-maturity investment	388,000	
Cash		388,000
Cash ($400,000 x .07 x 6 / 12)	14,000	
Held-to-maturity investment	1,200	
[($400,000 - $388,000) / 10]		
Interest revenue		15,200

IDEAS FOR YOUR STUDY TEAM

1. Rewrite each of the definitions of the key terms that appear at the end of the chapter using your own words. Imagine that you are trying to explain each key term to a friend who has not taken any accounting classes. Then, get together with the other members of your study team and compare your definitions.

Bond certificate

Bond discount

Bond premium

Bond principal

Bond sinking fund

Callable bonds

Convertible bonds

Coupon rate

Debenture

Effective-interest amortization

Effective-interest rate

Face amount

Financial leverage

Held-to-maturity portfolio

Indenture

Market interest rate

Net interest cost

Par value

Redeemable bonds

Stated rate

Straight-line amortization

Trustee

Yield

2. Each element of a company's capital structure has its advantages and disadvantages. Complete the table below by indicating whether each characteristic listed is an advantage (A) or a disadvantage (D). Then, get together with the other members of your study team, and compare your answers.

Characteristic	Stocks	Bonds
Liquid, traded on established exchanges.		
Dilutes ownership of the company.		
Cash payments limited to specified interest, regardless of net income growth.		
Payments are tax deductible.		
Positive financial leverage is possible.		
Interest payments must be made.		
Initial amount invested must be paid back.		
Investors receive a return only if earnings are satisfactory.		

3. Some years ago, the Tennessee Valley Authority (the TVA), a large power company, issued some 50-year maturity bonds, including zero coupon bonds. Although there were some doubts at the time about the company's ability to sell bonds with such a long life, the bonds sold very well. Most were purchased by pension plans. Answer the following questions. Then, get together with the members of your study team, and compare your answers.

Why would a company want to issue bonds with such a long-term maturity?

Why do you think the TVA needed the money?

Why might a 50-year bond might be difficult to sell?

Why do you think these 50-year bonds were so attractive to pension funds? (Refer back to chapter 9, if necessary.)

CHAPTER 11

REPORTING AND INTERPRETING OWNERS' EQUITY

CHAPTER FOCUS SUGGESTIONS

This chapter concludes the coverage of the right side of the balance sheet. As noted previously, a variety of business and accounting issues arise when managers need to obtain funds to finance the acquisition of assets and the operations of the business. The last two chapters addressed the reporting and interpretation of liabilities. This chapter addresses the issues that relate to owners' equity. Emphasis is placed on the two basic sources of owners' equity in a corporation: contributed capital and retained earnings. (Accounting and reporting issues that relate to sole proprietorships are addressed in Supplement A.)

You should be familiar with the process of incorporating a business, and the advantages and disadvantages of this form of business. Corporations issue two types of capital stock: common and preferred. You should be familiar with the characteristics, and advantages and disadvantages of each. You will need to know how to record transactions relating to the issuance (sale) of capital stock to investors for cash and/or noncash assets, and the purchase of treasury stock (stock previously issued by the corporation that is subsequently reacquired).

Corporate earnings that do not need to be retained in the business for growth and expansion are distributed to stockholders as dividends. Cash dividends, when formally declared by the board of directors, reduce total assets and total stockholders' equity. You should understand how current and cumulative dividend preferred stock preferences affect the declaration of dividends on common stock. Stock dividends, pro rata distributions of the corporation's stock to its stockholders, do not affect the total assets, liabilities or stockholders' equity of the corporation. Stock dividends only affect certain account balances within stockholders' equity. Stock splits do not affect total assets, liabilities or stockholders' equity, or any of the individual account balances within stockholders' equity. Stock splits affect only the par value of the stock and the number of shares outstanding. You should be familiar with the characteristics of cash dividends, stock dividends, and stock splits, and know how to record dividend transactions. You will also need to know how to compute the dividend yield ratio and dividend payout ratio.

READ AND RECALL QUESTIONS

BUSINESS BACKGROUND

What are the three factors that make is easy for individuals to participate in the ownership of corporations?

What does limited liability mean?

LEARNING OBJECTIVE

After studying this section of the chapter, you should be able to:
1. Describe the basic nature of a corporation.

OWNERSHIP OF A CORPORATION

What is a stockholder (or shareholder)? What information is stated on a stock certificate?

What three rights are granted to common stockholders?

What is a charter? What information is included on an application for a charter? What is another term for a charter? What is a board of directors? Who elects the members of the board of directors?

Dividend Yield

How is the dividend yield ratio computed? What does it measure? What is the other component of the return available to stockholders? Why do most investors purchase common stock?

How is the dividend payout ratio computed? What does it measure?

Authorized, Issued, and Outstanding Capital Stock

What is meant by the "authorized number" of shares? What does issued mean? What does outstanding mean? What does unissued mean?

What must a corporation do if it needs to sell more shares than authorized in its charter?

LEARNING OBJECTIVE
After studying this section of the chapter, you should be able to:
2. Compare and contrast the various types of capital stock.

TYPES OF CAPITAL STOCK

Common Stock

What is common stock? Why is common stock often called the residual equity? How is the dividend rate for common stock determined?

Why does common stock have more "upside potential" than preferred stock and more "downside risk?" What do these terms mean?

Par Value and Nopar Value Stock

What is par value? What is legal capital? What is nopar value stock?

Preferred Stock

What is preferred stock? Why doesn't preferred stock appeal to investors who want some control over the operations of the corporation?

313

Why is preferred stock generally less risky than common stock?

Special Features of Preferred Stock

What is convertible preferred stock? What is callable preferred stock?

LEARNING OBJECTIVE
After studying this section of the chapter, you should be able to:
3. Record transactions affecting capital stock.

ACCOUNTING FOR CAPITAL STOCK

What is contributed capital? What are the two distinct components of contributed capital?

What is additional paid-in capital? What are retained earnings?

Sale and Issuance of Capital Stock

What is an initial public offering (IPO)? What is a seasoned new issue? What is an underwriter?

What entry is used to record the sale of stock to the public for cash? How are the amounts that are credited to the common stock account and the capital in excess of par value account determined?

What are the two different approaches used to record the sale of common stock if a par value is not specified?

Secondary Markets

If one investor subsequently sells the stock of a corporation to another investor, how are the accounting records of the corporation affected? What are the three secondary markets, and what purpose do these markets serve?

Going Public

What are two common reasons for going public?

Capital Stock Sold and Issued for Noncash Assets and/or Services

When a company issues stock to acquire assets or services, how should the acquired items be recorded? What amount should be used if the market value of the stock issued cannot be determined?

Stock Options

What are stock options? Why is a stock option considered to be a risk free investment?

If the grant (option) price is equal to the current market price of the stock, how much compensation expense should be reported? How much compensation expense should be reported if the current market price exceeds the grant price?

LEARNING OBJECTIVE
After studying this section of the chapter, you should be able to:
4. Define and account for treasury stock.

TREASURY STOCK

What is treasury stock? What are two alternative approaches used to record purchases of treasury stock? Which method is more widely used?

Using the cost method, what entry is used to record the purchase of treasury stock in the open market? What type of account is the treasury stock account? Is treasury stock considered to be outstanding stock?

What entry is used to record the subsequent sale of treasury stock at a price greater than its purchase price?

vould this entry be affected if the treasury stock was sold at a price below its purchase price? What count would be used in the entry if there was an insufficient credit balance in the contributed pital account?

UNTING FOR CASH DIVIDENDS

nds Defined

ɔ wealthy investors in high tax brackets prefer to receive their return on stock investments in the ɪm of higher stock prices? Why do other investors, such as retirees, prefer to receive their return in e form of dividends?

What is the most common type of dividend? What is created when the board formally declares a dividend?

What are the two fundamental requirements for the payment of a cash dividend?

Dividend Dates

What is a declaration date? What is a date of record? What is a date of payment?

Financial Analysis

What is an ex-dividend date? Who receives the dividend if you buy stock before the ex-dividend date? Who receives the dividend if you buy the stock after the ex-dividend date?

Dividends on Preferred Stock

What are two types of dividend preferences made available to preferred stockholders?

318

Current Dividend Preference on Preferred Stock

What does a current dividend preference require?

Cumulative Dividend Preference on Preferred Stock

What does a cumulative dividend preference require? What are dividends in arrears? Why is preferred stock usually cumulative? How are dividends in arrears reported on the financial statements?

Impact of Dividends in Arrears

Why are analysts interested in information concerning dividends in arrears?

FOCUS ON CASH FLOWS

How is the sale of stock to investors for cash reported on the statement of cash flows? How is the payment of dividends to the stockholders reported on the statement of cash flows?

LEARNING OBJECTIVE
After studying this section of the chapter, you should be able to:
6. Contrast and account for stock dividends and stock splits.

ACCOUNTING FOR STOCK DIVIDENDS AND STOCK SPLITS

Stock Dividends

What is a stock dividend? What does "pro rata basis" mean?

Why isn't an investor who has received a stock dividend wealthier as a result? Why does a stock dividend make the stock more attractive to new investors? What terminology is required by the Securities and Exchange Commission whenever a stock dividend is 25% or more of the outstanding shares?

What is a "large" stock dividend? What is a "small" stock dividend?

What entry is used to record a large stock dividend?

What affect does a stock dividend have on the total amount of stockholders' equity? Why is the process of transferring an amount from retained earnings to contributed capital called "capitalizing earnings?"

How does the entry used to record a small stock dividend differ from that used to record a large stock dividend?

Stock Splits

What is a stock split? What happens to the total number of authorized shares in a stock split? What typically happens to the par or stated value so that the total par or stated value of all authorized shares is unchanged?

How is a stock split reported on the financial statements?

RETAINED EARNINGS

What is a prior period adjustment?

Why should an accounting error from a previous period be corrected by adjusting the beginning balance of retained earnings instead of making an adjustment to the current income statement?

Restrictions on Retained Earnings

Why would restrictions be placed on retained earnings? Why are analysts interested in information concerning restrictions on retained earnings?

ACCOUNTING AND REPORTING FOR UNINCORPORATED BUSINESSES

How does the typical account structure of a corporation differ from that of a sole proprietorship or partnership?

Accounting for Owners' Equity for Sole Proprietorships and Partnerships

Owners' Equity for a Sole Proprietorship

What is recorded in the capital account of a sole proprietorship? What is recorded in the drawing account?

Why don't the financial statements of a sole proprietorship reflect any income tax expense or income taxes payable?

Owners' Equity for a Partnership

What is the definition of a partnership? What five matters should be specified in a partnership agreement?

What are the three primary advantages of a partnership? What is the primary disadvantage?

What is recorded in the partners' capital accounts?

How does the income statement of a partnership differ from that of a corporation? Why don't the financial statements of a partnership reflect any income tax expense or income taxes payable?

SELF-TEST QUESTIONS AND EXERCISES

MATCHING

Match each of the key terms listed below with the appropriate textbook definition:

B	1.	Authorized number of shares	O	11.	Legal capital
I	2.	Common stock	H	12.	Nopar value stock
L	3.	Convertible preferred stock	P	13.	Outstanding shares
C	4.	Cumulative dividend preference	A	14.	Par value
F	5.	Current dividend preference	N	15.	Preferred stock
		Dividend dates:	K	16.	Prior period adjustment
S	6.	Declaration date	M	17.	Stock dividend
R	7.	Payment date	J	18.	Stock split
I	8.	Record date	E	19.	Treasury stock
Q	9.	Dividends in arrears	D	20.	Unissued shares
G	10.	Issued shares			

A. Nominal value per share of capital stocks specified in the charter, serves as the basis for legal capital.

B. Maximum number of shares of capital stock of a corporation that can be issued as specified in the charter.

C. Preferred stock preference that requires specified current dividends not paid in full to accumulate for every year in which they are not paid. These dividends must be paid before an common dividends can be paid.

D. Authorized shares of a corporation's stock that have never been issued.

E. A corporation's own stock that had been issued but was subsequently acquired and is still being held by that corporation.

F. The basic dividend preference on preferred stock for a particular year.

G. Total shares of stock that have been issued; shares outstanding plus treasury shares held.

H. Shares of capital stock that have no par value specified in the corporate charter.

I. The basic, normal, voting stock issued by a corporation, called residual equity because it ranks after preferred stock for dividend and liquidation distributions.

J. An increase in the total number of authorized shares by a specified ratio; does not decrease retained earnings.

K. Amount debited or credited directly to retained earnings to correct an accounting error of a prior period.

L. Preferred stock that is convertible to common stock at the option of the holder.

M. Distribution of additional shares of a corporation's own stock to current stockholders on a pro rata basis at no cost; decreases retained earnings.

N. Shares of stock that have specified rights over the common stock.

O. The permanent amount of capital defined by state law, that must remain invested in the business; provides a "cushion" for creditors.

P. Total shares of stock that are owned by stockholders on any particular date.

Q. Dividends on cumulative preferred stock that have not been declared in prior years.

R. Date on which a cash dividend is paid to the stockholders of record.

S. Date on which the board of directors officially approves the dividend.

T. Date on which the corporation prepares the list of current stockholders as shown on its records; dividends can be paid only to the stockholders who own stock on that date.

TRUE-FALSE QUESTIONS

For each of the following statements, enter a T or F in the blank to indicate whether the statement is true or false.

____1. The number of authorized shares in a corporation refers to the original number of shares issued when that company "went public."

____2. If a corporation only has one class of stock, it is common stock.

____3. Legal capital is a permanent amount of capital that owners cannot withdraw.

____4. Unlimited liability refers to the fact that creditors of a liquidated corporation can put claims on the assets of shareholders for debts that corporate assets are insufficient to pay.

____5. The chief advantage of preferred stock is that its dividends must be paid before any dividends can be given to common shareholders.

____6. Contributed capital from the sale of stock with a par value is usually divided between amounts received equal to par value of the shares sold, and amounts received in excess of par.

___7. When shareholders in a corporation sell all or part of their holdings to other private individuals, no entry is required on the part of the corporation.

___8. Treasury stock consists of unissued shares of the company's stock.

___9. When no other qualifying statements are made, the term "dividend" can mean either a cash or a stock dividend.

___10. A large stock dividend is recorded at the par value of the shares distributed.

___11. A stock split results in a decrease in the par value of the stock, and a proportionate increase in the number of shares outstanding.

___12. The full disclosure principle requires that any restrictions on retained earnings must be reported on the face of the balance sheet.

MULTIPLE CHOICE QUESTIONS

Choose the best answer or response by placing the identifying letter in the space provided.

_a_ 1.   A stockholder of a corporation is

    a.   one of the owners of the corporation.
    b.   a creditor of the corporation.
    c.   both an owner and a creditor of the corporation.
    d.   a manager of the corporation.
    e.   both c and d.

_b_ 2.   In order to create a corporation, it is necessary to apply to

    a.   the federal government.
    b.   the appropriate office in the state in which the corporation will be organized.
    c.   the SEC.
    d.   the FASB.
    e.   the IRS.

_b_ 3.   Outstanding shares of stock are those which

    a.   have been issued to investors.
    b.   have been issued, and have not been bought back by the company.
    c.   the company is permitted by its charter to issue.
    d.   are authorized, but have not yet been issued.
    e.   have been repurchased by the company.

_c_ 4.   Compact Corporation has 50,000,000 shares of common stock, par value $.01, authorized, and 16,697,000 shares issued and outstanding. Its total paid in capital is $199,623,000. If Compact rounds all dollar amounts on its financial statements to the nearest thousandth, the dollar amount reported as common stock on its balance sheet would be

    a. $500
    b. $200
    c. $167
    d. $199
    e. $333

C 5. Refer to the information in the preceding question. The average price received by Compact for a share of its stock was

   a. $.01
   b. $3.99
   c. $11.96
   d. $21.13
   e. cannot be calculated from the information given.

e 6. Quinn had one hundred shares of Compact common stock that she had purchased for $21 per share. She sold the shares to Randy for $28 per share. On Compact's books this would

   a. be shown as an increase in stockholders' equity of $2,800.
   b. be shown as an increase in stockholders equity of $700.
   c. be shown as an increase in retained earnings of $700.
   d. be shown as an increase to additional paid-in capital of $700.
   e. not be shown at all.

a 7. Cosmic Treats Co. purchased 40,000 shares of its own $1 par common stock on the open market for $600,000. Cosmic intends to hold the stock for employee bonuses. This stock would be carried on Cosmic's books in

   a. a contra equity account.
   b. the common stock account.
   c. an asset account, at cost.
   d. an asset account, at par value.
   e. a liability account.

d 8. On December 31, 1995, the board of directors of Ardent Inc. issued a press release to the newspapers stating that the company planned to pay a dividend of $.12 per share on its common stock. The date of this announcement is known as the date of _____; the company must record a liability _____.

   a. record; on the date of declaration.
   b. record; on the date of record.
   c. declaration; in the year in which the dividend will be paid.
   d. declaration; on the date of declaration.
   e. dividend; when the books are closed for the fiscal year.

e 9. Ardent Inc. had 1,000 shares of $100 par, 6% preferred stock outstanding, as well as 100,000 shares of $.01 par common stock. On March 31, 1996, their year-end, the board of directors declared a dividend of $9,500. In the past, they have tried to maintain a minimum dividend of $.10 per share on common stock. For the March 31 dividend, preferred stockholders would receive a total of _____ and common stockholders a total of

   _____.

   a. $6,000; $10,000
   b. $0; $9,500
   c. $4,750; $4,750
   d. $0; $10,000
   e. $6,000; $3,500

C 10. Refer to the information in the preceding question. Suppose the preferred stock is cumulative, and Ardent, having had a slow year, was unable to pay any dividends last year. In that case, preferred stockholders would receive _____ and common stockholders would receive _____ on March 31 of this year.

    a. $6,000; $3,500
    b. $12,000; 0
    c. $9,500; 0
    d. $12,000; $10,000
    e. $4,750; $4,750

e 11. A stock split, unlike a stock dividend,

    a. requires no journal entry.
    b. does not change total stockholders' equity.
    c. reduces the par value of the stock.
    d. increases the total number of shares outstanding.
    e. both a and c.

b 12. A prior period adjustment made to correct an error discovered after a previous year's results have been published is reflected in

    a. the ending balance of retained earnings.
    b. the beginning balance of retained earnings.
    c. a footnote, but not in the financial statements themselves.
    d. the income statement of the current period, as a extraordinary item.
    e. the statement of cash flows.

EXERCISES

Record your answers to each part of these exercises in the space provided. Show your work.

1. Tyler Corporation was organized in 19A. Its corporate charter authorized the issuance of 50,000 shares of common stock, par value $5 per share, and 10,000 shares of 8% preferred stock, par value $25 per share.

A. Prepare journal entries for each of the following transactions:

Jan. 1 Sold and issued 40,000 shares of common stock for cash at $25 per share.

Jan 1 Sold and issued 5,000 shares of preferred stock for cash of $75 per share.

Feb 1 Issued 5,000 shares of common stock in exchange for a tract of land. Assume the stock was selling at $26 per share at the time of this transaction.

June 1 Purchased 7,500 shares of common stock in the open market at $24 per share.

Aug 1 Sold 1,000 shares of the treasury stock at $26 per share.

Oct 1 Sold another 1,500 shares of the treasury stock at $22 per share.

Dec 31 Declared dividends totaling $100,000.

B. Compute the number of shares of common stock issued and outstanding at December 31, 19A.

C. Assuming that the market price of the common stock was $22.50 per share on December 31, 19A, calculate the dividend yield.

2. Core Corporation had 200,000 shares of common stock, par value $2 per share, authorized and 100,000 shares issued and outstanding on December 31, 19A. The market value of its common stock on that date was $100 per share. Prepare journal entries for each of the following independent transactions. If no journal entry is required, explain why, and indicate the effects, if any, on the financial statements.

A. Core Corporation declared a two-for-one stock split that will be accounted for as a 100% stock dividend.

B. Assume instead that Core Corporation declared a 25% stock dividend.

C. Assume instead that Core Corporation declared a five-to-four stock split (i.e., a 25% increase in the number of shares).

SOLUTIONS TO SELF-TEST QUESTIONS AND EXERCISES

MATCHING

1.	B	5.	F	9.	Q	13.	P	17.	M
2.	I	6.	S	10.	G	14.	A	18.	J
3.	L	7.	R	11.	O	15.	N	19.	E
4.	C	8.	T	12.	H	16.	K	20.	D

TRUE-FALSE QUESTIONS

1. F - The number of authorized shares is the maximum number of shares the corporation is permitted to offer for sale (as set forth in its corporate charter).

2. T

3. T

4. F - Unlimited liability applies to the owners of sole proprietorships and partnerships; not to corporations.

5. T

6. T

7. T

8. F - Treasury stock consists of shares of company stock that the company has repurchased.

9. F - Without a qualifier, "dividend" means a cash dividend.

10. T

11. T

12. F - Restrictions on retained earnings may be disclosed either on the financial statements themselves *or* in the footnotes to the financial statements.

MULTIPLE CHOICE QUESTIONS

1.	a	4.	c	7.	a	10.	c
2.	b	5.	c	8.	d	11.	e
3.	b	6.	e	9.	e	12.	b

EXERCISES

1A.

Jan 1	Cash (40,000 x $25)	1,000,000	
	Common stock (40,000 x $5)		200,000
	Capital in excess of par value		800,000
	(40,000 x $20)		
Jan 1	Cash (5,000 x $75)	375,000	
	Preferred stock (5,000 x $25)		125,000
	Capital in excess par value		250,000
	(5,000 x $50)		
Feb 1	Land (5,000 x $26)	130,000	
	Common stock (5,000 x $5)		25,000
	Capital in excess of par value		105,000
	(5,000 x $21)		
June 1	Treasury stock	180,000	
	Cash (7,500 x $24)		180,000
Aug 1	Cash (1,000 x $26)	26,000	
	Treasury stock (1,000 x $24)		24,000
	Contributed capital from		
	treasury stock transactions		2,000
	(1,000 x $2)		
Oct 1	Cash (1,500 x $22)	33,000	
	Contributed capital from		
	treasury stock transactions	3,000	
	(1,500 x $2)		
	Treasury stock (1,500 x $24)		36,000
Dec 31	Retained earnings	100,000	
	Dividends payable - preferred		10,000
	(5,000 x $25 x .08)		
	Dividends payable - common		90,000
	($100,000 - $10,000)		

1B.

Issued:			
Jan. 1		40,000	
Feb. 1		5,000	45,000
Less shares in treasury:			
Purchased:			
June 1		(7,500)	
Sold:			
Aug. 1	1,000		
Oct. 1	1,500	2,500	(5,000)
Issued and outstanding			40,000

1C.

Common dividends / Shares issued and outstanding = Common dividend per share
$90,000 / 40,000 = $2.25

Dividends per share / market value per share = Dividend yield
$2.25 / $22.50 = 10.0%

2.

A. Retained earnings   400,000
      Common stock   400,000
      (200,000 shares x $2 par value)

B. Retained earnings   5,000,000
      Common stock   5,000,000
      ((200,000 shares x .25) x $100)

C. No journal entry is required. In a stock split, the total number of authorized shares is increased by a specified amount and the par or stated value per share of all authorized shares is reduced so that the total par value of all authorized shares is unchanged.

Core Corporation's authorized shares would increase to 250,000 (200,000 + (200,000 x .25)) and its par value per share would decrease to $1.60 ($2 - ($2 x .25)). Before the stock split, the total par value of all authorized shares was $400,000 (200,000 shares x $2 par value per share). After the stock, split, the total par value of all authorized shares is still $400,000 (250,000 shares x $1.60 par value per share).

On the balance sheet, the amount of common stock would remain unchanged. Before the stock split, the total par value of the shares issued was $200,000 (100,000 shares x $2 par value per share). After the stock, split, the total par value of the shares issued is still $200,000 (100,000 shares + (100,000 shares x .25)) x $1.60 par value per share = 125,000 shares x $1.60 par value per share = $200,000).

IDEAS FOR YOUR STUDY TEAM

1. Rewrite each of the definitions of the key terms that appear at the end of the chapter using your own words. Imagine that you are trying to explain each key term to a friend who has not taken any accounting classes. Then, get together with the other members of your study team and compare your definitions.

Authorized number of shares

Common stock

Convertible preferred stock

Cumulative dividend preference

Current dividend preference

Dividend dates:
      Declaration date

      Payment date

      Record date

Dividends in arrears

Issued shares

Legal capital

Nopar value stock

Outstanding shares

Par value

Preferred stock

Prior period adjustment

Stock dividend

Stock split

Treasury stock

Unissued shares

2. Get together with the other members of your study team and discuss the following. Assume that a company has not retained earnings. Why it is not only illegal (generally), but also illogical, to declare a dividend and then pay that dividend out of additional paid in capital? Isn't the company still "giving something" to its shareholders?

3. Get together with the other members of your study team. Each member should choose a well-known publicly-held company. Assume that your study team owns 100 shares of each company's common stock. Do some research and answer the following questions.

What is the par value of your 100 shares?

What is the market value of one share of common stock? What is the total market value of your 100 shares?

What is the book value per share (total common stockholders' equity divided by the number of shares of common stock outstanding) of the company's common stock?

What percentage of the company does your "hundred block" represent?

How much influence will your 100 shares have in terms of voting in the shareholders' meeting?

What is the total amount of dividends that you would have received on your 100 shares during the past year?

CHAPTER 12
REPORTING AND INTERPRETING INVESTMENTS IN OTHER CORPORATIONS

CHAPTER FOCUS SUGGESTIONS

Corporations invest in the capital stock of other corporations for a variety of reasons. This chapter covers the reporting issues related to such long-term investments. Three methods are used: the market value, equity, and consolidated financial statements methods. The method used is determined by the percentage of shares owned in relation to the total number of shares outstanding. You will need to be familiar with each of the three methods. You will also need to know how to compute return on investment.

Under the market value method (investments less than 20%), the investment in the common stock of another corporation is initially recorded at cost. Thereafter, the investment is reported based on the current market value of the stock. Investments in common stock accounted for under the market value method must be classified as trading securities or available-for-sale securities. Unrealized gains and losses on trading securities are reported on the income statement; unrealized gains and losses on trading securities are reported as a component of stockholders' equity.

Under the equity method (investments between 20% and 50%), the investment is initially recorded at cost. Thereafter, the investment account is increased by the investor's proportionate share of the net income reported by the investee company and decreased by its proportionate share of the dividends declared by the investee company. The proportionate share of net income is reported on the income statement.

When a company acquires more than 50% of another company's outstanding voting stock, the investment is initially recorded at cost. However, for reporting purposes, consolidated financial statements must be prepared. The separate financial statements are combined each period to form a single set of consolidated financial statements. The consolidation process must include the elimination of the investment account in a five-step process. Depending on the terms of the acquisition, the ownership of a controlling interest of another corporation is accounted for as a pooling of interests (if stock is exchanged for stock) or combination by purchase (if cash is, or cash and stock, are exchanged for stock). The measurement of amounts reported in the consolidated financial statements is affected by the method used.

READ AND RECALL QUESTIONS

LEARNING OBJECTIVE
After studying this section of the chapter, you should be able to:
1. Discuss why corporations invest in each other.

BUSINESS BACKGROUND

What are the three categories of investments? What are the characteristics of each?

ACCOUNTING FOR INVESTMENTS IN SECURITIES

What is "significant influence?" What is "control?"

What measurement and reporting method should be used for a level of ownership characterized by "neither significant influence or control?" What measurement and reporting method should be used for a level of ownership characterized by "significant influence but not control?" What measurement and reporting method should be used for a level of ownership characterized by "control?"

If the investor can exercise no significant influence or control over the investee company, the market value method should be used. How is the investment measured at the date of acquisition? How is the investment reported on the balance sheet? How does the investor recognize revenue related to the investment?

338

If the investor can exercise significant influence, but not control, over the operating and financing policies of the investee company, the equity method should be used. How is the investment measured at the date of acquisition? How is the investment reported on the balance sheet? How does the investor recognize revenue related to the investment?

If the investor can exercise control over the operating and financing policies of the investee company, the consolidated financial statements method should be used. How is the investment measured at the date of acquisition? How is the investment reported on the balance sheet? How does the investor recognize revenue related to the investment?

MARKET VALUE METHOD

What method is used to account for all investments in nonvoting stock?

What is the maximum percentage of outstanding stock that can owned by an investor under the market value method? What are the two categories of investments in stock that are accounted for under the market value method?

What are trading securities? What are available-for-sale securities? What are the characteristics of each?

How is the trading securities portfolio reported on the balance sheet? How does the intent of management affect the manner in which the available-for-sale portfolio is reported on the balance sheet?

RECORDING INVESTMENTS AT MARKET VALUE

What type of asset is the only type of asset that is reported at fair market value on the balance sheet? What are the two primary factors for reporting this asset at fair market value?

Holding Gains and Losses

What other account is affected when the investment account is adjusted to reflect changes in fair market value? What does "unrealized" mean"

How are the unrealized holding gains and losses that relate to trading securities reported on the financial statements?

How are the unrealized holding gains and losses that relate to available-for-sale securities reported on the financial statements?

If management purchases a security as part of its available-for-sale portfolio, what account is used to record the cost of the securities? What account is used if management purchases the security as part of its portfolio of trading securities?

How is dividend income reported when the market value method is used?

How is the unrealized holding gain or loss determined at the end of the accounting period? What adjusting entry is used to record an unrealized holding gain? What adjusting entry is used to record an unrealized holding loss?

How is the allowance to adjust to market account reported on the balance sheet if it has a debit balance? How is it reported if it has a credit balance?

LEARNING OBJECTIVE

After studying this section of the chapter, you should be able to:

4. Record the sale of investments.

SALE OF AN INVESTMENT

Securities Sold from the Trading Portfolio

What entry is used to record the sale of stock from the trading portfolio at a gain? How is the gain computed? How is it reported on the financial statements?

The amount of the gain that is recognized on the sale of stock from the trading portfolio is not affected by any previous recording of unrealized gains. How is the double counting that results corrected? What adjusting entry is made at the end of the accounting period? How are adjustments for unrealized gains reported on the financial statements?

Securities Sold from the Available-for-Sale Portfolio

What two entries are used to record the sale of stock from the available-for-sale portfolio at a gain?

How is the gain recognized from the sale reported on the financial statements? How is the unrealized gains on investments account reported on the financial statements?

LEARNING OBJECTIVE
After studying this section of the chapter, you should be able to:
5. Use the equity method.

EQUITY METHOD

The market value method is used when investors are assumed to be passive. When are investors assumed to be "passive?"

What range of ownership (stated in percentages) indicates that the investor wants to be able to exert influence without becoming a majority owner? Why would a company want to exert influence over another company?

What method should be used when an investor can exert significant influence over an investee? What presumption is made in terms of the time frame of the investment?

What entry is used to record a purchase of stock under the equity method?

When dividends are paid on stock that is accounted for under the equity method, how are the dividends treated? What entry is used to record the dividends that are declared? How do the dividends affect the net income reported by the investor?

Assume that General Electric (the investor) purchased 30% of the outstanding stock of Davis Corporation (the investee). How would you compute General Electric's proportional share of the $40,000 of net income reported by Davis Corporation? What entry would an investor use to record its proportional share of an investee company's net income?

When the equity method is used, what entry would be used to record the proportionate share of a loss reported by the investee?

When the equity method is used, is the long-term investment account increased, or decreased, for the cost of shares that are purchased when an equity investment is made?

When the equity method is used, is the long-term investment account increased, or decreased, when the investee declares a cash dividend?

When the equity method is used, is the long-term investment account adjusted to reflect changes in the fair market value of the securities that are held?

Manager's Selection of Accounting Alternatives

Can managers choose between the market value method and equity method?

Why would managers want to avoid using the market value method? Why would they want to avoid using the equity method?

Improper Influence

What is "arm's length?" When one corporation is able to exert a significant influence over another (i.e., it owns 20% to 50% of the common stock), is it reasonable to assume that transactions between the two corporation's are at arm's length? What method is designed to overcome this problem? How does this method prevent manipulation?

INVESTING TO ACHIEVE A CONTROLLING INTEREST

What are the six reasons for acquiring control of another corporation?

What is vertical integration? What is horizontal growth?

What is synergy? What is diversification?

What are undervalued opportunities?

LEARNING OBJECTIVE

After studying this section of the chapter, you should be able to:

6. Explain the purpose of consolidated statements.

WHAT ARE CONSOLIDATED STATEMENTS?

What is a parent company? What is a subsidiary?

What are consolidated financial statements? What are intercompany items? Why must intercompany items be eliminated when consolidated financial statements are prepared?

METHODS OF ACQUIRING A CONTROLLING INTEREST

What is a pooling of interests? When does a pooling occur? What basis (cost or market value) is used to add together the assets of all of the affiliated companies under the pooling method?

What type of acquisition takes place when cash is offered to the owners of a company to acquire the stock in that company? Which method is used most often in practice to record an acquisition of the voting stock of a subsidiary?

LEARNING OBJECTIVE

After studying this section of the chapter, you should be able to:

7. Apply the purchase method and prepare elimination entries.

Purchase Method

Under the purchase method, what do the stockholders of the acquired company receive for the shares of stock that they sell? On the acquisition date, what does the investment account reflect?

Why would the parent pay more than book value when it acquires all of the stock of a subsidiary?

Why does the investment account need to be eliminated? What does the investment account balance represent?

What is goodwill? How is goodwill created? Can goodwill be recorded in a purchase transaction? Can goodwill be recorded in a pooling of interests? How is goodwill reported on the balance sheet?

How is the amount of goodwill that is recognized in a purchase transaction determined?

What are the five steps that must be completed to eliminate the investment account that is recorded on the parent's books? (Note that the first step may be different than that described depending on the market values of the various assets acquired. For example, the subsidiary may own other assets that have market values that are greater or less than cost.)

Financial Analysis

How is return on investment (ROI) computed? What does it measure?

Why could an acquisition accounted for under the purchase method have a large impact on ROI?

WHY ARE CONSOLIDATED FINANCIAL STATEMENTS USED?

When are consolidated financial statements used? Why do analysts prefer to see financial results reported on a consolidated basis?

Why would financial analysts be misled if they reviewed the operations of Acco separately from Allied Corporation?

CONSOLIDATION IN SUBSEQUENT ACCOUNTING PERIODS

What impact does the revaluation of assets have on future accounting periods? Why is it necessary to make a special entry during consolidation to record an additional amount of depreciation expense?

What impact does the creation of goodwill have on future accounting periods? When is the amortization of goodwill recorded? What is the maximum life permitted for amortization of goodwill? How does the amortization of goodwill affect cash flows?

Investments and Cash Flows

Under the market value method, how do unrealized holding gains or losses in the trading securities portfolio affect net income? How do they affect cash flows? Why are analysts interested in these items?

Should unrealized holding gains be added to, or subtracted from, net income to compute cash flows from operating activities? Should unrealized holding losses be added to, or subtracted from, net income to compute cash flows from operating activities?

350

Under the equity method, how does the investor's proportionate share of the investee company's net income affect the investor's net income? How does it affect cash flows?

Should the investor's proportionate share of the investee company's net income be added to, or subtracted from, the investor's net income to compute cash flows from operating activities?

Should the amortization of goodwill be added to, or subtracted from, the investor's net income to compute cash flows from operating activities?

SELF-TEST QUESTIONS AND EXERCISES

MATCHING

Match each of the key terms listed below with the appropriate textbook definition:

_____	1.	Available-for-sale securities	_____	8.	Pooling of interests
_____	2.	Consolidated financial statements	_____	9.	Purchase
			_____	10.	Significant influence
_____	3.	Control	_____	11.	Subsidiary
_____	4.	Equity method	_____	12.	Trading securities
_____	5.	Goodwill	_____	13.	Unrealized holding gains and
_____	6.	Market value method			losses
_____	7.	Parent			

A. The amount that was paid for the good reputation and customer appeal of an acquired company.

351

B. The ability of the investing company to determine the operating and financing policies of another company in which it owns shares of the voting stock; presumed to exist when more than 50% or the voting stock of an entity is owned by one investor.

C. Amounts recorded when there is a price change for securities which are currently held.

D. The ability of an investor to have an important impact on the operating and financing policies of another company (the investee).

E. All investments in stocks or bonds that are held primarily for the purpose of selling them in the near future; accounted for under the market value method.

F. The financial statements of two or more companies that have been combined into a single set of financial statements.

G. The company that has a significant investment in a subsidiary company.

H. All investments, other than trading securities, that are accounted for under the market value method.

I. An acquisition that is completed by purchasing subsidiary company voting capital stock for cash.

J. Method used by investor if 20% to 50% of the voting stock of the investee company is owned by the investor. It permits recording of the investor's share of investee's income.

K. Method used by investor if less that 20% of the voting stock of the investee company is owned by the investor, unrealized gains and losses are recorded based on changes in the prices of securities that are held.

L. The company that is owned by a parent company as evidenced by more than 50% of the voting capital stock.

M. An acquisition that is completed by exchanging parent company stock for subsidiary voting capital stock.

TRUE-FALSE QUESTIONS

For each of the following statements, enter a T or F in the blank to indicate whether the statement is true or false.

____1. Trading and available-for-sale securities are an exception to the cost principle.

____2. Available-for-sale securities are held primarily for the purpose of selling them in the near future.

____3. Long-term investments with no intent to exert influence are usually less than 20% of the investee company's stock.

____4. The market value method is only used when there is no significant influence or control.

____5. In order to have control, a company must acquire more than 50% of another company's stock.

____6. Unrealized holding gains would be reported in the investing section of the statement of cash flows.

___7. A company that acquired 35% of another company's stock would have a choice between accounting for the investment by the market value method, or the equity method.

___8. In simple terms, a consolidation is an adding together of each of the financial statements, line by line, of the parent company and the subsidiary.

___9. In a combination by purchase, the stock of the subsidiary is acquired from its current owners with cash by the parent, or acquiring, company.

___10. The amortization of goodwill has no cash impact, but can have a significant impact on earnings.

MULTIPLE CHOICE QUESTIONS

Choose the best answer or response by placing the identifying letter in the space provided.

___1. A company makes short-term investments in order to

   a. minimize investment risk.
   b. earn a high rate of return on funds that will be needed in the near future for operating items.
   c. accumulate funds for future investments in assets.
   d. have at least a small say in the management of another company.
   e. all of the above.

___2. The difference between significant influence and control in a long-term investment is mainly

   a. one of intent.
   b. Whether the investor company owns between 20% and 50% of the investee company's stock or more than 50%.
   c. a matter of how much control of the board of directors is achieved.
   d. a matter of how many management personnel it is possible to insert into the investee company.
   e. a question of the type of securities held.

___3. When there is neither significant influence nor control, the proper way to measure and report the investment and income from the investment is

   a. the market value method.
   b. the equity method.
   c. the consolidation method.
   d. either (b) or (c).
   e. either (a) or (b) or (c).

___4. All investments nonvoting stock are accounted for under

   a. the cost method.
   b. the equity method.
   c. the market value method.
   d. the investment method.
   e. the consolidation method.

___5. Trading securities are held primarily for

    a. influence in the management of another entity.
    b. their desirability to other companies, giving them a guaranteed high resale value.
    c. accumulating funds for the purchase of long-lived assets.
    d. sale in the near future.
    e. earning a return on funds that may be required for operating purposes in the future.

___6. When a trading security increases in value, it is necessary as part of the closing process to record _____ on the _____.

    a. income from investments; income statement
    b. income from investments; balance sheet
    c. no entry; financial statements.
    d. an unrealized holding gain; balance sheet
    e. an unrealized holding gain; income statement

___7. Available-for-sale securities differ from trading securities in that unrealized gains or losses are recognized

    a. as a separate component of stockholders' equity, rather than on the income statement.
    b. on the income statement, rather than as part of stockholders' equity on the balance sheet.
    c. only when the security is sold.
    d. differently; losses are recorded, but gains are not.
    e. as other income rather than as regular revenue items.

___8. The equity method presumes an investment was made

    a. to put temporarily excess cash to work in a high-return investment.
    b. as a sinking fund for bond retirement.
    c. for a long-term strategic purpose.
    d. for the purchase of a major asset.
    e. as a first step in purchasing another company.

Use the following information to answer the next three questions. Northeast Outdoor, Inc., a retailer, acquired 10,000 of the 40,000 outstanding shares of St. Charles Camping Equipment Company, a manufacturer, on the open market during July 19A. The $1 par value shares cost $220,000. By the end of 19A, the shares were worth $265,000. St. Charles earned net income of $1,200,000 during 19A. St. Charles Camping Equipment declared and paid a dividend of 10¢ per share on December 31, 19A.

___9. At the end of 19A, as a result of the increase in the market value of the investment, Northeast would

    a. record an unrealized holding gain on the income statement.
    b. record an unrealized holding gain as a separate item in stockholders' equity.
    c. record the unrealized holding gain as an addition to retained earnings.
    d. make no entry at all.
    e. record the unrealized holding gain as a contra-equity account.

___10. Northeast would record the dividend it receives from St. Charles Camping Equipment as

    a. a decrease in the long-term investment account.
    b. an increase in the long-term investment account.
    c. dividend revenue.
    d. an increase in retained earnings.
    e. an increase in unrealized holding gains.

___11. Northeast hopes at some point to purchase a controlling interest in St. Charles Camping Equipment. If they achieve this, it would be an example of a

    a. vertical integration.
    b. diversification.
    c. horizontal growth.
    d. synergy.
    e. a pooling of interests.

___12. A pooling of interests occurs when

    a. two companies are in a similar line of business.
    b. there is a stock-for-stock swap.
    c. more than 50% of a company's stock is bought for cash.
    d. two companies agree to become one company.
    e. bonds are redeemed for common stock.

___13. In a pooling of interests the assets of the acquired company are recognized at _____ and goodwill _____.

    a. their fair market value; is not recognized
    b. their historical cost; is recorded at the excess of cost over value of assets acquired
    c. their fair market value; is recorded at the excess of cost over value of assets acquired
    d. their fair market value; recognition is optional
    e. their historical cost; is not recognized

___14. Large Company paid $150,000 cash for 100% of the outstanding stock of Small Company. Small Company's machinery had a book value of $40,000, but an appraisal revealed that the equipment had a fair market value of $50,000. Small Company also had a small but very strong, loyal customer base. For these reasons, Large was willing to pay $150,000 for the net book value of Small's stockholders' equity of $128,000. The amount of goodwill reported on Large's consolidated balance sheet would be

    a. $10,000.
    b. $12,000.
    c. $22,000.
    d. $128,000.
    e. goodwill is not recorded in a combination by purchase.

___15. Goodwill is recorded as a(n) _____, to be amortized over a period not to exceed _____.

    a. asset; 17 years
    b. asset; 40 years
    c. asset; there is not a limit on the amortization period
    d. liability; 40 years
    e. equity account; 40 years

___16. In periods following the acquisition of another company, the presence of goodwill reduces _____ on the consolidated books of the parent company.

    a. cash
    b. total assets
    c. total equity
    d. net income
    e. total liabilities

___17. Many financial analysts use the return on investment ratio to evaluate

    a. the overall dividend rate of a company's investments.
    b. the effectiveness of the management of a company.
    c. how quickly assets are turned into cash.
    d. how efficiently long-lived assets are being used.
    e. how carefully a company controls expenses.

EXERCISES

Record your answers to each part of these exercises in the space provided. Show your work.

1. During 19C, Parker, Inc. acquired interests in Broderick, Inc. and Chadwick, Inc. Broderick has 100,000 shares of common stock outstanding, par value $2 per share. Chadwick has 250,000 shares of common stock outstanding, par value $10 per share. All three companies have calendar year-ends. The following transactions took place during 19C:

Jan. 1   Purchased 10,000 shares of Broderick common stock at $35 per share.

Jan. 2   Purchased 100,000 shares of Chadwick common stock at $50 per share.

Dec. 29   Broderick declared and paid a cash dividend of $1.00 per share.

Dec. 30   Chadwick declared and paid a cash dividend of $2.00 per share.

Dec. 31   Received the 19C annual financial statements of Broderick, Inc. that reported net income of $100,000.

Dec. 31   Received the 19C annual financial statements of Chadwick, Inc. that reported net income of $1,000,000.

Dec. 31   Market price of Broderick stock was $40 per share.

Dec. 31   Market price of Chadwick stock was $75 per share.

If applicable, assume that any securities purchased by Parker that would be accounted for under the market value method will be included in its trading securities portfolio, and that any securities that would be accounted for under the equity method are long-term investments.

A. What accounting method(s) should Parker use for its investments in Broderick and Chadwick?

B. Prepare journal entries for each of the transactions described above. If no entry is required, explain why.

357

C. (Refer to your answers to Part A.) If either investment is accounted for under the market value method, how would any unrealized gains or losses relating to those securities be reported in Parker's financial statements? How would your answer be different if these securities were included in Parker's available-for-sale securities portfolio?

2. On January 1, 19A, Davido Company purchased 5,000 shares of Venus Inc. common stock for $30 per share for inclusion in its trading securities portfolio. The price of Venus common stock was $29 per share on December 31, 19A. Davido sold all of its shares of Venus stock on January 31, 19B at $32 per share. Prepare the journal entries that are required by the information presented.

3. Refer to the information presented in the previous exercise. Assume instead that Davido purchased the Venus stock for inclusion in its available-for-sale securities portfolio instead of its trading securities portfolio. Prepare the journal entries that are required by the information presented.

4. On January 1, 19A, DPK enterprises acquired all of the outstanding stock of JMF Companies for $5 cash per share. An appraisal revealed that JMF's operational assets had a market value of $200,000 as of the date of acquisition. On that date (prior to the acquisition), the separate balance sheets (summarized) of the companies reported the following book values.

	DPK Enterprises	JMF Companies
Cash	$1,500,000	$200,000
Receivable from JMF Enterprises	25,000	
Operational assets (net)	50,000	150,000
Total assets	$1,575,000	$350,000
Payable to DPK Enterprises		$ 25,000
Other liabilities	$ 100,000	15,000
Common stock:		
DPK (no par)	1,000,000	
JMF ($1 par)		250,000
Retained earnings	475,000	60,000
Total liabilities and stockholders' equity	$1,575,000	$350,000

A. Should this combination be accounted for as a pooling of interest or a purchase? Explain.

B. Prepare the journal entry that would be recorded by DPK at the date of acquisition.

C. Determine the amount of goodwill that should be recognized.

D. Using the five-step elimination procedure, determine the adjustments that must be made in order to consolidate the two balance sheets.

E. Prepare a consolidated balance sheet immediately after the acquisition. (Hint: Complete the table below by reflecting the entry you prepared in part B in the journal entry column, then reflecting the adjustments that you determined to be necessary in Part D in the adjustments column, and completing the consolidated column by adding across each line.)

	DPK	JMF	Entry	Adjustments	Consolidated
Cash	$1,500,000	$200,000			.
Receivable from JMF	25,000				
Investment in JMF					
Operational assets (net)	50,000	150,000			
Goodwill					
Total assets	$1,575,000	$350,000			
Payable to DPK		$ 25,000			
Other liabilities	$ 100,000	15,000			
Common stock:					
DPK (no par)	1,000,000				
JMF ($1 par)		250,000			
Retained earnings	475,000	60,000			
Total liabilities and stockholders' equity	$1,575,000	$350,000			

SOLUTIONS TO SELF-TEST QUESTIONS AND EXERCISES

MATCHING

1. H	4. J	7. G	10. D	13. C
2. F	5. A	8. M	11. L	
3. B	6. K	9. I	12. E	

TRUE-FALSE QUESTIONS

1. T

2. F - Trading securities are held primarily for the purpose of selling them in the near future. The available-for-sale securities portfolio is not traded as actively as the trading securities portfolio. The purpose of the available-for-sale securities portfolio is to earn a return on funds that may be required for operating purposes in the future.

3. T

4. T

5. T

6. F - Unrealized holding gains represent increases in the market value of investments accounted for under the market value method and have no impact on the company's cash.

7. F - If the ownership level of voting shares is at least 20%, but not more than 50%, the equity method *must* be used.

8. T

9. T

10. T

MULTIPLE CHOICE QUESTIONS

1. b	5. d	9. d	13. e	17. b
2. b	6. e	10. a	14. b	
3. a	7. a	11. a	15. b	
4. c	8. c	12. b	16. d	

EXERCISES

1A. Parker should account for its investment in Broderick using the market value method because it owns 10% (10,000 / 100,000) of Broderick's outstanding stock. Parker should account for its investment in Chadwick using the equity method because it owns 40% (100,000 / 250,000) of Chadwick's outstanding stock.

1B.

Jan 1	Trading securities	35,000	
	Cash		35,000
	(10,000 x $35)		
Jan. 2	Long-term investment	5,000,000	
	Cash		5,000,000
	(100,000 x $50)		
Dec. 29	Cash	10,000	
	Dividend income		10,000
	(10,000 x $1)		
Dec. 30	Cash	200,000	
	Long-term investment		200,000
	(100,000 x $2)		
Dec. 31	No entry; equity in investee net income is not recorded under the market value method.		
Dec. 31	Long-term investment	400,000	
	Revenue from investments		400,000
	($1,000,000 x .4)		
Dec. 31	Allowance to adjust to market	50,000	
	Unrealized holding gain		50,000
	(10,000 x ($40 - $35))		
Dec. 31	No entry; unrealized gains and losses are not recorded under the equity method.		

1C. Assuming the Broderick securities are included in Parker's trading securities portfolio, the unrealized gain of $50,000 would be reported on Parker's income statement. On the other hand, if the Broderick securities are included in Parker's available-for-sale securities portfolio, the unrealized gain of $50,000 would be reported on Parker's balance sheet as a component of stockholders' equity.

2.

Jan 1, 19A		
Trading securities	150,000	
Cash		150,000
(5,000 x $30)		
Dec. 31, 19A		
Unrealized holding loss	5,000	
Allowance to adjust to market		5,000
(5,000 x ($29 - $30))		

Jan. 31, 19B

Cash (5,000 x $32)	160,000	
Trading securities (5,000 x $30)		150,000
Gain on sale of trading securities		10,000
(5,000 x ($32 - $30))		

Dec. 31, 19B (end of period adjustment)

Allowance to adjust to market	5,000	
Adjustment for unrealized loss		5,000
(from above)		

3.

Jan 1, 19A

Available-for-sale securities	150,000	
Cash		150,000
(5,000 x $30)		

Dec. 31, 19A

Unrealized holding loss	5,000	
Allowance to adjust to market		5,000
(5,000 x ($29 - $30))		

Jan. 31, 19B

Cash (5,000 x $32)	160,000	
Available-for-sale securities		150,000
(5,000 x $30)		
Gain on sale of trading securities		10,000
(5,000 x ($32 - $30))		

Dec. 31, 19B (end of period adjustment)

Allowance to adjust to market	5,000	
Unrealized losses on investment		5,000
(from above)		

4.A. This combination should be accounted for as a purchase because cash was exchanged for stock.

4B.

Investment in JMF Companies	1,250,000	
Cash		1,250,000
(250,000 x $5)		

4C.

Purchase price		$1,250,000
Net assets acquired, at market value:		
Book value of assets acquired	$350,000	
Plus market value increment of operational assets	50,000	
Market value of assets acquired	400,000	
Less book value of liabilities assumed	(40,000)	360,000
Goodwill		$ 890,000

4D.

Receivable from JMF (decrease)	$ 25,000
Operational assets (increase)	50,000
Investment in JMF Companies (decrease)	1,250,000
Goodwill (increase)	890,000
Payable to DPK (decrease)	25,000
JMF common stock (decrease)	250,000
JMF retained earnings (decrease)	50,000

4E.

	DPK	JMF	Entry	Adjustments	Consolidated
Cash	$1,500,000	$200,000	(1,250,000)		$ 450,000
Receivable from JMF	25,000			(25,000)	
Investment in JMF			1,250,000	(1,250,000)	
Operational assets (net)	50,000	150,000		50,000	250,000
Goodwill				890,000	890,000
Total assets	$1,575,000	$350,000			$1,590,000
Payable to DPK		$ 25,000		(25,000)	
Other liabilities	$ 100,000	15,000			$ 115,000
Common stock:					
DPK (no par)	1,000,000				1,000,000
JMF ($1 par)		250,000		(250,000)	
Retained earnings	475,000	60,000		(60,000)	475,000
Total liabilities and stockholders' equity	$1,575,000	$350,000			$1,590,000

365

IDEAS FOR YOUR STUDY TEAM

1. Rewrite each of the definitions of the key terms that appear at the end of the chapter using your own words. Imagine that you are trying to explain each key term to a friend who has not taken any accounting classes. Then, get together with the other members of your study team and compare your definitions.

Available-for-sale securities

Consolidated financial statements

Control

Equity method

Goodwill

Market value method

Parent

Pooling of interests

Purchase

Significant influence

Subsidiary

Trading securities

Unrealized holding gains and losses

2. . Euro Disney operates the Disneyland Paris theme park and resort near Paris, France. As of September 30, 1996, The Walt Disney Company owned 39% of Euro Disney. Note 3 to the consolidated financial statements in The Walt Disney Company 1996 Annual Report states, in part: "As of September 30, 1996, the company's recorded investment in Euro Disney was $430 million. The quoted market value of the Company's Euro Disney shares at September 30, 1996 was approximately $634 million." Get together with the other members of your study team and discuss the following.

Does the Walt Disney Company "own" Euro Disney? Is Euro Disney a subsidiary? Explain your answer. What is the corporate relationship?

What method of accounting does The Walt Disney Company use to account for its investment in Euro Disney? How can you tell?

What effect, is any, do the operating results of Euro Disney have on the financial statements of The Walt Disney Company?

367

3. Note 2 to the consolidated financial statements in The Walt Disney Company (the Company) 1996 Annual Report states, in part:

On February 9, 1996, the Company completed its acquisition of ABC. Pursuant to the acquisition, aggregate consideration paid to ABC shareholders consisted of $10.1 billion in cash and 155 million shares of Company common stock valued at $8.8 billion based on the stock price as of the date the transaction was announced.

The acquisition was accounted for as a _____ *(left blank here intentionally)* and the acquisition cost of $18.9 billion has been allocated to the assets acquired and liabilities assumed based on estimates of their respective fair values. Assets acquired totaled $4.8 billion (of which $1.5 billion was cash) and liabilities assumed were $4.4 billion. A total of $_____*(left blank here intentionally)*, representing the excess of acquisition cost over the fair value of ABC's net tangible assets, has been allocated to intangible assets and is being amortized over forth years."

Get together with the other members of your study team and work together to answer the following questions. (You can check your answers against those supplied at the end of this chapter.)

What method did The Walt Disney Company use to account for its acquisition of ABC? (Fill in the first blank in the footnote above.) Why did the company use this method?

What is "the excess of acquisition cost over the fair value of ABC's net tangible assets?"

How much goodwill was recorded in this transaction? Fill in the second blank in the footnote above.) How much amortization expense will be recorded annually as a result of this acquisition?

4. Each member of your study team should choose a recent corporate merger. (Make sure the merger has already been consummated, or completed.). Read about the merger, locate the financial statements of the surviving company, and answer the following questions. Then, get together with the other members of your study team and discuss what you found.

Did the companies merge, or did one buy the other? What kind of business combination was it (horizontal, vertical, synergy)? Explain.

How was the combination accounted for (as a purchase or a pooling of interests)? Explain the accounting implications of the method.

How much goodwill was recorded? Can you recompute the amount of goodwill using the information disclosed in the financial statements?

Selected answers relating to Ideas for Your Study Team No. 3: The Walt Disney used the purchase method to account for its acquisition of ABC. Goodwill in the amount of $18.3 billion (rounded) was recorded.

CHAPTER FOCUS SUGGESTIONS

This chapter covers the preparation and interpretation of the statement of cash flows. This required financial statement provides cash flow information in a manner that maximizes its usefulness to decision-makers.

The statement of cash flows has three main sections: cash flows from operating activities which are related to earning income from normal operations; cash flows from investing activities which are related to the acquisition and sale of productive assets; and cash flows from financing activities which are related to financing the enterprise. To develop the information to be reported in each section it is necessary to analyze the changes in selected accounts. The purpose of this analysis is to determine the cash flow effects of the transactions reflected in those accounts. You will need to be able to identify the accounts that must be analyzed to prepare each of the three sections of the statement.

The cash flows from operating activities section of the statement can be prepared using either the direct or indirect method. The amount of cash flow from operations reported is the same whether the direct or indirect method is used. Although the FASB prefers the direct method, the indirect method is used by most companies.

The direct method reports the components of the cash flows from operating activities as gross receipts (such as cash received from customers) and gross payments (such as cash paid for salaries and wages). The indirect method starts with net income and adjusts it to cash flow from operations. The adjustments are necessary because net income is an accrual basis number. Revenues are recorded when earned, and expenses when incurred without regard to when the related cash flows occur. For the most part, the adjustments convert net income to a cash basis number.

READ AND RECALL QUESTIONS

BUSINESS BACKGROUND

Why is cash flow critical? (Try to think of at least four reasons.)

What are the three main categories of activities that generate and use cash?

After studying this section of the chapter, you should be able to:
1. Classify cash flow statement items as part of net cash flows from operating, investing, and financing activities.

CLASSIFICATIONS ON THE STATEMENT OF CASH FLOWS

What is the basic purpose of the statement of cash flows?

What are cash equivalents? What two criteria must be met? How is the original maturity date considered? What types of investments qualify as cash equivalents? (Try to think of at least three types.)

Cash Flows from Operating Activities

What are cash flows from operating activities? What do these cash flows represent?

What are the two alternative approaches for presenting the operating activities section of the statement of cash flows?

What is the direct method? What two typical types of cash inflows and four typical types of cash outflows are reported as components of cash flows from operating activities when the direct method is used?

Which method is recommended by the FASB but rarely seen in practice? Why have many financial executives reported that they do not use this method?

What is the indirect method? What number does this method start with? Why are adjustments made to this number?

How can a company, such as Boston Beer, report positive net income but generate negative cash flows from operating activities?

Cash Flows from Investing Activities

What are cash flows from investing activities? What do these cash flows represent?

What two typical types of cash inflows and two typical types of cash outflows are classified as cash flows from investing activities?

Cash Flows from Financing Activities

What are cash flows from financing activities? What do these cash flows represent?

What two typical types of cash inflows and three typical types of cash outflows are classified as cash flows from financing activities?

RELATIONSHIPS TO THE BALANCE SHEET AND INCOME STATEMENT

What data is needed to prepare the statement of cash flows?

How can the change in cash be explained by a simple algebraic manipulation of the balance sheet equation?

LEARNING OBJECTIVE
After studying this section of the chapter, you should be able to:
2. Report and interpret differences between net income and cash flows from operating activities.

REPORTING AND INTERPRETING CASH FLOWS FROM OPERATING ACTIVITIES

Why do many analysts believe that the operating activities section of the cash flow statement is the most important section? What two management activities are the focuses of this section?

What is a common rule of thumb relating to net income and cash flow from operations that is followed by financial and credit analysts?

Which balance sheet accounts are normally analyzed when the operating activities section is prepared?

The cash flows from operating activities section of the statement of cash flows reports both the cash inflows and cash outflows that directly relate to income from normal operations reported on the income statement. As a result, the income statement is a natural starting point for this section of the statement of cash flows when the indirect method is used.

However, you must remember that the income statement is prepared using the accrual basis. When the accrual basis is used, cash is not necessarily received when revenues are recorded, and cash is not necessarily disbursed when expenses are recorded. By its very nature, the statement of cash flows is a cash basis statement. As a result, certain adjustments must be made to convert net income from an accrual basis number to a cash basis number when preparing cash flows from operating activities section. In addition, other adjustments must be made to ensure that the amounts reported in this section relate only to "normal" operations.

374

Noncash Expenses

Should noncash expenses be added to, or subtracted from, net income to convert net income to cash flow from operations?

Changes in Current Assets and Current Liabilities

Change in Accounts Receivable

When there is a net decrease in accounts receivable for the period, should the decrease be added to, or subtracted from, net income to convert net income to cash flow from operations? When there is a net increase in accounts receivable for the period, should the increase be added or subtracted?

Income Growth and Declining Cash Flows: A Warning Sign?

Increases in accounts receivable can cause net income to be greater than cash flows from operations. Why do many financial analysts view this situation as a warning sign?

Recall the rule of thumb followed by financial and credit analysts. Boston Beer's net income was $2,640 (in thousands), yet it reported a cash outflow from operations of $1,386 (in thousands). Why didn't beverage industry analysts interpret this as a warning sign?

Change in Inventory

When there is a net decrease in inventory for the period, should the decrease be added to, or subtracted from, net income to convert net income to cash flow from operations? When there is a net increase in inventory for the period, should the increase be added or subtracted?

Change in Prepaid Expenses

When there is a net decrease in prepaid expenses for the period, should the decrease be added to, or subtracted from, net income to convert net income to cash flow from operations? When there is a net increase in prepaid expenses for the period, should the increase be added or subtracted?

Analyzing Inventory Changes and Cash Flows from Operations

Boston Beer's increase in inventory was a major contributor to its negative cash flows from operations in the first quarter. Why didn't beverage industry analysts interpret this as a warning sign?

Changes in Other Current Assets and Other Assets

When should other current asset and other asset accounts be analyzed in connection with the calculation of cash flow from operations?

When other current assets and other assets include operating items, and there is a net decrease in these accounts for the period, should the decrease be added to, or subtracted from, net income to convert net income to cash flow from operations? When there is a net increase in these accounts for the period, should the increase be added or subtracted?

Change in Accounts Payable

When there is a net increase in accounts payable for the period, should the decrease be added to, or subtracted from, net income to convert net income to cash flow from operations? When there is a net decrease in accounts payable for the period, should the increase be added or subtracted?

Change in Accrued Expenses

When there is a net increase in accrued expenses for the period, should the decrease be added to, or subtracted from, net income to convert net income to cash flow from operations? When there is a net decrease in accrued expenses for the period, should the increase be added or subtracted?

Summary

Should adjustments that involve *an increase in an asset or a decrease in a liability* be added or subtracted to reconcile net income to a cash basis? Should adjustments that involve *a decrease in an asset or an increase in a liability* be added or subtracted to reconcile net income to a cash basis?

Net Income vs. Cash Flow from Operations

How is the quality of income ratio computed? What does it measure? When this ratio is not equal to one, what three questions do analysts ask to determine the significance of the findings?

Additional Issues in Interpreting Cash Flows from Operations

Why must gains and losses on sales of property, plant, and equipment be eliminated from the operating section of the statement of cash flows? What would happen if they were not eliminated from the operating section? Should gains be added to, or subtracted from, net income? Should losses be added or subtracted?

When there is an increase in a deferred tax liability for the period, should the increase be added to, or subtracted from, net income to convert net income to cash flow from operations? When there is a decrease in a deferred tax liability for the period, should the decrease be added or subtracted? (Hint: This account follows the same rules as accounts payable and accrued expenses.)

When the equity method is used to account for an intercorporate investment, should equity profits be added to, or subtracted from, net income to convert net income to cash flow from operations? Should equity losses be added or subtracted?

Errors and Irregularities and Cash Flow From Operations

How might an astute analyst interpret a growing difference between net income and cash flow from operations?

A Comparison of the Direct and Indirect Methods

What is the difference between the direct method and the indirect method of reporting cash flows from operating activities?

Boston Beer Company used the indirect method to report a net cash outflow from operating activities of $1,386 (in thousands). Assume that the company decided to use the direct method. What impact, if any, would this choice have on the *amount* of the net cash outflow from operating activities?

LEARNING OBJECTIVE
After studying this section of the chapter, you should be able to:
3. Report and interpret cash flows from investing activities.

REPORTING AND INTERPRETING CASH FLOWS FROM INVESTING ACTIVITIES

Which balance sheet accounts are normally analyzed when the investing activities section is prepared?

What are the four typical investing activities?

Manufacturing Strategy, Outsourcing, and Cash Investments

What ratio do analysts use to assess a company's ability to finance purchases of plant and equipment from operations? How is it computed?

Boston Beer Company's capital acquisitions ratio was 2.74 for the period 1993 through 1995. Minnesota Brewing's was –1.42 for the same period. How would this information be interpreted by an analyst?

LEARNING OBJECTIVE
After studying this section of the chapter, you should be able to:
4. Report and interpret cash flows from financing activities.

REPORTING AND INTERPRETING CASH FLOWS FROM FINANCING ACTIVITIES

Which balance sheet accounts are normally analyzed when the financing activities section is prepared?

What are the five typical financing activities? Would each type be characterized as an inflow or outflow?

Financing Growth

What are the three sources of funds that are normally used to finance the long-term growth of a company?

> **LEARNING OBJECTIVE**
> *After studying this section of the chapter, you should be able to:*
> 5. Explain the impact of noncash financing and investing activities.

PRESENTATION OF THE STATEMENT OF CASH FLOWS

Noncash Investing and Financing Activities

What are noncash investing and financing activities? How should they be reported?

Supplemental Cash Flow Information

When companies use the indirect method of presenting cash flows from operations, what two additional figures must be reported? What are the two alternative approaches to reporting this information?

Adjustment for Gains and Losses

How should transactions that cause gains and losses be classified on the statement of cash flows?

Assuming that a transaction that causes a gain or loss will be classified as an investing or financing activity, why must an adjustment be made for the gain or loss in the operating activities section of the statement of cash flows?

Should gains be added to, or subtracted from, net income to convert net income to cash flow from operations? Should losses be added or subtracted?

Spreadsheet Approach – Statement of Cash Flows, Indirect Method

How do most companies organize the data that is required to prepare a statement of cash flows? What are the benefits of this approach?

Why is preparation of a statement of cash flows more difficult than preparing an income statement or balance sheet?

SELF-TEST QUESTIONS AND EXERCISES

MATCHING

Match each of the key terms listed below with the appropriate textbook definition:

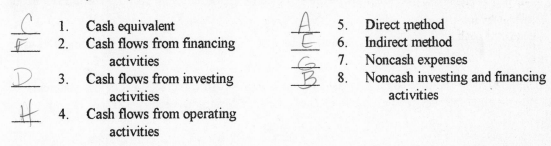

C 1. Cash equivalent
F 2. Cash flows from financing activities
D 3. Cash flows from investing activities
H 4. Cash flows from operating activities

A 5. Direct method
E 6. Indirect method
G 7. Noncash expenses
B 8. Noncash investing and financing activities

A. Reports components of cash flows from operating activities as gross receipts and gross payments.

B. Transactions that do not have direct cash flow effects; reported as a supplement to the statement of cash flows in narrative or schedule form.

C. A short-term highly liquid investment with original maturity of less that three months.

D. Cash inflows and outflows relating to the acquisition or sale of productive facilities and investments in the securities of other companies.

E. The method of presenting the operating section of the statement of cash flows that adjusts net income to computer cash flows from operating activities.

F. Cash inflows and outflows related to how cash was obtained from external source (owners and creditors) to finance the enterprise.

G. Expenses that do not cause an immediate cash outflow; for example, depreciation expense.

H. Cash inflows and outflows directly related to earnings from normal operations.

TRUE-FALSE QUESTIONS

For each of the following statements, enter a T or F in the blank to indicate whether the statement is true or false.

___1. The amount of the cash flow from operating activities that is reported under the direct method is usually less than the amount reported under the indirect method, as a result, more companies use the indirect method.

___2. When the indirect method is used to preparing the operating activities section of the statement of cash flows, net income is reported first as a positive amount.

___3. When the indirect method is used, an increase in accounts receivable is added to net income.

___4. When the indirect method is used, a decrease in inventory is added to net income.

___5. When the indirect method is used, an increase in accounts payable is subtracted from net income.

___6. When the indirect method is used, a decrease in accrued liabilities is subtracted from net income.

___7. When the indirect method is used, depreciation expense should be added back to net income.

___8. When the indirect method is used, gains from the sales of operating assets should be subtracted from net income.

___9. Interest expense related to bonds payable would be reported in the cash flow from financing activities section.

___10. The declaration of a dividend would be reported in the cash flow from financing activities section.

___11. The sum of the individual increases or decreases for all three sections of the statement of cash flows equals the change in cash and cash equivalents during the year.

MULTIPLE CHOICE QUESTIONS

Choose the best answer or response by placing the identifying letter in the space provided.

_a_1. A significant amount of net income is not a guarantee of future success because net income is a(n) _____ number, and does not necessarily reflect the company's ability to generate _____.

    a. accrual basis; cash.
    b. cash; sales.
    c. cumulative; cash.
    d. deceptive; sales.
    e. estimated; actual income.

_c_2. The statement of cash flows is divided into the following sections:

    a. current and noncurrent.
    b. inflows and outflows.
    c. operating, investing, and financing.
    d. operating and non-operating.
    e. assets, liabilities, and equity.

_d_3. Cash flows from operating activities represent

    a. cash inflows from sales of goods or services.
    b. purchases and disposals of operating assets.
    c. ordinary income items.
    d. cash inflows and outflows from normal operations.
    e. cash income before accounting changes and taxes.

_b_ 4. Cash flows from investing activities are normally determined by analyzing

    a. all non-cash asset accounts.
    b. long-lived asset accounts.
    c. long-term liability accounts.
    d. shareholders' equity accounts.
    e. both (a) and (b).

_b_ 5. All of the following would be reported as cash flows from financing activities except the

    a. sale of additional shares of the company's stock.
    b. income for the period.
    c. payment of a cash dividend.
    d. repayment of the principal of a bond payable.
    e. borrowing of cash on a long-term note payable.

_d_ 6. The purchase of machine in exchange for a 5-year note payable would

    a. not be reported on the statement of cash flows, because it involves no cash.
    b. be included in investing activities as a cash outflow.
    c. be included in financing activities as a cash inflow.
    d. be reported in a footnote or supplemental schedule to the statement of cash flows.
    e. both (b) and (c).

_b_ 7. The direct method and the indirect method are alternative methods of preparing

    a. the statement of cash flows.
    b. the operating activities section of the statement of cash flows.
    c. the worksheet for the statement of cash flows.
    d. the net income calculation.
    e. cash inflows.

_C_ 8. A company's sales for its latest fiscal year were $1,500,000, all on account. Beginning accounts receivable for the year were $180,000. Accounts receivable at the end of the year totaled $200,000. Collections from customers were

    a. $1,500,000.
    b. $1,520,000.
    c. $1,480,000.
    d. $1,300,000.
    e. $180,000.

_a_ 9. The beginning balance of salaries payable was $5,000. The company paid $200,000 cash for salaries during the year. At the end of the year, salaries payable had a balance of $8,000. Salaries expense reported on the income statement was

    a. $203,000.
    b. $200,000.
    c. $197,000.
    d. $208,000.
    e. $192,000.

d__ 10. Office supplies expense amounted to $322,000 for the year. The office supplies account had a beginning balance of $20,000, and an ending balance of $28,500. Purchases of office supplies amounted to

    a. $322,000.
    b. $313,500.
    c. $342,000.
    d. $330,500.
    e. $293,500.

d__ 11. Interest receivable decreased from $5,000 to $3,000 during the year, and the company reported interest revenue of $35,000 for the year. Cash collections of interest totaled

    a. $33,000.
    b. $35,000.
    c. $32,000.
    d. $37,000.
    e. $38,000.

C__ 12. Accrued income taxes payable at the end of the year amounted to $30,000. Income tax expense was reported to be $52,000, and payments for the year for income taxes were $40,000. The beginning balance of income taxes payable was

    a. $10,000.
    b. $12,000.
    c. $18,000.
    d. $42,000.
    e. indeterminable from the information given.

a__ 13. Depreciation expense for a company was $215,000 for the year. Using the indirect method for cash flow from operations, this expense would be

    a. added back to net income.
    b. subtracted from net income.
    c. not listed on the statement of cash flows.
    d. reported in the investing section as a deduction.
    e. reported in the investing section as an inflow.

C__ 14. A company with a calendar yearend purchased an asset for $90,000 on January 1, 19A. On January 1, 19D, when accumulated depreciation was $52,000, the company sold the asset, reporting a gain of $5,000 on the income statement. If the company used the indirect method for cash flow from operating activities, it would need to _____ to reconcile net income to cash flow from operations.

    a. add $5,000
    b. add $43,000
    c. deduct $5,000
    d. deduct $43,000
    e. exclude this item

_e_ 15. Refer to the information in the preceding question. This transaction should be recorded in the _____ section, as an _____ of _____.

    a. operating; outflow; $5,000.

    b. investing; inflow; $5,000.

    c. investing; outflow; $5,000.

    d. supplementary schedule; inflow; $43,000.

    e. investing; inflow; $43,000.

_____ 16. Debt with a net book value of $20,500,000 was retired early at a loss of $250,000. The company would report this item on the statement of cash flows in the _____ section as a(n) _____ of _____.

    a. investing; outflow; $20,250,000

    b. financing; outflow; $20,250,000

    c. financing; outflow; $20,750,000

    d. financing; inflow; $20,250,000

    e. financing, inflow; $250,000

EXERCISES

Record your answers to each part of these exercises in the space provided. Show your work.

1. Indicate whether each of the following transactions affect cash flows from operating activities (O), cash flows from investing activities (I), or cash flows from financing activities (F), and whether the effect is an inflow (+) or an outflow (-). If necessary, indicate that the transaction does not affect cash flows from operating, investing, or financing activities (none).

		A.	Recording and payment of salaries and wages.
		B.	Proceeds from sale of bonds for cash.
		C.	Purchase of equipment for cash.
		D.	Cash purchases of office supplies.
		E.	Cash interest payments to bondholders.
		F.	Prepayment of insurance for first six months of year.
		G.	Payment of principal to bondholders.
		H.	Cash sales.
		I.	Purchase of long-term investment for cash.
		J.	Payment of dividends to stockholders.
		K.	Receipt of cash in exchange for signing long-term note payable to bank.
		L.	Issuance of common stock for cash.
		M.	Recording and payment of monthly interest due on note payable.
		N.	Issuance of common stock for land.
		O.	Repurchase of common stock on open market for cash.
		P.	Payment of principal amount due on long-term note payable.
		Q.	Acquisition of land in exchange for note payable.
		R.	Recorded adjusting entry for expiration of prepaid insurance.
		S.	Receipt of dividend income on long-term investment.
		T.	Proceeds from sale of long-term investment.

2. Assume that the indirect method is used to determine net cash flows from operating activities. Indicate whether each of the following would be added to (add) or subtracted from (subtract), net income to reconcile net income to cash flow from operations.

	A.	Increase in accounts receivable
	B.	Decrease in accounts payable
	C.	Decrease in inventory
	D.	Increase in accrued expenses
	E.	Gain on sale of investments
	F.	Depreciation expense
	G.	Loss on retirement of bonds
	H.	Increase in prepaid expenses
	I.	Increase in deferred tax liability
	J.	Equity in net income of investee

3. Compute the amount of net cash flows from operating activities using the information provided below.

Net income	$500,000
Increase in accounts receivable	14,000
Increase in accounts payable	32,000
Decrease in inventory	35,000
Decrease in accrued expenses	16,000
Loss on sale of investments	42,000
Amortization expense	12,000
Gain on retirement of bonds	25,000
Decrease in prepaid expenses	5,000
Equity in net loss of investee	2,000

4. Compute the amount of net cash flows from investing activities, and then the net cash flows from financing activities using the information provided below. If any of the items listed are not used, explain why.

Proceeds from sale of bonds for cash	$1,000,000
Cash interest payments to bondholders	25,000
Conversion of bonds into preferred stock	1,000,000
Purchase of long-term investment for cash	300,000
Payment of dividends to stockholders	75,000
Proceeds from long-term note payable	500,000
Issuance of common stock for cash	5,000,000
Payment of interest due on long-term note payable	50,000
Issuance of common stock for land	250,000
Repurchase of common stock on open market for cash	125,000
Payment of principal amount due on long-term note payable	250,000
Acquisition of land in exchange for note payable	900,000
Receipt of dividend income on long-term investment	40,000
Proceeds from sale of building	525,000
Proceeds from sale of long-term investment	2,500,000
Purchases of equipment	125,000

SOLUTIONS TO SELF-TEST QUESTIONS AND EXERCISES

MATCHING

1.	C	3.	D	5.	A	7.	G
2.	F	4.	H	6.	E	8.	B

TRUE-FALSE QUESTIONS

1. F - The amount of cash flows from operations that is reported under the direct method is the same as that reported under the indirect method.

2. T

3. F - When the indirect method is used, an increase in accounts receivable is subtracted from net income.

4. T

5. F - When the indirect method is used, an increase in accounts payable is added to net income.

6. T

7. T

8. T

9. F - The *payment* of dividends would be reported as a financing activity.

10. T

11. T

MULTIPLE CHOICE QUESTIONS

1. a

2. c

3. d

4. b

5. b

6. d

7. b

8. c $180,000 + $1,500,000 - x = $200,000, x = $1,480,000.

9. a $5,000 + x - $200,000 - $8,000, x = $203,000.

10. d $20,000 + x - $322,000 = $28,500, x = $330,500.

11. d $$5,000 + $35,000 - x = $3,000, x = $37,000.

12. c   x + $52,000 - $40,000 = $30,000, x = $18,000.

13. a

14. c

15. e $43,000 is the amount of cash received.

16. c $20,500,000 + $250,000 = $20,750,000.

EXERCISES

1.

O	-	A.	Recording and payment of salaries and wages.
F	+	B.	Proceeds from sale of bonds for cash.
I	-	C.	Purchase of equipment for cash.
O	-	D.	Cash purchases of office supplies.
O	-	E.	Cash interest payments to bondholders.
O	-	F.	Prepayment of insurance for first six months of year.
F	-	G.	Payment of principal to bondholders.
O	+	H.	Cash sales.
I	-	I.	Purchase of long-term investment for cash.
F	-	J.	Payment of dividends to stockholders.
F	+	K.	Receipt of cash in exchange for signing long-term note payable to bank.
F	+	L.	Issuance of common stock for cash.
O	-	M.	Recording and payment of monthly interest due on note payable.
None		N.	Issuance of common stock for land.
F	-	O.	Repurchase of common stock on open market for cash.
F	-	P.	Payment of principal amount due on long-term note payable.
None		Q.	Acquisition of land in exchange for note payable.
None		R.	Recorded adjusting entry for expiration of prepaid insurance.
O	+	S.	Receipt of dividend income on long-term investment.
I	+	T.	Proceeds from sale of long-term investment.

2.

Subtract	A.	Increase in accounts receivable
Subtract	B.	Decrease in accounts payable
Add	C.	Decrease in inventory
Add	D.	Increase in accrued expenses
Subtract	E.	Gain on sale of investments
Add	F.	Depreciation expense
Add	G.	Loss on retirement of bonds
Subtract	H.	Increase in prepaid expenses
Add	I.	Increase in deferred tax liability
Subtract	J.	Equity in net income of investee

391

3.

Operating Activities:

Net income	$500,000
Adjustments:	
Change in accounts receivable	(14,000)
Change in inventory	35,000
Change in prepaid expenses	5,000
Change in accounts payable	32,000
Change in accrued expenses	(16,000)
Amortization expense	12,000
Gain on retirement of bonds	(25,000)
Loss on sale of investments	42,000
Equity in net loss of investee	2,000
Net Cash Flow from Operating Activites	$573,000

4.

Investing Activities:

Proceeds from sale of building	$ 525,000
Purchases of equipment	(125,000)
Proceeds from sale of long-term investment	2,500,000
Purchase of long-term investment	(300,000)
Net Cash Flow from Investing Activities	$2,600,000

Financing Activities:

Proceeds from long-term note payable	$ 500,000
Payment of long-term note payable	(250,000)
Proceeds from sale of bonds	1,000,000
Proceeds from issuance of common stock	5,000,000
Repurchase of common stock on open market for cash	(125,000)
Payment of dividends to stockholders	(75,000)
Net Cash Flow from Financing Activities	$6,050,000

The following items would be classified as cash flows from operating activities:

Cash interest payments to bondholders	$25,000
Payment of interest due on long-term note payable	50,000
Receipt of dividend income on long-term investment	40,000

The following items would be reported as noncash investing and financing activities:

Conversion of bonds into preferred stock	$1,000,000
Issuance of common stock for land	250,000
Acquisition of land in exchange for note payable	900,000

IDEAS FOR YOUR STUDY TEAM

1. Rewrite each of the definitions of the key terms that appear at the end of the chapter using your own words. Imagine that you are trying to explain each key term to a friend who has not taken any accounting classes. Then, get together with the other members of your study team and compare your definitions.

Cash equivalent

Cash flows from financing activities

Cash flows from investing activities

Cash flows from operating activities (cash flows from operations)

Direct method

Indirect method

Noncash expenses

Noncash investing and financing activities

2. Analysts might interpret a large increase in accounts receivable as an indicator of a problem for a company, which must be investigated. What about a decrease in accounts receivable? Get together with the members of your study team, and discuss the following question. Can you think of instances where a decrease in accounts receivable is also an indication of a problem?

3. Charles Co. purchased an asset early this year for $150,000. They are debating about whether to use straight-line or double declining balance depreciation. If they use straight line, their depreciation expense for the first year will be $14,000. If they use double declining balance, depreciation expense will be $30,000. Their revenues for the year were $850,000. Other expenses, all paid in cash, were $720,000. Answer the following questions with figures as support. Then get together with the other members of your study team, and compare your answers.

Which method will produce greater net income?

Which method will produce greater cash flows from operations?

4. Get together with the other members of your study team and locate two or three publicly-held companies that have recently fallen into financial difficulties. Locate recent copies of their annual reports to stockholders. Look carefully at the statements of cash flows. What items can you list that seem to be indicators of potential cash flow problems?

CHAPTER 14
ANALYZING FINANCIAL STATEMENTS

CHAPTER FOCUS SUGGESTIONS

This chapter emphasizes the analytical uses of information contained in financial statements. You should be familiar with each of the five categories of commonly used financial ratios. You will need to know how to compute each of the ratios that are set forth in the chapter, and understand what each ratio measures. Although many ratios are often calculated for a given company, not all of the ratios may be relevant to the decision being made. You should be familiar with the various types of standards that are used to evaluate the results of relevant ratios, and be able to identify situations in which further investigation and evaluation are required.

READ AND RECALL QUESTIONS

LEARNING OBJECTIVE
After studying this section of the chapter, you should be able to:
1. Identify the major users of financial statements and explain how they use statements.

BUSINESS BACKGROUND

What are the two broad groups of users of financial statements?

What three types of information are of interest to users of financial statements?

When considering a stock investment, what three factors should investors consider as they evaluate the future income and growth potential of the business?

UNDERSTANDING A COMPANY'S STRATEGY

What do you need to know before you can evaluate how a company is doing? How can you obtain this information?

FINANCIAL STATEMENT ANALYSIS

What are the two types of benchmarks for making financial comparisons? Why is it difficult to find comparable companies?

LEARNING OBJECTIVE
After studying this section of the chapter, you should be able to:
2. Explain the objectives of ratio analysis.

RATIO AND PERCENTAGE ANALYSES

What does a ratio or percent express? What does the use of ratio analysis help decision makers to do?

Component Percentages

What does a component percentage express? What is the base amount for the income statement? What is the base amount for the balance sheet?

COMMONLY USED RATIOS

When an income statement account is compared with a balance sheet amount, what should be done to the balance sheet amount? When is it appropriate to simply use data from the ending balance sheet?

What are the five categories of commonly used financial ratios?

TESTS OF PROFITABILITY

What does profitability measure?

Return on Owners' Investment

How is the return on owners' investment ratio computed? What does it measure? What would cause a negative return?

Return on Total Investment

How is the return on total investment ratio computed? What does it measure? Would the return on total investment usually be larger or smaller than the return on owners' investment?

Financial Leverage

How is the financial leverage ratio computed? What does it measure? When does positive leverage occur? Why do most companies obtain a significant amount of resources from creditors rather than obtaining resources only from the sale of their capital stock?

Earnings per Share (EPS)

Why are some analysts critical of the return-on-investment ratios? How is the earnings per share ratio computed? What does it measure?

Quality of Income

How is the quality of income ratio computed? What does it measure? What does a quality of income ratio above one indicate? What does a ratio below one represent?

Profit Margin

How is the profit margin percentage computed? What does it measure? Why is it difficult to compare profit margins for companies in different industries? Is a larger profit margin percentage always better?

Fixed Asset Turnover Ratio

How is the fixed asset turnover ratio computed? What does it measure?

How is the asset turnover ratio computed? What does it measure?

What ratio results when you multiply the asset turnover ratio by the profit margin ratio?

TESTS OF LIQUIDITY

What is liquidity? How do analysts evaluate the short-term financial strength of a company?

Cash Ratio

How is the cash ratio computed? What does it measure? Why should a company be careful not to have a cash ratio that is too high? Why do analysts become very concerned if this ratio deteriorates over a period of time?

Current Ratio

How is the current ratio computed? What does it measure? What is another name for this ratio?

What current ratio would analysts consider to be conservative? What might be indicated by a very high current ratio?

Quick Ratio (Acid Test)

How is the quick ratio computed? What does it measure? Why is the quick ratio considered to be a more conservative test of liquidity?

Receivable Turnover

How is the receivable turnover ratio computed? Why is this ratio called a turnover ratio?

What does the receivable turnover ratio measure? What does a high ratio usually suggest? Why might a high ratio suggest the opposite? What would cause this ratio to be low?

How is the average age of receivables computed? What does it measure? What is the rule of thumb for the relationship between the average age of receivables and the credit terms granted to customers?

The average age of receivables for Home Depot was calculated as 6.6 days. Why isn't this a reasonable estimation? What amount was not known when the receivable turnover ratio was computed for Home Depot?

Inventory Turnover

How is the inventory turnover computed? What does it measure? Why is an increase in this ratio usually considered to be favorable? Why might a high inventory turnover ratio indicate a problem?

How is the average days' supply in inventory computed? What does it measure?

Why do companies in the food industry (grocery stores and restaurants) have high inventory turnover ratios? Why do companies that sell expensive merchandise (automobile dealers and high-fashion clothes) have much lower ratios?

TESTS OF SOLVENCY AND EQUITY POSITION

What is solvency? What do tests of solvency measure?

Times Interest Earned Ratio

How is the times interest earned ratio computed? What does it measure? What does a very high ratio indicate?

Cash Coverage Ratio

How is the cash coverage ratio computed? What does it measure? Why might interest payments be a better measure of the company's obligation than accrued interest expense?

Debt/Equity Ratio

How is the debt/equity ratio computed? What does it measure? Why is debt risky for a compnay?

MARKET TESTS

What do market tests measure?

Price/Earnings (P/E) Ratio

How is the price/earnings ratio computed? What does it measure?

How is the capitalization ratio computed? What does it measure?

Dividend Yield Ratio

How is the dividend yield ratio computed? What does it measure? Would higher dividend yields be offered by stocks with high or low growth potential?

MISCELLANEOUS RATIO

Book Value per Share

How is the book value per share computed? What does it measure? Will the book value per share be greater than or less than the market value per share for most companies?

OTHER ANALYTICAL CONSIDERATIONS

Does growth in total sales volume always indicate that a company is successful? Why or why not?

What causes uneconomical expansion?

LEARNING OBJECTIVE
After studying this section of the chapter, you should be able to:
5. Interpret accounting ratios.

INTERPRETING RATIOS

What should analysts do before using ratios computed by others?

When are comparisons of ratios for different companies appropriate?

How could an optimal current ratio obscure a short-term liquidity problem?

LEARNING OBJECTIVE
After studying this section of the chapter, you should be able to:
6. Describe how accounting alternatives affect ratio analysis.

IMPACT OF ACCOUNTING ALTERNATIVES ON RATIO ANALYSIS

What is perhaps the most important first step in analyzing financial statements? Where can the related information be found?

Insider Information

What is insider information? What can happen if you buy or sell stock based on insider information?

Information in an Efficient Market

What is an efficient market? What does the price of a security reflect in an efficient market?

SELF-TEST QUESTIONS AND EXERCISES

MATCHING

Match each of the key terms listed below with the appropriate textbook definition:

____ 1. Component percentage   ____ 4. Ratio (percentage) analysis
____ 2. Efficient markets   ____ 5. Tests of liquidity
____ 3. Market tests   ____ 6. Tests of solvency

A. A securities market in which prices fully reflect available information.

B. Ratios that measure a company's ability to meet its currently maturing obligations.

C. A percentage that expresses each item on a particular financial statement as a percentage of a single base amount.

D. Ratios that measure a company's ability to meet its long-term obligations.

E. An analytical tool designed to identify significant relationships; measures proportional relationship between two financial statement amounts.

F. Ratios that tend to measure the market worth of a share of stock.

TRUE-FALSE QUESTIONS

For each of the following statements, enter a T or F in the blank to indicate whether the statement is true or false.

____1. The past performance of a company can be useful in forecasting future results.

____2. Economy-wide factors affect all companies in the same way.

____3. Time series analysis involves comparing information for a single company for the current and the previous year.

____4. The standard industrial classification codes established by the government are a source of potentially comparable companies to be used for analytical purposes.

____5. Return on owners' investment relates the company's net income (or, if applicable, its income before extraordinary items) to the capital invested by the owners of the company.

____6. Return on total investment is the same as return on owners' investment.

___7. Financial leverage is the advantage, or disadvantage, the occurs as the result of earning a return on owners' investment that is different from the return earned on total investment.

___8. Ratios save the analyst time, because as long as the ratios are calculated, the figures underlying them do not have to studied in such great detail.

___9. Book value per share reflects the amount of long-lived assets represented by one share of stock.

___10. The formulas used in calculating the various financial ratios are established by the FASB, and, as a result, can be relied upon to be used uniformly by all companies.

MULTIPLE CHOICE QUESTIONS

Choose the best answer or response by placing the identifying letter in the space provided.

___1. An example of an economy-wide factor that might affect any company is

   a.   a hurricane.
   b.   the price of wheat.
   c.   gross national product.
   d.   increased import tariffs on automobiles.
   e.   a winter with relatively little snow.

___2. When the balance sheet is expressed in component percentages, all amounts are stated as a percentage of

   a.   working capital.
   b.   total assets.
   c.   cash.
   d.   sales.
   e.   total equity.

___3. Return on investment is a test of

   a.   profitability.
   b.   liquidity.
   c.   solvency.
   d.   market strength.
   e.   capital structure.

___4. Equity capital is considered to be less risky than debt capital because

   a.   there is no legal requirement to declare and pay dividends, and it has no maturity date.
   b.   equity ownership can be purchased by investors in smaller quantities.
   c.   stock can be repurchased more easily.
   d.   equity capital distributes ownership of the company more widely.
   e.   equity provides more opportunities for financial leverage.

___5. Despite the risks of debt financing, companies obtain significant resources from creditors because of the

    a. benefits of financial leverage.
    b. ease of selling bonds.
    c. ability to deduct interest from taxes, but not dividends.
    d. convertibility of debt.
    e. both a and c.

___6. The dividend yield ratio is meant to measure the

    a. average dollar amount of dividends that the company pays.
    b. return based on the current market price of the stock.
    c. proportion of earnings per share paid out in dividends.
    d. proportion of dividends to interest on debt.
    e. growth in the value of the stock.

___7. An significant increase in total sales reported by a retailer may not be an indicator of success if

    a. it is caused by opening more outlets, and same-store sales are decreasing.
    b. accounts receivable is increasing too rapidly.
    c. cost of goods sold is increasing.
    d. collection efforts are not sustained.
    e. all of the above.

___8. An efficient market

    a. responds immediately to new information.
    b. uses automated systems to update information.
    c. reacts to new information quickly and in an unbiased manner.
    d. takes into account old as well as new information.
    e. processes transactions as quickly as possible.

___9. Solvency tests are designed to forecast the company's ability to

    a. avoid bankruptcy.
    b. meet long-term obligations.
    c. meet currently maturing obligations
    d. avoid running short of cash.
    e. both (b) and (c).

EXERCISES

Record your answers to each part of these exercises in the space provided. Show your work.

1. You have worked with Pixar's financial information in various chapters in this Study Guide. Pixar has a calendar yearend. Presented below are the income statement (assume that it covers the year ended December 31, 19B) and comparative balance sheets (assume that they are as of December 31, 19B and 19A) from a recent annual report published by Pixar. Note that the *dollar* amounts shown in Pixar's financial statements are in thousands.

Other information reported by Pixar in its 19B Report to Shareholders included the following. Cash flows from operating activities totaled $24,226 (in thousands) during 19B. The note payable and accrued interest owed at the end of 19A were paid during January 19B. (The amount of interest expense recorded during 19B was not separately reported in the financial statements. As such, because the amount was not material, assume that no interest expense was recorded that year.) Pixar did not declare any dividends during 19B.

Assume that Pixar's common stock closed at $13 on December 31, 19B.

Pixar
Income Statement
for the year ended December 31, 19B
(in thousands)

Revenues:		
Software	$ 6,306	
Animation	3,947	
Film	18,847	
Patent licensing	9,127	
Total revenues		$38,227
Cost of revenues		4,703
Gross margin		33,524
Operating expenses::		
Research and development	$ 6,985	
Sales and marketing	1,768	
General and administrative	5,577	
Total operating expenses		14,330
Income from operations		19,194
Other income, net		8,031
Income before income taxes		27,225
Income tax expense		1,906
Net income		$25,319

Pixar
Balance Sheets
December 31, 19B and 19A
(in thousands)

	19B	19A
Assets		
Current assets		
Cash and cash equivalents	$ 44,648	$ 97,286
Short-term investments	116,321	47,002
Trade accounts receivable, net	929	784
Other receivables	5,390	1,969
Prepaid expenses and other current assets	982	309
Capitalized film production costs	1,372	1,446
Total current assets	169,642	148,796
Property, plant and equipment, net	4,655	1,552
Capitalized film production costs, net of current portion	1,578	2,170
Other assets	1,588	497
Total assets	$177,463	$153,015
Liabilities		
Current liabilities		
Accounts payable	$ 1,060	$ 742
Note payable and accrued interest		2,373
Film production costs payable		3,324
Accrued liabilities	5,262	3,400
Unearned revenue	337	269
Total current liabilities	6,659	10,108
Stockholders' equity		
Common stock; no par value; 10,000,000 shares authorized; 38,286,500 and 39,413,102 shares issued and outstanding as of December 31, 19A and 19B, respectively)	187,308	185,845
Unrealized gain (loss) on investments	(48)	49
Deferred compensation	(1,049)	(2,261)
Accumulated deficit	(15,407)	(40,726)
Total stockholders' equity	170,804	142,907
Total liabilities and stockholders' equity	$177,463	$153,015

A. Compute the following ratios for 19B and, if possible, for 19A, using the information set forth above. If you are not able to compute one or more of the ratios using the formula(s) set forth in the textbook, clarify how you altered the formula(s), and indicate the effect on the ratio calculation.

TESTS OF PROFITABILITY

Return on Owners' Investment

Return on Total Investment

Financial Leverage

Earnings per Share (EPS)

Quality of Income

Profit Margin

Fixed Asset Turnover Ratio

Asset Turnover Ratio

TESTS OF LIQUIDITY

Cash Ratio

Current Ratio

Quick Ratio (Acid Test)

Receivable Turnover

Average Age of Receivables

TESTS OF SOLVENCY AND EQUITY POSITION

Cash Coverage Ratio

Debt/Equity Ratio

MARKET TESTS

Price/Earnings (P/E) Ratio

Capitalization ratio

MISCELLANEOUS RATIO

Book Value per Share

B. Look through the list of ratios set forth in Part A and list any commonly used ratios that were not included in that list. Indicate why each ratio was excluded from the list, identify its type (profitability, liquidity, etc.) and give the formula for each.

C. Answer the following questions by reference to the ratios that you calculated in Part A.

  i) Does Pixar have positive or negative financial leverage?

ii) What does Pixar's profit margin mean?

iii) What does Pixar's fixed asset turnover ratio mean?

iv) What does Pixar's asset turnover ratio mean?

v) Would an analyst be concerned with the decrease in Pixar's cash ratio? Why or why not?

vi) Would an analyst be concerned with Pixar's high current ratio in 19B? Why or why not?

D. Compute the percentage changes in total assets, total liabilities, and total shareholders' equity.

E. Compute the component percentages for total current assets at the end of 19B and 19A.

F. Compute the component percentages for cost of revenues and gross margin for 19B.

G. What other information is required to interpret Pixar's ratios?

2. Allied American had inventories totaling $4,300, $4,800, and $4,700 at the end of 19A, 19B, and 19C, respectively. Allied's net credit sales were $117,000, $123,000, and $115,000 during 19A, 19B, and 19C, respectively. Allied's cost of goods sold were $70,000, $73,000, and $69,000 during 19A, 19B, and 19C, respectively. Compute the following tests of liquidity ratios for 19B and 19C for Allied, and then comment on the results.

Inventory Turnover

Average Days' Supply in Inventory

Comments

SOLUTIONS TO SELF-TEST QUESTIONS AND EXERCISES

MATCHING

1.	C	3.	F	5.	B
2.	A	4.	E	6.	D

TRUE-FALSE QUESTIONS

1. T

2. F - Economy-wide factors may affect all companies, but not necessarily at the same time or to the same extent. (For example, increases in interest rate often slow economic growth because consumers are less willing to buy merchandise on credit when interest rates are high. Retailers may suffer the effects well before firms that provide services to businesses.)

3. F - Time series analysis is generally performed over a *number of* years.

4. T

5. T

6. F - Return on total investment is computed by dividing the sum of net income (or, if applicable, income before extraordinary items) and interest expense (net of tax) by average total assets. Return on owners' investment is computed by dividing the sum of net income (or, if applicable, income before extraordinary items) and interest expense (net of tax) by average total stockholders' equity.

7. T

8. F - Most ratios represent averages; therefore, they may obscure underlying factors that are of interest to the analyst. (For example, an optimal current ratio may obscure a short-term liquidity problem if the company has a minimal amount of cash and a large amount of inventory. The inventory needs to be sold to customers and the resulting receivables collected before the company's bills can be paid.)

9. F - Book value per share is computed by dividing *common stockholders' equity* by the number of common shares that are outstanding.

10. F - With the exception of earnings per share, the computation of any particular ratio is not standardized. Neither the accounting profession or analysts have prescribed the exact manner in which a ratio must be computed.

MULTIPLE CHOICE QUESTIONS

1.	c	4.	a	7.	a
2.	b	5.	e	8.	c
3.	a	6.	b	9.	b

EXERCISES

1A.

TESTS OF PROFITABILITY

Return on Owners' Investment

19B

$25,319 / [($142,907 + $170,804) / 2] = $25,319 / $156,855.50 = 16.1%

Return on Total Investment

19B

($25,319 + $0) / [($153,015 + $177,463) / 2] = $25,319 / $165,239 = 15.3%

The denominator should be net income (or, if applicable, income before extraordinary items) and interest expense (net of tax). As noted, Pixar did not separately report its 19B interest expense. As such, interest expense (net of tax) could not be added back to net income. The return on total investment shown here is somewhat lower than it would be if the amount of interest expense (net of tax) had been factored in.

Financial Leverage

19B

16.1% (from above) - 15.3% (from above) = .8%

Earnings per Share (EPS)

19B

$25,319 / [(38,286 + 39,413) / 2] = $25,319 / 38,849.5 = $.65

Note that this computed amount of earnings per share ($.65) is different from the amount actually reported by Pixar ($.53). This difference is caused by some additional complexities in the computation of EPS that are covered in more advanced accounting courses.

Quality of Income

19B

$24,226 / $25,319 = .96

Profit Margin

19B

$25,319 / $38,227 = 66.2%

Fixed Asset Turnover Ratio

19B

$38,227 / [($1,552 + $4,655) / 2] = $38,227 / $3,103.5 = 12.32

Asset Turnover Ratio

19B

$38,227 / [($153,015 + $177,463) / 2] = $38,227 / $165,239 = .23

TESTS OF LIQUIDITY

Cash Ratio

19B

$44,648 / $6,659 = 6.7

19A

$97,286 / $10,108 = 9.6

Current Ratio

19B

$169,642 / $6,659 = 25.5

19A

$148,796 / $10,108 = 14.7

Quick Ratio (Acid Test)

19B

($44,648 + $116,321 + $929 + $5,390) / $6,659 = $167,288 / $6,659 = 25.1

19A

($97,286 + $47,002 + $784 + $1,969) / $10,108 = $147,041 / $10,108 = 14.5

Receivable Turnover

19B

$38,227 / [($929 + $784) / 2] = $38,227 / $856.5 = 44.6

Average Age of Receivables

19B

365 / 44.6 = 8.2 days

TESTS OF SOLVENCY AND EQUITY POSITION

Debt/Equity Ratio

19B

$6,659 / $170,804 = 3.9%

19A

$10,108 / $142,907 = 7.1%

MARKET TESTS

Price/Earnings (P/E) Ratio

19B

$13 / $.65 (from above) = 20

Capitalization ratio

19B

$.65 (from above) / $13 = 5.0%

MISCELLANEOUS RATIO

Book Value per Share

19B

$170,804 / 39,413 = $4.33

19A

$142,907 / 38,286 = $3.73

1B.

The inventory turnover ratio (computed by dividing cost of goods sold by average inventory) and average days' supply in inventory (computed by dividing 365 by the inventory turnover ratio) were not listed under the tests of liquidity. Pixar does not have inventory.

The times interest earned ratio (computed by dividing the sum of net income, interest expense and income tax expense by interest expense) and cash coverage ratios (computed by dividing the sum of cash flow from operating activities, interest expense and income tax expense by interest expense paid) were not listed under tests of solvency. Pixar did not separately report the amount of interest expense on its income statement.

The dividend yield ratio (computed by dividing dividends per share by market price per share) was not listed under market tests. The dividend yield for 19B would be zero; Pixar did not declare any dividends during 19B.

1C.

i) Pixar has positive financial leverage. Its return on owners' investment of 16.1% is slightly higher than its return on total investment of 15.3%.

ii) Pixar's profit margin of 66.2% means that each dollar of revenue earned by the company generated 66.2 cents of net income.

iii) Pixar's fixed asset turnover ratio of 12.32 means that the company generated an average of $12.32 of revenues for each dollar invested in fixed assets.

iv) Pixar's asset turnover ratio of .23 means that the company generated an average of 23 cents of revenues for each dollar invested in total assets.

v) Initially, an analyst might be concerned with the decrease in Pixar's cash ratio from 9.6 at the end of 19A to 6.7 at the end of 19B. However, Pixar has a significant amount of short-term investments that could be converted to cash.

vi) An analyst probably would not be concerned with Pixar's high current ratio of 25.5 in 19B. Most of the company's current assets are comprised of cash and cash equivalents, and short-term investments. Pixar does not have a significant amount of receivables and has no inventory. Pixar's quick ratio of 25.1 at the end of 19B is only slightly lower than its current ratio.

1D.

Percentage change in total assets

($177,463 - $153,015) / $153,015 = $24,448 / $153,015 = 16.0

Percentage change in total liabilities

($6,659 - $10,108) / $10,108 = ($3,449) / $10,108 = (34.1%)

Percentage change in shareholders' equity

($170,804 - $142,907) / $142,907 = $27,897 / $142,907 = 19.5%

1E.

19B

$169,642 / $177,463 = 95.6%

19A

$148,796 / $153,105 = 97.2%

1F.

Component percentage for cost of revenues

$4,703 / $38,227 = 12.3%

Component percentage for gross margin

$33,524 / $38,227 = 87.7%

or 100% - 12.3% (from above) = 87.7%

1G. Analysts must understand Pixar's operations and the accounting policies that it uses. They might use rules of thumb to interpret the meaning of some ratios. Other ratios might be evaluated using a time series analysis (comparing this year's ratios to those of previous years). Analysts would also compare Pixar's ratios to those of its direct competitors (which may be difficult if its competitors are different in terms of size, are owned by other companies, have subsidiaries, operate in other lines of business, and/or use alternative accounting policies) and industry averages (which also may be difficult for the same reasons). Because many of the ratios represent averages, analysts need to be aware of any underlying factors that might be of interest.

2A.

Inventory Turnover

19C

($69,000 / [{$4,800 + $4,700) / 2] = $69,000 / $4,750 = 14.5

19B

($73,000 / [{$4,300 + $4,800) / 2] = $73,000 / $4,550 = 16.0

Average Days' Supply in Inventory

19C

365 / 14.5 (from above) = 25.2 days

19B

365 / 16.0 (from above) = 22.8 days

The decrease in Allied's inventory turnover and increase in its average days' supply in inventory appears to be unfavorable. But further investigation might be warranted. For example, the company may have decided to keep higher levels of inventory on hand so that sales are not lost because of items that are out of stock. In addition, these ratios represent averages. As such, they may obscure underlying factors that are of interest.

IDEAS FOR YOUR STUDY TEAM

1. Rewrite each of the definitions of the key terms that appear at the end of the chapter using your own words. Imagine that you are trying to explain each key term to a friend who has not taken any accounting classes. Then, get together with the other members of your study team and compare your definitions.

Component percentage

Efficient markets

Market tests

Ratio (percentage) analysis

Tests of liquidity

2. At this point in the course, you probably feel that you cannot possibly handle any more information. Now, you are expected to memorize a long list of ratios, and understand what each of the ratios measures. Feeling overwhelmed? Practice will help. The ratios will start to sink in as you complete exercises and problems. What else can you do? Get together with the other members of your study team. Try to come up with memory device for each ratio (a chart, a picture, a list) to help each other remember how to calculate each ratio and understand its meaning.

TESTS OF PROFITABILITY

Return on Owners' Investment

Return on Total Investment

Financial Leverage

Earnings per Share (EPS)

Quality of Income

Profit Margin

Fixed Asset Turnover Ratio

Asset Turnover Ratio

TESTS OF LIQUIDITY

Cash Ratio

Current Ratio

Quick Ratio (Acid Test)

Receivable Turnover

Average Age of Receivables

TESTS OF SOLVENCY AND EQUITY POSITION

Times Interest Earned Ratio

Cash Coverage Ratio

Debt/Equity Ratio

MARKET TESTS

Price/Earnings (P/E) Ratio

Capitalization ratio

Dividend Yield Ratio

MISCELLANEOUS RATIO

Book Value per Share

3. Now that the course is over, take a few minutes to "recap." List at least ten things that you learned in this course that you truly believe you will use sometime in the future (in another course, during an internship you have lined up, when you are succeeding in the career that you are striving for, or in your life outside of work). Maybe you are already using some of the things that you have learned! Be specific; indicate *how* you will use what you have learned (don't just jot down, "how to read financial statements). Then, get together with the other members of your study team, and compare your lists.